St. Louis Lost

By Mary Bartley

VIRGINIA PUBLISHING

ST. LOUIS, MO

Library of Congress Catalog Card Number: 94-61846

Virginia Publishing Co.
232 N. Kingshighway, Suite 205
St. Louis, MO 63108
(314) 367-6612

CONTENTS

Introduction

Epilogue

Bibliography

Introduction

For many years, St. Louis' preservationists and historians and some of the public have been concerned about the numbers of historic buildings that have been torn down and have made efforts to save at least some of them. Literally all of the city's early Creole buildings are gone, and almost every vestige of the fur-trading days has disappeared. The magnificent stock of 19th-century buildings, in various styles, has been severely depleted, destroying the work of the many well-recognized architects who were considered among the best of their day. Their buildings were nationally recognized as beautiful and innovative in design and construction. These buildings were monu-

ments to a time when St. Louis was among the five largest urban centers in the United States. A time when the city sponsored some of the nation's most successful fairs and expositions and civic leaders vied with the neighbor to the north, Chicago. Some even thought St. Louis should be the nation's capital because of its location, rail center capacity, fine buildings, and economic growth.

Some years ago, when Manhattan's Grand Central Terminal was threatened with demolition, Jacqueline Kennedy Onassis spoke at a fund-raising event on behalf of saving it. "If you don't care about the past," she said, "you can't take care of the future." She

Courtesy Landmarks Association of St. Louis.

believed it important for the present generation of leaders, and those who follow, to know and appreciate the history of their cities and their historic buildings as they plan the future of 21st-century metropolitan areas.

In 1991, Mrs. Onassis wrote, "We are the only country in the world that trashes its old buildings, old neighborhoods. Too late we realize how much we need them." She was writing about many urban centers, including St. Louis, where beautiful, old, and useful buildings have been cavalierly squandered.

A city's historic buildings should stand as tangible testament to its past riches and greatness, and provide a template for its strong future. The eagerness to find the lowest common denominator in this country parallels efforts to tear down the structures that make each city unique, when they are perceived to be in the way of some seemingly grand scheme. Instead of incorporating that which has been well designed and successful into a modern plan, the simplistic approach has been taken and the buildings have been obliterated, in what seems to be a race to make our city look like many others — a race to grab the plastic ring of mediocrity.

Unlike Europeans, Americans have always torn down old buildings to build new ones, viewing demolition as being as much a part of progress as new construction. We welcome the new structures, built on the ruins of the old, as evidence of economic growth. But in the late 20th century, we are recognizing that a sense of place and past is lost in the rubble, and there is growing sentiment to preserve some historic and architecturally significant structures.

The cities that have understood their historic roles, in addition to immediate economic considerations, have been successful in retaining many important elements of the past. Some have built successful tourist industries and maintained their civic pride. New York, Boston, Philadelphia, Charleston, Savannah, San Francisco, and New Orleans come to mind — some having done a better job than others. What these cities have in common is an understanding of their role in history and their responsibility to it.

St. Louis also has a great, varied, and rich history, having played important roles in the outcomes of both the Revolutionary and the Civil Wars, as well as in lesser conflicts including the War of 1812 and the Mexican War. The city was of critical importance to the opening of the West, from the explorations by its early fur traders and its support of the Lewis and Clark Expedition to supplying the legions of settlers headed west to vast open lands and untold mineral riches. The city's history was influenced first by the various Indian tribes who used the land, and then by the French, Spanish, African-Americans, Americans, Germans, Jews, Irish, Czechs, and Italians who settled here. St. Louis was home base to some of the best American architects of the 19th century, and much of their work helped St. Louis grow into a beautiful city.

Many of the city's great buildings have been torn down in the name of progress. The nationally recognized Title Guaranty and Buder Buildings were destroyed to accommodate the amorphous Gateway Mall plan; others were razed to create a redundance of surface parking. Carolyn Toft, executive director of the Landmarks Association of St. Louis, points out that in St. Louis and elsewhere "the life span of office buildings has been and will continue to be controlled by economics." The issue that must be addressed is whose economics are benefited by demolition. Taking down one great building to provide surface parking for tenants and customers of another does not necessarily serve the interests of the city as a whole.

Other structures, singly and in groups, have disappeared because there was no overall planning for future growth of the city when they were built and their original context was destroyed. Vandeventer Place, for instance, was victim of a rapidly expanding city where there were no controls on noise, industrial zoning, or air pollution. Those who built some of the great houses simply walked away from them when the surroundings declined. They just built an equally grand house elsewhere.

There has been a willingness in St. Louis to ignore our own history — somehow the history of other cities is more impressive to us. The houses of important historical figures have been demolished, including those of William Tecumseh Sherman and William Clark, as well as the house where U.S. Grant married Julia Dent. In the Mill Creek Valley, literally thousands of beautiful, well-built 19th-century houses were demolished, along with 42 of 43 historic churches. Yet St. Louisans appreciate similar historic buildings and sites elsewhere, and have happily trooped off to eastern cities to view their row houses and historic monuments, have admired the great houses and gardens of the Hudson River Valley and Virginia's James River, have traveled to Mississippi and Louisiana to tour the plantation houses, and have gone to Chicago to appreciate its fine commercial buildings.

We had more than our share of all these things in St. Louis. It is fortunate that despite the staggering amount of demolition that has occurred here, many historic structures and sites remain. Grand residential areas — the Central West End and portions of North and South St. Louis — have been fought for before and will be fought for again. Others will become endangered for the first time.

Public response to the destruction of a significant building or neighborhood is now heeded, thanks to the existence of the Landmarks Association of St. Louis and the city's Heritage and Urban Design Commission, the latter having the mandate to review demolition proposals and provide a forum for the timeless debate about the value and cost of change. The city's appearance will continue to change, regardless of the rights and wrongs of historic preservation, as old structures make way for new ones. It is up to those who care about St. Louis' heritage to make sure that the costs of change are not prohibitive.

St. Louis Lost tells the stories of a few of the buildings that are gone. The subjects were selected for their architectural, historic, and/or social interest. The book is not intended to be a complete listing of all that have been lost, and it is not an architecture textbook. It is a plea for better urban planning, serious consideration of the value of our historic structures and sites, and reevaluation of our collective definition of progress.

Some subjects are well known, and others are more obscure. One section discusses semirural life in North St. Louis before the Civil War — a way of life that existed for only 35 years, gone because of the unplanned development of that part of the city. That development was remarkably rapid, though not nearly as rapacious as that of West County in the 1970s. Subjects range from the early French houses to downtown office buildings, Vandeventer Place to the Mill Creek Valley, halls and convention centers to Sportsman's Park. All have had a role in the city's history.

In writing this book, I have been fortunate to have the generous assistance and cooperation of many people. Three readers, or editors, have been invaluable. Ella Rena Chapman has guided me through a maze of commas and convoluted sentences to clarity. William G. Seibert has kindly and patiently made sure that historic contexts are accurate, and Gina Hilberry

Courtesy Norman Champ

has helped me correct the error of my ways in describing architectural styles. She has also been extremely generous in allowing me the use of her extensive architectural history library.

Duane Sneddeker, curator of the Photograph and Print Collections at the Missouri Historical Society, has been generous with his time and encouragement, and his knowledge of the collection has been essential. The Collections staff, including Kirsten Hammerstrom, Debbie Brown, Steve Call, and David Schultz, were great in helping me find just the right images.

The Library staff, headed by Emily Miller and Stephanie Klein, has been wonderful. Many thanks to Sherrie Evans, John Furlong, Dennis Northcott, Debra Schraut, Edna Smith, Barbara Stole, Carol Verble, and Dorothy Woods for their patience, kindness, and efficiency. Archivist Martha Clevenger and then-assistant archivist Wendi Perry have been wonderful in helping find various important documents.

I am also grateful for the assistance of various friends and family and those to whom I was referred. I was fortunate to be able to interview Anne W.

Newhard a few years ago about her grandfather's house on Portland Place and William Glasgow Bowling about the general subject before they died. William Julius Polk, Jr., was very helpful with descriptions of his family's house on Westmoreland Place and of how difficult it was to keep the grand old houses during the Depression years. Family papers from Merrill Glasgow of Houston, Texas, and Violet W. Bowling of St. Louis were invaluable resources, as were interviews with Martin Ludington, Joel Cooley, Esley Hamilton, Charles Kindelberger, Daniel J. McGuire, and Robert Moore, historian for the Jefferson National Expansion Memorial. Additional thanks are in order to Wayne Goeke; Frederick Medler; Margaret Priest; William Vollmar, archivist for the Anheuser Busch Companies; Kate Shea and Jan Cameron of St. Louis' Heritage and Urban Design Commission; Ed Machowski and Jeannie Head in the Microfilm Division of the St. Louis Comptroller's office; the staff in the St. Louis Assessor's Records office; and Carolyn Toft, executive director of the Landmarks Association of St. Louis. I am also grateful for the support of Kathleen Hamilton and the Central West End Bank.

Last, but certainly not least, my thanks to Suzanne Goell, who was the managing editor of the *West End Word* when the original columns of *St. Louis Lost* were published, and to Jeff Fister, the paper's current publisher, for his continuing interest and support.

If it is appropriate to dedicate this book to anyone, it would be to my husband, Jock, for his patience, support, and tolerance of late dinners, and to our children — Doug, Lulu, and Wizzie — for their interest and concern, even though the subject matter is history.

I

The Creole Era

A lithograph of the early St. Louis riverfront, showing the market and city hall, looking north from Walnut Street, 1840s. *Courtesy Missouri Historical Society.*

Humans may have drifted into the Mississippi Valley as long as 20,000 years ago. There is evidence of ancient cultures, and even now at Cahokia we can see the massive ritual and burial mounds of the far-flung and sophisticated Mississippian Indian culture that populated the region from 700 A.D. to the 16th century.

The Mississippians were followed by the Siouan-speaking Plains tribes of the Missouri and Osage, along with their kinfolk, the Kansas, Otoe, Iowa, Omaha, and Illinois Indians who hunted, trapped, cultivated, and gathered in the Mississippi and Missouri River valleys. They had separated from the Winnebago nation and left their Great Lakes homes to escape the pressures of French military and colonizing activities in Canada.

The Osage established a village on the Missouri River 180 miles west of St. Louis and ranged east to the Mississippi River and as far south as the Arkansas River valley. Their truculence, power, and numbers made them a force the Europeans had to respect. The Missouri, who were closely related to the Osage in language and appearance, were allied with them against incursions of the Woodland Fox and Sauk tribes from northern Wisconsin. The Missouri were much admired as boatmen and were great hunters.

In 1673, Pere Jacques Marquette and Louis Jolliet traveled down the Mississippi River in birch bark canoes from the Fox River in Wisconsin as far south as the Quapaw Indian village at the mouth of the Arkansas River. They concluded that the Mississippi River emptied into the Gulf of Mexico and did not turn west to the Pacific Ocean as had been fervently hoped. They began the French exploration of the vast North American interior. In that era, the British claimed much of the eastern seaboard, while the French claimed the southern and eastern reaches of Canada and the Great Lakes. The Spanish were entrenched in Mexico, parts of the Gulf Coast, the southwestern territories, and California. The rival European powers all wanted to claim more North American land and find a water passage to the riches of the Far East.

Nearly 20 years after the Marquette and Jolliet expedition, Rene Robert Cavalier — Sieur de la Salle — traveled the length of the Mississippi River and found its vast delta as it flowed into the Gulf of Mexico. He claimed the entire territory for Louis XIV of France.

From 1698 to 1722 France rivaled Spain in the lower Mississippi Valley. In 1700, Jesuit missionaries briefly established a village with some Kaskaskia Indians north of the River des Peres near the Mississippi River's western bank south of the Missouri confluence. The French founded Mobile, Alabama, in 1702 and New Orleans in 1722. There were French settlements along the Gulf Coast, and Kaskaskia, Cahokia, Ste. Genevieve, and Fort de Chartres were established to the north in the Illinois Country.

The stage was set for an international competition to settle which nation would control the vast interior — the rich Upper and Lower Louisiana Territories — of North America.

CREOLE ST. LOUIS

Various military and political events influenced the founding of St. Louis. The Seven Years' War of 1756 to 1763, the last of the French and Indian Wars, had curtailed exploration of the Mississippi and Missouri valleys and had created a stagnant economy in New Orleans and other parts of North America.

In an effort to stimulate economic activity, Jean Jacques Blaise d'Abbadie, the last French governor of the Province of Louisiana, granted six-year monopolies in various commodities and territories to several New Orleans businessmen. Exclusive fur-trading rights with the Indians of the Missouri River and the western

The home owned by Pierre Laclede, Antoine Maxent, and Auguste Chouteau, shown after it was enlarged and remodeled by Chouteau in 1789. *Courtesy Missouri Historical Society.*

banks of the Mississippi were granted to Gilbert Antoine Maxent and his partner, Pierre Laclede de Liguest. Maxent was the financier of their enterprises, and Laclede agreed to establish a trading post and manage it in the expectation it would become a great city.

In 1763, Laclede left New Orleans with his young lieutenant, Auguste Chouteau, and a party of 30 men to travel up the Mississippi River to its confluence with the Missouri in search of the ideal site for a trading post. They stopped at the settlement of Ste. Genevieve, which they discarded as a potential site because it was "insalubrious"; it was too prone to flooding and disease and was too far from the confluence. As there was inadequate space to store their supplies and wares in Ste. Genevieve, the party continued upriver to Fort de Chartres on the east bank, where they could stay for the winter and scout the western bank. It was there that Laclede learned of the 1763 Treaty of Paris, which ended the French and Indian Wars, ceding all French claims to territory east of the Mississippi to the British. France retained, it was thought, claims to its lands west of the Mississippi

River, along with New Orleans and Florida. Some 40 or 50 families in Fort de Chartres and other French settlements on the east bank of the Mississippi decided to follow Laclede to his new settlement, as they feared life under British rule.

At the time, Laclede did not suspect that France had also ceded, in secret, the lands of the Louisiana Province west of the Mississippi River to Spain in 1762.

Laclede found the ideal site for his trading post below the confluence of the Missouri and Mississippi Rivers. It had a gently sloping plateau that terminated at a limestone bluff safely above the flood plain, and a gap in the bluff gave easy access to the river. The site offered an abundance of timber for firewood and lumber, outcroppings of stone for building, and plenty of clean water, with no deep ravines to hinder future growth. The site had previously been appealing to Indian tribes, as evidenced in the 27 ceremonial mounds arranged parallel to the river.

The site was also one that could eventually control the mid-Mississippi Valley in terms of commerce and military advantage. Aside from its proximity to the

Missouri River, it was near the confluences of both the Illinois and Ohio Rivers, giving St. Louis the opportunity to trade with the cities in the East. Various smaller rivers, including the Osage, made it possible to ship iron and lead to St. Louis from the rich mines south and southwest of the new village.

After wintering at Fort de Chartres, Laclede sent Auguste Chouteau, then only 14 years old, to the previously marked site on February 15, 1764. Chouteau and his crew began to clear the site and to lay out streets according to Laclede's detailed plan, which provided for three 38-foot-wide north and south streets called La Grande Rue (First Street), Rue d'Eglise (Second Street), and Rue de la Grange (Third Street). Several streets were to run west from the river, including today's Walnut, Market, and Chestnut Streets. The streets formed a grid, and the blocks so created measured 240 feet by 300 feet. A group of three blocks was left open for use as a communal gathering place and an open drill field.

Other areas reserved for communal use were common fields for cattle grazing and procurement of building timber and firewood, and five separate tracts set aside for food cultivation. The former fields were fenced and maintained by inhabitants, and the latter were divided into strips approximately 192 feet wide and one and a half miles long, each assigned to an inhabitant as an equitable means of assuring that all village landowners had access to prime farmland.

A large shed for tools and supplies was quickly completed, as were cabins for living quarters. They then began construction on a large house to serve as Laclede's home and as a center of commerce and government. It would be the first of St. Louis' great buildings.

In April 1764, Laclede returned to the site and named it St. Louis, after King Louis XV, whose patron saint was the Crusader King, Louis IX.

After Laclede's departure, a party of 150 Missouri Indians descended on Chouteau and the other settlers, declaring their intention to become permanent residents of the settlement. The eastern bank Creole families that had been attracted to St. Louis fled across the river. Chouteau sent for Laclede, who persuaded the Indians to live elsewhere, but not before the basement of the large house had been dug out by the Missouri women and children — who were paid for their labors in vermilion, awls, and verdigris.

Laclede's house stood on the block between Rue d'Eglise and the public market. It was 60 feet wide and 23 feet deep, as measured by Colonial French standards, which varied according to the reported length of the French king's foot. In St. Louis, the measure could be nine inches and up, and in the case of the Chouteau house, it was reported to be 13 inches.

The house was designed to provide as much comfort as possible in the extreme river valley climate. The stone basement extended ten feet above ground in the New Orleans fashion, and covered galleries — or porches — lined the sides to help cool the interior during the hot summer months and protect the plaster walls from the rain. The architecture was reminiscent of that of the Colonial French and Creole houses of the day. The roof was high-hipped to facilitate drainage, but the Laclede house was wider than the usual folk house. The change was probably due to availability of long timbers for rafters, which made a wider house feasible.

The first floor consisted of a large center room with two smaller rooms on each side. Government and trading business was conducted in the center room, while the other four rooms were used for living purposes.

Laclede's house was luxurious by frontier standards. It had highly polished black walnut floors, laid with walnut used previously at Fort de Chartres and removed as the British took over. The walls were of upright logs, hewn square, plastered, and whitewashed.

The entire property was surrounded by a high cedar or mulberry fence — similar to today's stockade fence — as were all the lots granted to the new residents. This was required in Laclede's plan for the city as part of its defenses. With all the properties thus protected, only the streets had to be closed off to defend the village from attack.

As large as Laclede's house was, it was crowded. Laclede had sent for Madame Marie Therese Bourgeois Chouteau — Auguste's mother — to come to St. Louis from New Orleans with her four younger children. Madame Chouteau was estranged from her husband, Rene Auguste Chouteau, and there was talk as to the paternity of the younger children. Although Madame Chouteau and Laclede were known to have a liaison, he never acknowledged any of her children as his.

Laclede, Madame Chouteau, and all the children occupied the house, as did Louis St. Ange de Bellerive, the last French governor of the Louisiana Territory. It took the Spanish six years after gaining the territory to send a governor to St. Louis, and when Don Pedro Piernas replaced the highly disliked first governor, Don Francisco Riu, he also lived in Laclede's house for a brief time.

Laclede built a second, equally impressive house for Madame Chouteau and her children to show his appreciation for the services of young Auguste and his regard for the rest of her offspring. Its style was typical of French houses of the day, with many exterior doors and stairways.

He deeded the original house and its land to his old partner, Maxent, to keep him from financial ruin.

Pierre Laclede died in 1778 when returning upriver from a business trip to New Orleans. He was buried near the mouth of the Arkansas River, and his grave was never found again.

Maxent was not a good steward, and the house and land fell into disrepair. It was further damaged when Maxent rented it to Piernas, who had been promoted to governor of all the western Louisiana Territory, for use as his headquarters.

In 1789, Auguste Chouteau bought the Laclede/Maxent house and its land at a public sale and proceeded to repair, improve, and enlarge it so that it became the showplace of the growing village. It was St. Louis' first rehabilitation project.

Chouteau added a second floor and garret to the original house. He repaired and added to its stone walls so that they were two and one-half feet thick. Additionally, he replaced the stockade fence with stone walls that had narrow slits at regular intervals so that muskets could be fired through it. He improved the stables, slave cabins, and service buildings, and added a large stone warehouse that measured 50 by 30 feet. He also sank a well near the house, the first in St. Louis.

The interior appointments were elegant. After years of neglect, the walnut floors were polished " 'til they shone like mirrors" and were ready at all times for dancing.

The furniture was either imported from France or made to order by talented Creole craftsmen. Huge cherry-wood armoires were in the bedrooms; cabinets, tables, and chairs made of cherry wood, rosewood, and walnut decorated the other rooms. There were also many mirrors from France. China of excellent quality graced the dining room table, along with fine German crystal, and an abundance of sterling silver added a festive air to the many Chouteau dinner parties.

Chouteau's library contained more than 500 volumes. While local schools were still virtually nonexistent, the first families were well-educated, well-read, and intellectually curious.

A kitchen was added to the main structure; it had been an outbuilding in previous years.

Chouteau had more than two dozen slaves to maintain the establishment. Although frontier life was difficult for many, it was comparatively pleasant for him and his family.

Chouteau lived there for more than 40 years in elegant style. He continued to prosper with his monopoly of the fur trade with the Osage, and Spanish rule did not hinder his activities.

In July 1803, word finally came to St. Louis that in 1800, Spain had secretly retroceded the Lower and Upper Louisiana territories to France by the Treaty of Ildefonso and that France had sold all the land to the United States under the Treaty of Cession for four cents an acre, or $15 million.

The Creoles were appalled! They had had their own way under the benign Spanish rule and were annoyed that they had become part of the United States without their knowledge or consent. They dreaded what they perceived to be a dictatorial government run by fearless officials they had observed east of the Mississippi River. The Americans of the Upper Louisiana Territory were also opposed, as they had come west to find free land and hunting, and to escape a nosy, interfering government with its taxes, courts, and ubiquitous lawyers.

In 1804, Captain Amos Stoddard came to St. Louis as United States agent and commissioner to the French government. He was impressed by the town, Chouteau, and Chouteau's house. He wrote to his mother that "it was the most prominent in St. Louis."

Stoddard also wrote that he "found the French very friendly, if somewhat expensive." He had been given a public dinner on his arrival, and the citizens had honored him with another dinner and a ball. The party that Stoddard felt compelled to give in return cost him $622.75.

"The French...study to render their entertainments sumptuous," Stoddard wrote. "Their tables are covered with a great variety of dishes; almost every sort of food dressed in all manner of ways is exhibited in profusion. The desserts are no less plentiful, and there is no want of delicacy in their quality or variety."

After Chouteau died in 1829, his widow, Marie

Therese Cerre, lived there for several more years. Chouteau's house was torn down in 1841, despite strong pleas to save it, to make way for commercial buildings. It was the first of the grand St. Louis houses to meet that fate, but certainly not the last.

Another of the classic French houses torn down to make way for progress was located somewhat south of the center of town between Third and Fourth Streets, Gratiot and Lombard Streets.

The house was notable as the residence of St. Louis' first physician, Dr. Antoine Francois Saugrain, who was born at Versailles, outside Paris, in 1763.

He was a member of a prominent intellectual family that had been engaged in the book selling and publishing business since the reign of Henry IV of France. One of his sisters married Henri Didot of the famed Paris publishing house, another married the well-known painter Antoine Charles Horace Vernet, and a third wed the prominent physician and surgeon Joseph Ignace Guillotin, who invented the guillotine as a fast and painless method of execution.

Saugrain was educated in Paris as a chemist, physician, mineralogist, and natural philosopher. In 1783, he made his first trip to the Americas in his role as a mineralogist in the employ of Don Bernardo de Galvez, the viceroy of Mexico.

His second trip, four years later, brought him to the United States with a letter of introduction to Benjamin Franklin. He joined an expedition led by the famed botanist, Picque, to explore the Ohio River, study its natural history, and scout a site for a settlement.

The expedition left Pittsburgh on March 19, 1788, and was attacked by Indians two days later. Picque and another man were killed and Saugrain was seriously wounded. He managed to get to Louisville, Kentucky, the closest settlement, where he recovered and later returned to Pittsburgh. He traveled to Philadelphia to spend time with Franklin before returning to Paris at the outbreak of the French Revolution.

Saugrain, a Royalist, returned to America in 1790 and was one of the founders of a French emigre settlement at Gallipolis, Ohio, where he married Genevieve Rosalie Michau.

In 1797, Saugrain settled in St. Louis, wooed in

The home of Dr. Antoine Saugrain, the city's first physician, had gardens that were the first in St. Louis cultivated with non-native plant materials. *Courtesy Missouri Historical Society.*

great part by a 17,000-acre Spanish land grant. Part of the granted land was the three-acre site at Third and Gratiot Streets in the village of St. Louis.

Saugrain moved into the classic French stone house that had been built in 1767 and became St. Louis' first physician. As the village's only physician until 1806, he was appointed Surgeon of the Garrison by the Spaniards and was paid $30 per month.

His house, though not as large as the Laclede and Chouteau houses, was a fine one. It measured 40 by 30 feet and had three outbuildings. Its roof was thatched as some were in the early days, but it did not extend over surrounding porches as many on early Creole houses did. Saugrain established an orchard, several gardens, and greenhouses. He grew both medicinal and kitchen herbs, and Mme. Saugrain's flower garden was widely renowned, as she cultivated rare and unusual plants from seeds sent to the doctor by friends from all over the world.

The gardens had many visitors. Saugrain saw patients at the house, which was also used as a post office, and many came to share his 450-volume library. Others came to see the village's first truly cultivated garden. Governmental flags — Spanish, French, and then United States — flew from a pole on the Saugrain roof. In 1798, the doctor built a seven-foot stone wall around his city property to protect his family from Indian attacks.

Saugrain relied almost entirely on herbal remedies for the sick, though he viewed the then-popular herb, calomel, as a poison — an advanced notion for his time. He performed surgery when necessary and continued to make measuring instruments and conduct scientific experiments. He supplied the Lewis and Clark Expedition with their medical provisions, he blew the glass for and calibrated the barometers and thermometers they took on the trip, and he made and supplied their phosphoric matches.

In 1803, Thomas Jefferson appointed Saugrain as Surgeon's Mate in the U. S. Army and assigned him as post surgeon at Jefferson Barracks — a salaried position. While Saugrain had no interest in making a fortune in the wilderness, he did accrue land, and by 1805 he was listed as paying $3,000 in real estate taxes.

In 1809, Saugrain brought the smallpox vaccine to St. Louis, and a notice he placed in *The Missouri Gazette* promised to vaccinate "indigent persons, paupers, and Indians gratuitously."

Saugrain continued to practice medicine until his death in 1820, but there was no thought that his house and office were worth preserving. The French-style houses, especially the most common poteaux en terre, or post-in-ground buildings, were being removed to build more modern residences and commercial buildings.

MOUND CITY

Among the changes wrought in the name of progress was the gradual, but systematic, removal of the 27 earthen ritual and burial mounds that were part of the St. Louis landscape when Chouteau and Laclede arrived. Nineteenth-century archaeologists found that there was a chain of mounds running the length of the Mississippi and its tributaries and that their builders were part of a sophisticated society that maintained a system of travel and communication that extended as far as Mexico.

Fortunately, a Major Long made a drawing of the St. Louis mound locations near the river before there was much building in those areas. It shows a circle of mounds near the center of the future town, a large

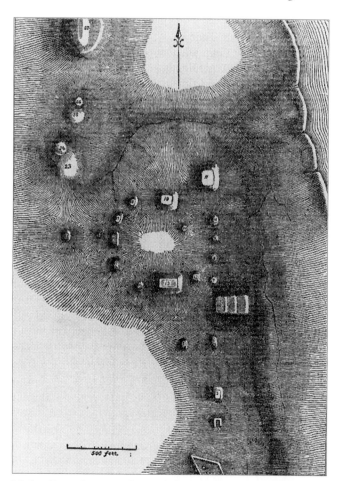

Major Long's map showed the St. Louis mounds.
Courtesy Missouri Historical Society.

square mound to the circle's southeast, groupings of small mounds, a few mounds west of the city, and a very large mound to the north. A map made from his drawing was included in the Smithsonian Report for 1861. While Long's drawing was not to scale, it does show that the mounds were man-made and not formations caused by the ebb and flow of the Mississippi River.

The St. Louis mounds were similar to the large mound at Cahokia built by the Mississippian Indians, though some early residents could not believe that "primitives" could have created them. Some early 19th-century denizens, holding to the belief that the Irish and Welsh found America before Columbus, speculated that the mounds were built by Celtic predecessors. Some tried to strike up conversations with the Native Americans in Old Welsh to prove their discovery theory, but they were unsuccessful.

St. Louis gained its nickname "Mound City" in the late 18th century from river travelers who used the two largest mounds as landmarks. The largest, La Grange de Terre (earthen barn), as it was called by the Creoles, was located on land bounded by Broadway, Second Street, Mound Street, and Brooklyn Street.

As St. Louis grew, the mounds were gradually destroyed to accommodate buildings and streets. In 1842, a British traveler, James S. Buckingham, observed, "The indifference manifested by almost all classes of Americans towards these antiquities of their own country renders it almost certain that in a few years the great number of them will disappear."

Early St. Louisans did not view the mounds as important antiquities. In the very early days, residents would climb the larger ones to view the faraway fires that had been set to burn off prairie grass. A mound near Ashby Street was pressed into service in 1838 as the city's first reservoir, and in 1844, an entrepreneur leveled part of the top of La Grange de Terre and built

La Grange de Terre, the "earthen barn" or big mound, which was destroyed in 1868. *Courtesy Missouri Historical Society.*

a small tavern. Although the views were grand, the tavern soon failed and the building was razed.

By 1855, streets cut through both the north and south ends of La Grange de Terre, and in 1866, Archbishop Peter Kenrick sold the major portion of the site to a group of New York investors for $18,000. The remainder of the mound site was sold to a blacksmith for $12,000. Destruction began in earnest in 1868 with workers carrying away cartloads of the mound, including bones and artifacts, which were used as fill dirt in a construction project of the Northern Missouri Railroad.

One newspaper writer noted sadly that "to all intents and purposes the Mound is gone. What should have been purchased by the City and preserved inviolate, will soon be known only in local tradition."

Other mounds were located west of the City and they, too, were leveled. One, located near Kingshighway and Martin Luther King Drive, was known as Cote Brilliante (Shining Hill). It was destroyed in 1877, in conjunction with construction of the Christian Brothers College. Two smaller mounds, located in Forest Park, were destroyed during construction for the 1904 Louisiana Purchase Exposition.

After 1804, the influx of Americans began to change the French village. While French culture and

The fur warehouse built by Manuel Lisa in 1818 was constructed of native limestone. *Courtesy Missouri Historical Society.*

ways would remain evident for some years, they were destined to be submerged by a larger American and immigrant population by 1840. The Creoles continued to prosper, especially in the boom fur trading years of the 1820s and 1830s, but the American changes, including "boorish public behavior," were overwhelming the French and their Colonial culture. Tastes in architecture were becoming Americanized — the French styles were considered quaint, ungainly, and outdated. English was eclipsing French as the dominant language, and the Creoles were losing influence.

St. Louis continued to grow, and some 326 structures were built between 1804 and 1821, among them a stone warehouse that fur trader Manuel Lisa built in 1818.

Lisa, a Spaniard, was born in New Orleans in 1772 and came to St. Louis in the late 1790s. He was bold and aggressive and intended to make his fortune quickly in the fur trade. Lisa managed to wrest the long-held Missouri River Osage monopoly from the Chouteaus in 1802, by using the influence of relatives in the New Orleans bureaucracy and by pleading poverty and the needs of the large hungry families of his partners Charles Sanguinet, Gregoire Sarpy, and Francois Benoist. Lisa's victory proved to be hollow, as the Chouteaus convinced Osage Chief White Hair to move half his people south to the Arkansas River where they could legally engage in trade with the tribe.

Lisa became the master fur trader of the Upper

Missouri; his brilliant, aggressive, and litigious traits served him well. He gained unprecedented ascendancy among the Omaha, Ponca, Teton and Yankton Sioux, Mandan, and Arikara tribes by being bold and fearless. He kept brass cannons at the ready and did not hesitate to use them. He took Mitain, a beautiful Omaha woman, as his consort and included their children as his heirs. Lisa dominated the fur trade for 20 years — making more enemies than friends. But no one doubted his genius and courage.

In 1804, when Thomas Jefferson wrote to Meriwether Lewis to suggest that he open commerce with any Indian tribes he met during his expedition, Lisa felt threatened. He and his partner, Francois Benoist, did all they could to create as many difficulties as possible for Lewis, with little success.

Lisa's reputation improved somewhat during the War of 1812, when he used his influence to keep the Santee Sioux and other pro-British tribes from attacking Missouri and St. Louis.

He gained further respectability in 1818 when he married Mary Hempstead, the widowed daughter of Presbyterian minister Stephen Hempstead.

Lisa joined the growing scale of commercial enterprise when he built his large stone warehouse at Main and Chestnut Streets in 1818. It measured 26 by 67 1/2 feet and was two stories high. Plain in appearance, the warehouse had a gabled front, quoins at the corners, and windows with straight lintels.

The structure, which became commonly known as the Old Rock House, served various purposes over its long life. It was used to store furs as well as U.S. Army provisions. In 1821, the Missouri Fur Company stored $31,875 in furs there, including 7,010 buffalo robes, 4,089 half beaver skins, 4,063 deer hides, 1,800 raccoon pelts, and other furs. After Lisa died in 1820, apparently as the result of a brawl, the warehouse was owned by other fur trading interests until that trade died out.

The Old Rock House subsequently underwent a number of transformations, including use as a sailmaking establishment. It was barely singed in the great fire of 1849, and only a corner of it had to be removed to accommodate a drop inlet when Chestnut Street was extended to the Mississippi River. In the 1880s, an incongruous mansard roof was added to it, and the building became a saloon and night club where such notables as W.C. Handy performed.

At the time the National Park Service acquired it in 1936, there was a saloon on the first floor and a nightclub on the second. The third floor, created with the addition of the mansard roof, was divided into many small bedrooms for "entertaining."

The historic value of the Old Rock House was well understood in 1939, when it was evacuated and carefully dismantled — each stone being numbered — for historic restoration. It was the last vestige of St. Louis' fur-trading and steamboat era, and no existing building associated with the early history of St. Louis had a greater claim to preservation.

According to Robert Moore, historian of the Jefferson National Expansion Memorial, the supposed restoration was really a reconstruction because the limestone and other materials had seriously deteriorated. "Only ten to twenty percent of the original building was left," Moore said. "When the project was completed in 1941, the Rock House looked as it had in 1818, but only 150 of the stones, saved from the west wall, were from the original building."

The Rock House was again dismantled in the 1950s to allow the relocation of some railroad tracks in conjunction with construction of the Jefferson National Expansion project. Park Service spokespeople assured those concerned that the building would be rebuilt as part of the project. When the Expansion Memorial was completed, the site of the Rock House was occupied by the stairs on the north side of the Arch. The Park Service incorporated the then-remaining 119 stones into an exhibit to give an idea of the building's architecture and importance to St. Louis history. It can be seen in the northwest gallery of the Old Courthouse.

Some of the beams that were hewn to replace originals in 1940 were used as part of the decor of the Nantucket Cove Restaurant, when it was located at Kingshighway and West Pine boulevards.

The warehouse as the "Old Rock House," shown with its incongruous mansard roof addition. *Courtesy Missouri Historical Society.*

The Early Private Places

Missouri Park, which protected the eastern flank of Lucas Place, featured formal flower beds that were much admired in the 1850s. *Courtesy of a private collection.*

There is some debate concerning the origin of the St. Louis private places, including the theory that they are a derivation of the French "place," or town square. Another theory looks to the Colonial St. Louis custom of surrounding residential town lots with a palisade to protect against invasion by the British via Detroit or the Illinois Territory.

It is more likely that the places, while influenced by European and eastern United States precedents, were a local reaction to the extraordinary and uncontrolled growth of early 19th-century St. Louis. Residential neighborhoods were relentlessly undermined by commercial and industrial interests. The complete lack of zoning protection was a major problem for residential areas, though the free-for-all approach to city growth created a great climate for lucrative real estate speculation.

One of the first attempts at creating and controlling a desirable residential area was that of Anne Lucas Hunt when she established Summit Square in 1828. Summit Square covered a square block bounded by Fifth and Sixth Streets on the east and west and by Olive and Pine Streets on the north and south.

Mrs. Hunt and her brother, James H. Lucas, inherited extensive real estate holdings. Their father was Jean Baptiste Charles Lucas, the largest land owner in early St. Louis, where he settled after Thomas Jefferson had appointed him land commissioner for the Louisiana Territory.

This view of Lucas Place is from 1860. *Courtesy Missouri Historical Society.*

Summit Square, a restricted block, not a private place, was owned by the City. It declined, starting in the 1840s, as there was no control over adjacent properties.

One of the most important of the Summit Square houses was built in 1829 for Bartholomew Berthold, whose charm, intelligence, education, and advantageous marriage led to his status as a prominent citizen.

Berthold, born in 1780, was a native of the Italian Tyrol. As a very young man he served as secretary to General Willet, with whom he fought at the Battle of Marengo against Napoleon. When General Willet found it advisable to leave France in the face of Napoleon's rising power, Berthold accompanied him to the United States.

Berthold was 18 when he arrived in this country. He detached himself from military life and, after living in Philadelphia and Baltimore, came to St. Louis in 1809. He was successful here, and in 1811 he married Pelagie Chouteau, a daughter of the founding family.

Berthold went into the fur trading business with his brother-in-law, Pierre Chouteau, Jr. The two were very successful and eventually formed a partnership with John Jacob Astor to control a major portion of this nation's fur trade.

Soon after his marriage, Berthold bought a large tract of land near the intersection of Fifth and Pine Streets from Bernard Pratte, who had bought it from Anne Lucas Hunt. He paid $5 plus other considerations, which must have been generous, as Pratte had paid nearly $4,000 for the parcel.

Berthold built a handsome mansion on the then-isolated site over the protests of his friends, who feared he and his young family would be victims of the savages assumed to be lurking in the nearby woods and ravines.

The design of the Berthold house is attributed to Gabriel Paul. It was an adaption of a 1769 Classical Revival plantation house in Charleston, South Carolina, a style that migrated west through Tennessee and Kentucky and remained popular for several decades.

The brick mansion had a well-proportioned Palladian portico supported by four Ionic columns. Broad halls on both the first and second floors led to

The design of the Berthold mansion was attributed to Gabriel Paul. *Courtesy Missouri Historical Society.*

centrally placed doors to the veranda. The house was spacious, as the Bertholds had seven children, and it was a popular rendezvous for the Creole families.

The house was elegant, the food and drink were said to be superb, and the company was erudite. Berthold was respected as an educated conversationalist and as a linguist. He was fluent in English, French, German, and Italian, and his fluency was useful when foreign dignitaries — such as Marquis de Lafayette — came to visit.

Berthold died in 1831 at the age of 51. His widow continued to live in the house with various of their children until 1859, when she moved west to Olive Street between 9th and 10th Streets. Her move was prompted by the increased commercial activity encroaching on her property.

The fine old house became the local headquarters for the Johnson and Douglas party. After they were defeated for the presidency by Abraham Lincoln, the rent-free use of the mansion was given to a group of Confederate sympathizers called the Minute Men. That group had been formed in opposition to a German-backed military society called the Wide Awakes, who were avidly partisan to the Union cause.

During the Minute Men's tenure, the house was known as Fort Berthold and was considered by many to be a Confederate stronghold. On March 4, 1861, the first partisan Confederate flag in St. Louis was flown from the roof of the mansion, resulting in the formation of a large crowd of interested citizens.

A sentry was posted on the second-floor veranda, and feelings among the divided crowd ran high. The Wide Awakes decided to storm the house. The Minute Men, who had managed to acquire a cannon, placed their loaded weapon in the doorway and dared anyone to try to enter. No attack was attempted.

After the Civil War, in 1866, Madame Berthold leased the corner of Pine Street and Broadway (its name had just been changed from Fifth Street) to a confectioner for $7,020 per year. The house was destroyed to make room for a commercial building.

In 1885, the corner property, which ran 58 feet north on Broadway and 127 feet west on Pine Street, was sold by Pelagie Berthold's heirs to Gerard B. Allen for $127,000. The remaining frontage on Broadway was sold later that year to the St. Louis National Bank for $90,000. The property sale represented a generous return on Berthold's $5 investment, no matter what the additional considerations might have been.

Summit Square failed as a long-term residential neighborhood, but those who invested there profited handsomely, as the property succumbed to the onslaught of commercial development.

Other early attempts to control the fate of a residential area through restrictions included John O'Fallon's Union Addition, Thomas Allen's Soulard development, and William C. Carr's Carr Square. In each case, the development was deeded to the city and functioned as a restricted, not private, area. None met the success of the later private places, which were controlled by either a developer or place residents.

William C. Carr, born in 1783 in Albermarle County, Virginia, came to St. Louis in 1804, when a wave of Anglo-Americans joined the French Creoles to make their fortunes in the newly purchased Louisiana Territory. Carr, educated as a lawyer, had a strong influence from the moment he arrived here. He married Anna Marie Elliot, the daughter of a prominent citizen, and became involved in the community. In 1808, four years after he left Virginia, he was elected

William Carr's Hazelwood was located on 2,300 acres in the vicinity of Wash and Eighteenth streets. *Courtesy Missouri Historical Society.*

to the Board of the Trustees of the newly incorporated town of St. Louis. His peers on that board were Edward Hempstead, Jean Cabanne, Auguste Chouteau, and William Christy.

Over the years, Carr practiced law successfully and served as U.S. land marshal for the Missouri Territory. In 1826, he was appointed circuit court judge, which meant he traveled around five Missouri counties dispensing the only available justice. His large circuit extended all the way to the Arkansas border.

It was also in 1826 that his wife died, leaving him with three young daughters. Three years later, he married Dorcas Bent, daughter of Silas Bent.

Carr retired from the circuit court after eight grueling years. The rigorous travel demands — and a move to impeach him on the part of those who disagreed with some of his decisions — combined with the needs of his family to influence his decision to return to the private practice of law in St. Louis.

Between 1820 and 1830 Carr acquired nearly 2,300 acres west and north of the then-city limits and built a luxurious country estate he called Hazelwood.

The house was located in the vicinity of today's Wash and Eighteenth Streets. It was surrounded by a large park with tall, stately trees bounded by a white-washed board fence.

There was a good-sized lake at the front of the property.

Many of the plants and trees in the park and the garden were imported from England by Carr and his close friend, Henry Shaw.

The large, late-Georgian-style house was built of white-painted brick. It was said to be a grand, but comfortable, house, filled with furnishings brought from England and from Virginia.

The 1840 census lists Carr as having "more than ten slaves," and there were quarters behind the house for those who took care of the house, gardens, park, greenhouses, and stable of race horses. The latter were a long-time avocation of Carr, and his animals often competed with those belonging to the Lucas family.

In 1842, Carr established his exclusive residential area, Carr Square, near Hazelwood. The new enclave extended from 14th Street to 17th Street between Biddle Street and Franklin Avenue. Subsequently, Carr Square extended to Jefferson Avenue. Carr deeded his development to the city and established deed restrictions to forbid nuisances such as factories, nine-pin alleys, and other offensive institutions.

Within the development, Carr established Carr Park between 14th and 15th Streets with the intention of protecting his residential area. He deeded it also to the city with the provisions that it was "to remain vacant and serve forever for a pleasure ground and public square and for no other purpose."

Carr School, currently adjacent to the park, was named for William Carr, who was a member of the first school board in St. Louis, along with Alexander McNair, Thomas Hart Benton, William Clark, and Auguste Chouteau. The fact that the board accomplished little did not affect the honors they received.

Although Carr Square attracted some notable residents, including Confederate General Daniel M. Frost, the area's early success was due to the support of family members, including C. Bent Carr, Mrs. Peters (a daughter of Judge Carr), and Walter Carr.

But the city was growing faster than Judge Carr had anticipated. Carr Square was soon surrounded, and by the time the area was platted by Compton and Dry in their 1875 publication, no vestige was left.

As the 1850s dawned, St. Louis was expanding very rapidly; it was no longer a bucolic frontier town. The city had weathered a decimating cholera epidemic in 1849 — the same year that the steamboat *White Cloud* exploded, setting the riverfront afire and destroying a majority of the city's commercial buildings and its few remaining examples of early French architecture. The disaster resulted in a building frenzy to meet the demands of a river trade which was booming with 600 steamboats operating from the levee. Over 400 wholesale houses supplied the surge of travelers who passed through St. Louis on the way west to dreams of limitless land and California gold.

The prime residential areas near Fourth and Fifth Streets were being swallowed up by the inexorable commercial growth; immigrants were arriving at the rate of 10,000 new residents a year. Change was occurring more rapidly than was liked by many.

In 1851, James H. Lucas and his wife Marie sold a city block located immediately east of Fourteenth Street to the City for $95,000 for use as a park. They then donated an adjacent city block, bounded by St. Charles, Locust, Thirteenth and Fourteenth Streets, to "contribute to the ornament and health of the city," stipulating that the gift "forever be maintained as a public promenade for the inhabitants of St. Louis." Both transactions were part of Lucas' plan to establish a private, protected residential neighborhood that became the first private street in St. Louis.

Lucas, working with George I. Barnett, had no intention of repeating his sister Anne's mistakes at Summit Square. The donated and purchased land was combined by the City to create Missouri Park, which would form a protective buffer for the new Lucas Place. There were no gates to Lucas Place, as the park formed a barrier on the east and there was no development to the west at the time the enclave was established.

Unlike preceding efforts to create an exclusive enclave, Lucas Place was not ceded to the City. Lucas executed all deeds for Lucas Place property. These contained restrictions which prohibited objectionable or commercial uses, established a building line 25 feet from the street line, mandated that only private vehicles be permitted on the street, and provided that the restrictions could be abrogated by the action of a majority of the property owners after a lapse of 30 years. The latter provision recognized the strong likelihood that Lucas Place would not last — Lucas was a shrewd pragmatist who did not want to preclude any opportunities. The restrictions also stipulated that property owners were responsible for street and lighting maintenance. Unlike those of future private places, Lucas' restrictions did not prevent the establishment of three institutional uses in his subdivision: the First Presbyterian Church, which moved from Fourth Street; Mary

Institute, a girls' preparatory school connected with Washington University; and after the Civil War, the Second Presbyterian Church.

These institutional uses were reinforced by the construction of the first public high school building in Missouri. Built at the corner of Fifteenth and Olive Streets, the school overlooked Lucas Place. Designed in the Gothic style by William Rumbold, it was completed in 1856. It was roughly square in plan with four octagonal towers at its corners. The towers were topped with pointed onion domes, and a tall, square castellated tower extended outward and upward from the main facade of the building. In the mid-19th

Central High School was the first public high school in Missouri. *Courtesy Missouri Historical Society.*

century, Gothic architecture was considered the most appropriate for schools, and this building was thought to be a fine expression of St. Louis' leadership in public education. With its rich mixture of pinnacles, window tracery, finials, and battlements, the building was a grand example of a much-maligned style. It set the standard for St. Louis' tradition of good design for public school buildings.

Lucas filed a plat map with the City showing regular 25-foot-wide lots. Though narrow by today's standards, the width was acceptable at the time, and the regularity and density were reminiscent of the exclusive row-house developments in East Coast cities. But the actual development of Lucas Place took a radically different turn. The lots that were ultimately purchased ranged in width from 27 feet to 110 feet. Lucas' plan showed 78 possible sites. With the broad variation in lot widths, 26 structures were built within the original Fourteenth to Seventeenth Street boundaries. Lucas Place was extended along with the City Limits, first to Eighteenth Street and then to Grand Avenue, but the restrictions were not applied west of Seventeenth Street.

Lucas Place marked a St. Louis trend which eschewed row houses and preferred deep setbacks from the street, and it established the model for the later private places with their "parklike" settings. Of the 26 structures built within the original confines, 17 had open space on all four sides.

Architectural styles ranged from the Greek Revival style used for the City's earliest houses to the newly fashionable Italianate, which prevailed when the concept of spaciousness became more entrenched. Though Lucas Place evolved with a mixture of styles and spaces that lacked coherence, this architectural experimentation influenced the standards used later in private places and other subdivisions.

The residents of Lucas Place included H.C. Creveling, Benjamin Farrar, J. B. Sickles, Louis A. LaBeaume, General William S. Harney, William Morrison, Oliver Hart (architect for the nearby First Presbyterian Church), Robert Campbell, Thomas Gantt, Governor Trusten Polk, Mrs. George Collier, Daniel B. Gale and his business partner Carlos Greely, Giles Filley, and James How. The latter built the largest and most expensive of the houses within the early boundaries.

All the residents were wealthy. Undeveloped lots sold at one time for $250 per front foot, deterring some influential citizens whose background and social status exceeded their

The Sarah Collier house on Lucas Place was built in 1858. *Courtesy Missouri Historical Society.*

tangible means. According to Richard Allen Rosen, writing in the *Gateway Heritage Magazine* (Summer, 1992), "...as the city bounded with new money, and as surnames became insufficient evidence of a person's wealth or status, identification by neighborhood became increasingly important. Lucas Place, actually more a settlement of new rich than of the city's old families, took on the aura of an elite enclave."

Among the houses that were built with space on all four sides were those of Mrs. George Collier and James How. The house built for Mrs. Collier, whose husband was the owner of the Collier White Lead Company, was considered one of the finest in Lucas Place. Designed by George I. Barnett in the Italianate style, it was stone with horizontal belt courses and quoins; it had a projecting Doric portico and an elegant Palladian window at the second-story level. The first-story windows were fully arched, while the second-floor windows had segmental arches, and those on the third had rectangular upper sashes.

James How, who was in the leather and hide business, was also president of the Phoenix Insurance Company and the State Savings Institution. He bought his 100-foot-wide lot at 1515 Lucas Place from James Lucas in 1854. He paid a relatively modest $12,000 for the land, on which Lucas held a deed of trust of $11,500 at 6 percent interest. How's large Italianate mansion was completed in 1858. Three stories high and faced in stone, it was five bays wide and had arched windows at the first and second stories. An extraordinary iron veranda, wrought by the St. Louis firm of Schickel and Harrison, surrounded three sides of the house, in the manner seen in earlier French architecture.

How sold this house to James H. Lucas in 1867 for the princely sum of $87,000. Lucas moved from the

The How-Lucas mansion in Lucas Place. *Courtesy Missouri Historical Society.*

large mansion, which he had built in 1848 at Ninth and Olive Streets. Katherine Lindsay Franciscus wrote in her article "Social Customs of Old St. Louis" that the Lucases were "dispensers of that characteristic charming hospitality which seemed to be the peculiar portion of the French element of society."

During the postbellum years, Lucas Place was the most conspicuously elegant street in St. Louis. Even though the Civil War had slowed its development, the economic privations brought on by the conflict probably helped its builders avoid excesses.

As similar residential opportunities developed to the west, Lucas Place's deed restrictions protected the subdivision's integrity but could do nothing to prevent commercial intrusion on surrounding streets. Among the intruders was a small soap factory owned by a Nicholas Schaeffer, located near Twenty-second Street and Washington Avenue. James Lucas tried to buy Schaeffer's property to protect Lucas Place. After a period of tough negotiation, the two men were within $1,000 of an agreed price. But both became obstinate and refused to budge from their respective positions. The uncharacteristic inability to make a deal on Lucas' part cost millions in lost real estate values for him and his friends, while Schaeffer's soap factory prospered, producing soap from rendered animal fat and a malodorous effluvia that made the quality of life downwind less than desirable.

By the late 1880s, the area of the original Lucas Place was in serious decline. Some of its residents had moved to Vandeventer Place, others to Chouteau Avenue and the western reaches of Lucas Place near Grand Avenue, and the truly adventurous went all the

Another view of Lucas Place. *Courtesy of a private collection.*

way west to the new streets being developed near Forest Park.

Among those who chose to move farther west on Lucas Place were Mary Scanlan and her family. Mrs. Scanlan was considered the era's leading hostess, and in addition to being a descendant of the prominent Christy family, she was an heiress to the Wiggins Ferry fortune.

The Wiggins Ferry was, for many years, the only available transportation across the Mississippi River at St. Louis. The business was established in 1797 by James S. Piggott, a Revolutionary War officer who became county judge in St. Clair County, Illinois. The privilege of establishing a ferry was granted by Spanish Lieutenant Governor Don Zenon Trudeau, who also gave Piggott substantial land grants on both sides of the river. After Piggott died, Samuel Wiggins acquired the ferry business and started to amass a fortune. By 1820, he had sold the business to group of prominent businessmen, although he retained a minority ownership position and continued to control operations. The group included both Andrew and Samuel Christy.

The Wiggins Ferry prospered during the high cotton-shipping and trading days of the 1840s and 1850s, through the Civil War as a link between East and West, and on to the turn of the century. Construction of the Eads Bridge ended the monopoly which the company had enjoyed, but there was ample business for both. The land the ferry company owned on both sides of the river grew more and more valuable as the city emerged as a major commercial and shipping center.

In 1902, when the ferry company and its land were being purchased by the Chicago, Rock Island and Pacific Railroad, the Terminal Association entered the bidding and bought the largest individually held block of stock from Mary Scanlan. Already a wealthy woman, she received $2.14 million for the 1,400 shares she inherited from her Christy ancestors.

Mrs. Scanlan's pattern of residences was typical of the wealthy of her era. She established herself as a leading hostess at her large town house in the eastern section of Lucas Place and then followed the migration west. She built a mansion at 3535 Lucas Place, near Grand Avenue, that caused the whole town to sit up and take notice.

The exterior of the white stone house was described as massive and important. Inside, no luxury was forgone and no detail overlooked. It had a broad entry hall with a grand carved staircase crowned by a magnificent stained glass window. A reception room, dining room, and breakfast room were arranged on the west side of the hall, and the large kitchen was in the basement. A formal grand salon occupied the entire east side of the first floor. The room was a nearly exact copy of the salon at Emperor Victor Emanual's main palace.

Its predominant colors were pale Empire blue and gold. The parquet floor, a mosaic of rare woods, was polished to a high gloss. Oriental rugs blossomed like flowers at intervals across the floor. A large cut-crystal chandelier hung in the center of the room's elaborately frescoed ceiling.

The portieres and window draperies, also pale blue and gold, were made of imported French satin damask. The lace under-curtains at the windows were hand-wrought lace with roses and fuchsias in the colors of the natural flowers.

The room was richly and comfortably furnished with chairs and sofas upholstered in either pale blue or gold. The rich materials showed through the antique lace coverings on the arms and backs. The walls were covered with brocade interspersed with wood paneling, and a magnificent Mexican onyx mantel which framed the fireplace was topped by a tall, French gilt mirror.

While the grand salon drew a great deal of attention, the reception room was also described in glowing terms. One writer said the room displayed "the best ideas of American taste in elegance and comfort." The room was richly carpeted, and the walls were covered with portraits and pictures. Sections of the walls that did not have the latter were decorated with brocade hangings. The room contained all manner of bric-a-brac and objets d'art in the best Victorian manner.

Mrs. Scanlan entertained the elite of St. Louis and famous world figures at her Lucas and Grand mansion. President Grover Cleveland was a guest, as were descendants of Rochambeau, DeGrass, and Lafayette, who were visiting the United States as guests of the nation in an ongoing celebration of the revolutionary centennial and the victory at the Battle of Yorktown.

Mary Scanlan died in 1903, and the Scanlan mansion went the way of the rest of Lucas Place when Grand Avenue became a major commercial and entertainment district.

But a few Lucas Place residents, including the prominent banker Rufus Lackland, clung stubbornly to their homes after 1890. Some of the mansions con-

verted to "high-toned" boarding houses quickly became seedy. Lackland, who died in 1910, lived to see the spire removed from the First Presbyterian Church and its transformation to the Gayety Theater.

Isaac Lionberger, recounting the memories of the Lucas Place of his 1870s childhood, wrote, "We who have lived a little while, recall the quiet charm of Lucas Place: the pleasant park on the east, the rows of stately trees and stately houses, the aristocratic tide which streamed from its doors, the smart carriages, and the constant hospitality of its generous inhabitants."

The final blow for Lucas Place came with the decision by city leaders to break the agreement governing use of Missouri Park, which had protected the neighborhood's eastern flank. In 1883, the St. Louis Exposition Association was formed with the expressed purpose of holding an annual exposition that would attract visitors from all over the country to see displays of new machinery, inventions and designs, mineral and agricultural products, artwork, and paintings. It was assumed that masses of visitors would provide a boost to the St. Louis economy, and no one thought much about its effect on Lucas Place.

The Association was organized with capital stock of $600,000. Each of the 24,000 shares issued had a par value of $25. Samuel M. Kennard served as president, R.M.Scruggs was vice president, and Henry V. Lucas was secretary. The group lost no time in getting James Lucas' heirs to agree to break the restrictive covenant governing the use of Missouri Park, as they planned their first exposition for 1884. An ordinance was passed that permitted commercial use of the land for 50 years.

Excavation at the Missouri Park site began on August 23, 1883. Over 60,000 cubic yards of earth were moved for the foundation and huge basement. When it was completed in September 1884, the new Exposition Hall was 438 feet long, 338 feet wide, and 108 feet high. It required 9 million bricks and 600 tons of iron and steel in its construction.

The architect was J.B. Legg, whose monumental Second Empire/Classical design included three grand entrances facing Olive Street, arched windows, and stone-bordered rose windows. The building was considered a precursor of the styles and pretensions of those to follow at the 1898 Exposition in Chicago.

The speed and efficiency of the Exposition Hall's construction, which took place in a little over a year, was considered as remarkable as its size, design, and mechanical equipment. Four groups of 250-horse-power Heine Improved Boilers heated the facility, which was lighted by power produced by eight Edison dynamos.

For local citizens, the large music hall was a major point of interest. It seated 3,524 people and had standing room for an additional 2,000. Its large, ornately framed stage was said to accommodate a cast of up to 1,500. In 1888, the music hall was the site of the national Saengerfest, billed as the greatest music convention in the world. Ambitious grand opera productions were consistently popular. Gilmore's Famous Band played daily concerts in the hall until 1892, when Gilmore died. John Philip Sousa's band played often in the mid-1890s, and, in 1896, Gilmore's band played again — this time under the direction of a young musician named Victor Herbert.

The Exposition Hall was also the scene of national political conventions, and at their 1888 convention, the Democrats nominated Grover Cleveland and Alan G.

Thurman. The Democratic Convention returned to the Exposition Hall in 1904.

But the building's main purpose was to serve as the site of the 16 annual St. Louis Expositions, held for six weeks each fall, starting in 1884. The St. Louis Expositions were unique in that they made money each year. In 1895, the Association paid a 50-cents-per-share dividend to its stockholders when shareholders of other expositions across the country were taking losses. In 1896, the Association was able to donate $8,000 to the victims of the great cyclone that had devastated parts of the city.

In 1887, the Association added a coliseum wing to the hall that could easily seat 7,000 people. The room could accommodate 12,000 when the 112-by-222-foot arena space was used for seating. The addition cost $150,000 and added more than 60,000 square feet to the complex.

Around the turn of the century there was talk of discontinuing the successful expositions, and writers in

The Exposition and Music Hall, now site of the main public library. *Courtesy Missouri Historical Society.*

W. M. Reedy's *The Mirror* sensed a move on the city's part to raze the Exposition Hall and let its site revert to park land.

But in 1902, philanthropist Andrew Carnegie offered to give the city $1 million to build a library system. Half of Carnegie's gift was earmarked for a central library building and the balance was designated for branches. The only requirement of the City was that it provide the land free of charge.

The Exposition and Music Hall site was deemed the most appropriate location for the main library building.

By 1906, when Lucas Place was fading into memory, the Exposition and Music Hall was disintegrating. The impressive heating and lighting plants had been removed, and there were gaping holes in the roof and the floor. Demolition had been delayed so that a group touting the construction of a new coliseum could explore the possibilities of using the building's 600 tons of steel in the new structure.

The Exposition and Music Hall was demolished in 1906, and construction of the existing main library building, designed by Cass Gilbert, was begun.

James Lucas, who died in 1873, did not live to see the decline of his dream and destruction of the park he had thought would exist forever. In 1893, Ordinance Number 1094 was passed, changing a long list of street names, among them that of Lucas Place to Locust Street.

All that remains of Lucas Place is the handsomely restored home of fur trader Robert Campbell, which is now a museum.

Commerce, Growth, & a Plan of Sorts

A model for a plaster cap at the St. Nicholas Hotel. *Courtesy Missouri Historical Society.*

By the 1830s and 1840s, St. Louis was meeting the great commercial expectations of its founders and early leaders. The fur trade was prospering as a result of the British and European demand for pelts for fashionable beaver hats. Other businessmen were diversifying in many directions, and the steamboat era was in full sway. The village had become a city, and numerous buildings were being erected to meet the burgeoning commercial needs. The population was growing rapidly, and housing, for all economic levels, was in high demand. Since there was no overall planning beyond Laclede's original grid, buildings were built wherever landowners wanted them.

Pierre Laclede's dream of a prominent city that could command the Mississippi Valley seemed to be coming true. St. Louis had played an important role in preventing the British from attacking the colonies from the west during the Revolutionary War. It was taking a major part in the opening of the great western lands. And it had established itself as a leading transportation and manufacturing center.

Having achieved such status, it became obvious that first-class hotel accommodations would be necessary if the historically hospitable city was to maintain its reputation. Several fine hotels were built during the first half of the 19th century — the Southern, the

The third Planter's Hotel was representative of St. Louis' 19th-century hospitality. At left is the Old Courthouse. *Courtesy Missouri Historical Society.*

The Turkish Den was an amenity in the Planter's House Hotel. *Courtesy Missouri Historical Society.*

Lindell, the Virginia, and the Barnum were among them — but the most famous was the Planter's House Hotel.

The first establishment to bear that name opened in 1817 in a frame trading post on the riverfront, where it remained until 1840, when civic leaders saw the need to build a top-flight hotel that would be counted among the finest in the nation.

The building of the second Planter's House Hotel was financed through the investment of private citizens. Contributors to the venture selected Pierre Chouteau, James Lucas, John Kerr, and Peter Powell to represent them as trustees.

Begun in 1837 and designed by Henry Spence, the new 300-room, four-story hotel was located at Fourth and Pine Streets, removed from the hurly-burly and odor of the riverfront. It had a classic, dignified exterior and shops and offices at the ground level. There was a huge main dining room, and three addi-

tional restaurants were associated with it. The grand ballroom featured decorative details copied from the Temple of Erectheus in Athens, Greece. The Planter's House Hotel was considered the finest in the West and was seen by civic leaders as a symbol of the new St. Louis. It became the gathering place for politicians and businessmen and was the byword for luxury and good service. A room cost $4.25 per person per day, and the rate included four sumptuous meals. The trustees leased the facility to various operators over the years for the then-considerable sum of $7,000 per month.

Landowners from both the north and the south appreciated the hospitality and brought their families to spend the winter. One evening in 1841, the menu offered an imposing array of foods including filet de boeuf, fried oysters, broiled grouse, saddle of antelope, and wild duck. Desserts included custard pudding and apple, plum, and pumpkin pies.

Famous visitors were often in residence. Jefferson

Davis, Abraham Lincoln, Andrew Jackson, Henry Clay, U.S. Grant, and William F. Cody — among others — all signed the register at one time or another, and Charles Dickens stayed there during his American tour. Dickens, who was notably critical of this country and of St. Louis, wrote favorably about the Planter's House.

"We went to a large hotel called the Planter's House, a building like an English hospital, with long passages and skylights above the room doors to allow for circulation of air," Dickens wrote. "There were many fine boarders in it and as many lights sparkled and glistened from the windows down into the street below when we drove up as if it had been illuminated on some occasion of rejoicing.

"It is an excellent house and the proprietors have the most bountiful notions of providing the creature with comforts. Dining alone with my wife in the room one day I counted fourteen dishes on the table at once."

The second Planter's House continued as the city's beacon of hospitality for many years until 1887, when a fire severely damaged the building and it was closed. The old building, called an architectural nightmare by some, was demolished in 1891 to make room for a new, even grander, Planter's House Hotel.

The new building was financed in an unusual way. When St. Louis was a candidate for the Columbian Exposition, civic leaders secured pledges of $5 million, plus an additional $1 million for entertainment at the fair. When the Exposition was awarded to Chicago, the group decided to offer a $1 million bonus to any corporation or individual who could and would build a first-class, fireproof hotel in the city.

The bonus attracted investors who chose the Fourth and Pine Street site and retained Isaac Taylor to design the hotel.

Taylor's original design was for an Italian Renaissance building, but his plans were modified to an adapted Renaissance style to permit the inclusion of some French Rococo Renaissance rooms, which were considered the last word in elegance.

The 400-room hotel was built in an inverted "E" shape to allow natural light to pour into every room. The first and second floors were built of Ohio stone and granite, while the upper stories were of light-beige-colored brick trimmed with cut stone. Molded bricks were used around the principal entrances in the front.

The magnificent front portico, made of cast iron, featured Ionic columns. It was crowned by an elaborate cast-iron balustrade.

Inside, grandeur and elegance were the order of the day. The lobby rotunda measured 50 feet from north to south and 122 feet from east to west. Colored marble lined the walls to a height of ten feet. The 20-foot ceiling was decorated with medallions of choice heraldic design. A large grand staircase stood at one end, topped by a large bronze guardian lion. At the base, a pair of bronze, human-size sprites held lamps aloft on each of the newel posts.

The main restaurant was considered the most elegant room in the city. It had many Doric columns and was decorated in tones of Empire green and silver. The hotel offered other elegant public rooms — the ladies' dining room, a sumptuous Moorish room, and various meeting and banquet rooms were much admired.

The main bar was well-known to civic leaders, politicians, and gentleman visitors. The bar measured 45 by 47 feet and was designed in a semicircle. It was there that bartender Charles Dittrich invented a cool and delicious lime, lemon, and gin drink called a Tom Collins — named after a regular and favored customer. Dittrich followed the footsteps of a predecessor who, years earlier, had given the world the Planter's Punch to enjoy.

For all its elegance and history, the Planter's House did not thrive during World War I. The doors closed on its present, past, and future in 1922. The building was converted for use as offices and was called the Planter's Building until 1930. It was then renamed the Cotton Belt Building.

It was finally torn down in 1976 to make way for construction of the Boatmen's Tower.

Another noteworthy 19th century hotel in St. Louis was the New St. Nicholas Hotel, located at 407 North Eighth Street. Designed by the great Louis Sullivan, it has been called a "Victorian wonder that lost its integrity" before it was finally destroyed.

The New St. Nicholas, like two other Sullivan buildings in St. Louis — the Union Trust Building and the Wainwright Building — was considered a marvel of modern construction in 1893 because of its precedent-setting steel frame skeleton. Its elegant terra-cotta detail and massive round-arched entrances were typical of Sullivan's designs. The building was considered a

The St. Nicholas Hotel was designed by Louis Sullivan. *Courtesy Missouri Historical Society.*

The same building was remodeled to be the Victoria building by the firm of Eames and Young. *Courtesy Gina Hilberry.*

triumph of engineering and design and was the site of the 1895 national meeting of the American Institute of Architects. Rooms cost $1.50 to $2.00 a night without a private bath and $2.50 to $4.00 if the amenity was included.

But in 1905 a fire severely damaged the hotel. New owners decided to convert it to use as an office building and retained the firm of Eames and Young to oversee and design the remodeling project. When they had finished, little of Sullivan's design remained. Its name, too, was gone as the property had been rechristened the Victoria Building.

The steep, gabled roof disappeared to accommodate extra floors topped by a flat roof. The arched windows of the seventh-floor ballroom were sacrificed in the name of additional space, and the deeply carved terra-cotta balconies also disappeared. Sullivan's arched openings at the ground floor were obscured by shop additions and remodeling.

The building was demolished in 1973 — the economic victim of obsolescence and unwieldy interior arrangements. George McCue, architectural historian of the *St. Louis Post-Dispatch*, could find few reasons to save the building, but hoped that the original elevator

cages might be recovered from the rubble. Only Sullivan's grand terra-cotta snowflake panels that decorated four spandrels and pieces of the upper friezes were saved by architectural historians from Washington University and Southern Illinois University at Edwardsville.

In 1836 — the beginning of St. Louis' maturation period — 25 leading merchants, who were dissatisfied with the disorganized trade practices on the levee, formed a new organization — a Chamber of Commerce. Edward Tracy was president, Henry von Phul was vice president, and John Ford was secretary.

The new group quickly gained members and began to bring order to chaos by adopting a tariff of commissions for buying and selling produce, setting a schedule of fees for arbitration, and establishing rates for steamboat agents.

The group was loosely organized until 1848, when it merged with the Millers' Exchange, began to have regular meetings, and took the name of the Merchants' Exchange. The group met in borrowed quarters and moved often when the need for additional space for the growing membership became apparent. It took nearly 20 years before commercial growth dictated the need for permanent headquarters. In 1855, Exchange members bought five parcels of land when the City sold its remaining holdings in Block 7, which included frontage on Main Street. Barnett and Weber designed the first Merchants' Exchange Building, the first in the country built to exclusively serve a civic organization.

Some 20 years later, *Missouri Republican* publisher George Knapp suggested that the organization's quarters had become inadequate because of commercial and membership growth. When he proposed the membership build a new, larger building, his idea was enthusiastically endorsed.

Francis Lee and Thomas Annan were retained as architects, and the magnificent commercial High Victorian/Italianate-style second Merchants' Exchange Building was completed in 1875 at a cost of nearly $2 million. Located at Third and Pine Streets, it appeared as a monolith from the exterior but was essentially two buildings, set parallel to one another, joined at the ends and separated by a courtyard.

The frontage on Pine Street stretched for 235 feet and provided office space, while the back section accommodated the grand trading hall.

When the new Merchants' Exchange was opened, Masons' president Web Samuels extolled its virtues in his dedicatory speech, calling the building the result of Missouri soil and skill.

"Foundations of granite, walls of sandstone and brick, framework of iron and wood, lead and iron plumbing and heating apparatus, a large portion of glass, and even the very paint that decorates its ceilings and graceful columns come from the surface and bosom of our state and are chiseled into beauty and molded into form by our own artisans and manufacturers," Samuels said.

Although Samuels' remarks were full of pride and poetry, he neglected to mention that a great deal of the glass had been imported from Belgium and that the marble came from Georgia.

The Merchants' Exchange Building was expected to make St. Louis an important convention center, and indeed, the Democratic Convention was held in its grand hall in 1876. The convention nominated Samuel Tilden, who garnered 250,000 more votes than his Republican opponent, Rutherford B. Hayes, who won the presidency by one electoral vote.

The grand hall was also the scene of the first Veiled

The Merchants' Exchange Building was called the "result of Missouri soil and skill." *Courtesy Missouri Historical Society.*

The trading floor of the Merchants' Exchange Building was the nation's largest unobstructed space in 1875. *Courtesy Missouri Historical Society.*

Prophet Ball, and succeeding balls were held there until 1900.

Although the entire building was a marvel of grandeur — there was a massive carved walnut staircase, the black walnut doors were as thick as a telephone directory, and the brass doorknobs were the size of small cantaloupes, and there were acres of black walnut paneling on its walls — it was the grand hall that was universally admired.

The hall measured nearly 235 feet long by 98 feet wide. The ceiling was 65 feet high. The room was brightened by 62 windows arranged in two tiers, and a gallery extended around the hall between the two rows of windows. At the time, the unobstructed space was the largest in the nation, made possible by iron truss construction which supported the roof.

The expansive ceiling was decorated with three

frescoes. The central figure, symbolic of our great city of the West, was surrounded by groupings representing the agricultural, mineral, and industrial products of the Mississippi Valley. Another group of figures represented the four corners of the Earth bringing their various offerings to "The West," which, with outstretched arms, offered its products in return.

Business was conducted from an ornate black walnut rostrum flanked by two large wrought-iron maidens, each holding a globe aloft. Exchange members met every day from 9:15 to 11:15 a.m. to display their grain on marble-topped tables and to make deals.

In the 1880s, the grand hall was further embellished with a huge fountain replete with water nymphs and sprites. A gift from John A. Scudder, it sat in the middle of the trading floor. After 20 years, in 1903, the fountain was dismantled and removed to reclaim additional space to transact business. The fountain was re-erected in Fountain Park.

The exterior of the building, with its pedimented entry, arched windows, pilasters, and elaborate frieze, did not change for 72 years — until 1947 — when the stone balustrade, copings, and cornices were removed for safety reasons. The years had loosened them, and it was feared they might fall to the sidewalk. This removal was a bellwether of the future — or lack of it.

In 1957, the members of the Merchants' Exchange, the oldest grain market in the United States, decided to move to new headquarters in the 5200 block of Oakland. Their magnificent landmark was sold to the Pierce Corporation — which owned the neighboring Pierce Building — for $500,000.

The new owners "found it impractical" to repair or convert the old Merchants' Exchange Building. The annual tax bill of $14,000 probably influenced their decision to demolish it.

Strong pleas were made to save the building. Charles van Ravensway, then director of the Missouri Historical Society, argued that it and the Eads Bridge were all that remained in St. Louis of the architectural monuments of the period following the Civil War. It was widely held among historians that few, if any, 19th-century St. Louis buildings were more significant in terms of excellence of design and historic importance.

But preservationist sentiments were ignored and demolition was completed in March 1958, after many artifacts had "migrated" all over the country. Parts went to Chicago, Detroit, Dallas, and Tucson. The Belgian glass windows, with their half-inch-thick panes and 16-foot frames, were installed in a manufacturing firm's building in Flat River, Missouri. It took four men to carry half a sash.

Other artifacts — paneling, brass elevator cages, and the like — ended up in St. Louis houses and bars.

The site was used as a parking lot until construction began on the Adam's Mark Hotel.

St. Louis' growth and maturity were recognized on the federal level in 1850, when Congress voted its first appropriation for a new Post Office and Custom House to be built in the river city. At the time, it was the largest

federal building project west of the Mississippi River and would be the site of all federal business in the Mississippi Valley during the Civil War and the two decades that followed it.

That the project carried controversy and political intrigue was not unusual for federal building projects of the era. Contention became obvious when there was no clear consensus as to its location. The government selected a site at Second and Chestnut Streets occupied by Meriwether Lewis Clark's failed St. Louis Theatre and the *Intelligencer* newspaper where Mark Twain once worked as a printer. The location was close to the business district, and promoters felt that it would strengthen commerce there. But Thomas Hart Benton and John O'Fallon — both powerful men — preferred a more westerly location, at Third and Olive Streets; and a third faction, led by James Clemens, favored a location at Second and Carr Streets because it was clear to them that the city would grow in a distinctly

The Old Post Office and Custom House was completed in 1859. *Courtesy Missouri Historical Society.*

northern direction.

After intense behind-the-scenes lobbying, the location at Third and Olive Streets was chosen.

George I. Barnett was appointed as the supervising architect in 1852, and the site was cleared. Barnett sent his plans to Washington, D.C., for approval and received, instead, on September 20, a detailed list of specifications for the building from W. L. Hodges, the Acting Secretary of the Treasury. Antedating, by several years, the extensive use of cast iron and fire-proofing materials, Hodges' specifications gave specific instructions for the foundation and brick piers, support-ing arches in the basement, and a variety of uses for cast iron. Iron was to be used for the stairs and all orna-ments, including shells of the columns, bases, capitals, antae, belts, courses, balustrades, windows, and win-dow fittings. All exterior doors were to be finished in wrought iron. Interior uses of cast iron included columns, both round and square, used from basement to roof to support floorings and the roof. All were to be hollow and proportioned to their respective posi-tion, purpose, and required weight-bearing capacity. Floors of the entrance, second, and third floors were to be composed of iron girders, running lengthwise, resting on columns and walls, which supported iron beams.

Barnett started drawing plans in accordance with Hodges' directives, only to find that Hodges had been replaced by A. B. Young on September 25, 1852. Young approved the final, modified plans (some of which survive in the custody of the National Park Service at the Old Courthouse) in 1853, and initial contracts were let. Excavation finally began in 1854 for a building that represented one the earliest examples of the extensive use of cast iron in a major federal building.

In 1856, Barnett was accused of engaging in political intrigue and unspecified improprieties. He was removed from his position and replaced by Tho-mas Walsh, one of his principal competitors.

When the Post Office and Custom House was completed in 1859, it asserted a monumental presence in the Third Street business district. Its style was described, in the nomenclature of the era, as Anglo-Italian. Today, it would be called Greek Revival. Its Third Street facade, with a projecting portico consist-ing of six Corinthian columns supported by a rusticated base punctuated by five arches, was an important addition to the downtown streetscape. It was reported that the columns were a remnant of the St. Louis Theatre — commissioned by M. L. Clark but stored underneath the stage until he could afford to have them installed.

The building was used as a post office and custom house and accommodation for the Federal Courts. In this latter capacity, it became famous as the site of the Whiskey Ring trials which stunned the nation during the second Grant administration. The scandals started in St. Louis as a well-organized conspiracy originally conceived to fight a perceived Liberal Republican political threat. The scam quickly developed into a gold mine for the conspirators. The major figures included William McKee, a patronage boss and principal owner of the *Globe Democrat*; John McDonald, supervisor for the Internal Revenue Service for Missouri and the Southwest (who owed his appointment to McKee); William Avery, chief clerk of the Internal Revenue Department; John A. Joyce, the St. Louis Collector of Revenue; and Orville Babcock, Grant's secretary. In all, 213 indictments were handed down, bringing to trial the ring leaders, distillers, gaugers who examined the whiskey, rectifiers who affixed the federal revenue stamps, and various politi-cians. A Merchants' Exchange publication, which revealed that three times as much whiskey had been distilled in St. Louis as showed on Treasury reports, called attention to the nationwide frauds, which had caused the government to lose more than $4 million in revenues from 1873 to 1875.

A major result of the scandal was the loss of St. Louis' distillery industry. Several distillers moved their plants to Kentucky; others went out of business or became wholesalers of distilled spirits and wines.

Even during the Whiskey Ring trials, the Post Office and Custom House building was considered too small. The Federal Government had selected a site for a new facility on Olive Street between Eighth and Ninth Streets — another controversial decision because it diminished the role of the river and the riverfront district in the business community and encroached on a fashionable residential area.

The new (now old) Post Office was not completed until 1884. From 1884 until after the turn of the century, the Third Street building was used to house the United States Appraiser's Office, the Marine Hospital Service, the Pension Examiner's Office, the Army Recruiter's Office, and the Assay Office. In its later years, the building was used as a warehouse.

There were protests in 1939 when the National Park Service announced that the Third Street Post Office and Custom House would be demolished to accommodate the Jefferson National Expansion Memorial project. Various suggestions were made — including that the building would be an ideal site for a science museum or other cultural use — all to no avail. The Park Service announced it would save and renovate the Old Courthouse and that it would be impossible to preserve both buildings. There were then suggestions that the columns be saved because of their long association with the city. It was thought they could be incorporated in the planned memorial. Newton B. Drury, then-director of the National Park Service, said that "portions will be saved for later display."

The Post Office and Custom House was demolished in 1939. According to an article in the April 6, 1941, *Post-Dispatch*, the stone arches and three Corinthian columns were being re-erected at Laurel Hill Memorial Gardens. They are a long way from the St. Louis riverfront.

The post-Civil War years brought considerable energy to St. Louis — to the point that individualism, boosterism, and no small measure of pomposity were the order of the day. The war had restricted most river trade in and out of St. Louis, and it was a divisive time for the city. Leaders viewed the postwar years as a period to promote the city and to negate the gains made by rival Chicago, where economic development had not been impeded by the hostilities.

One manifestation of boosterism and individualism was brief enthusiasm for commercial buildings designed in the Second Empire style of architecture for commercial buildings, though the Second Empire residential buildings became ubiquitous after 1866. The style was imitating the latest French fashions and reminiscent of Paris — a city that some leaders hoped would be rivaled by St. Louis.

In 1873, George Knapp, publisher of the *Missouri Republican*, erected a large Second Empire-style build-

The *Missouri Republican* **building was designed by Thomas Walsh and Edward Jungenfeld.** *Courtesy Missouri Historical Society.*

The McLean Tower was a heavy-handed example of Second Empire architecture. *Courtesy Missouri Historical Society.*

ing at the southeast corner of Third and Chestnut Streets to house his newspaper business and provide office space to rent to others.

Two previous locations of the newspaper had been destroyed by fire — the first in the great fire of 1849 and the second in 1870. Neither fire was set by an irate reader, but experience dictated that not only must the new building make an important statement, it needed to be fireproof.

Designed by Thomas Walsh and Edward Jungenfeld, the new *Missouri Republican* Building incorporated many of the specifications for the Third Street Post Office and Custom House. It had cast-iron facades on its two street sides in wedding cake layers, while the rest of it was faced with hydraulic-pressed brick. The building rose 125 feet to its extravagantly articulated mansard roof.

The main stairway was of iron, and the interior was finished in either black walnut or white ash. Hard pine floors were laid on top of fireproof cement. In addition, an iron tank containing 26,000 gallons of water was placed on the roof in case of an emergency,

This wood engraving from 1857 shows the B'nai El Synagogue. *Courtesy Missouri Historical Society.*

Museum of Fine Arts, forerunner to the Art Museum. *Courtesy Missouri Historical Society.*

and every floor was equipped with fire hoses. The *Missouri Republican* was swallowed by the *St. Louis Globe Democrat* in 1919 and the building was demolished thereafter.

Among the more prominent Second Empire buildings was the McLean Tower located at Fourth and Market Streets, directly across from the Old Courthouse, which it overwhelmed architecturally. Described by architectural historian Lawrence Lowic as "the most egregious display of brash individualism," the building was designed by James Stewart in collaboration with Edward Jungenfeld. It was financed by James McLean, patent medicine manufacturer, entrepreneur, and inventor. McLean was well-known for his antiwar sentiments and designed several machine guns, believing they were such terrible weapons that no one would ever go to war again. He was especially proud of his design of "The Annihilator," a machine gun that could fire 120 rounds per minute.

The McLean Tower had a pretentious, apparently uncoordinated and ungainly facade that included a plethora of statuary and intricate ornaments. In this case, more was considered best. Pretension and ornament did not guarantee a long life, and the McLean Tower was demolished. The Whipple Insurance Map of 1897 does not carry an identifying label for the McLean Tower at Fourth and Market Streets.

Whereas the majority of downtown St. Louis' important 19th-century buildings were built as monuments to commerce and government, the maturing city also had religious and cultural buildings that were notable.

The 1850s brought an era of extensive ecclesiastical construction. Variations of the Gothic and Romanesque styles were dominant, with Protestant congregations often favoring the Gothic Revival style. The new Church of the Messiah, built by the Unitarians in 1852, was located at the relatively tranquil intersection at Ninth and Olive Streets. It was designed by John Johnston in a simplified Gothic style reflecting a national trend espoused by leading ecclesiologists. Its exterior was brick with restrained

This old French Renaissance mantel was exhibited in the Museum of Fine Arts. *Courtesy Missouri Historical Society.*

Immanuel El.

The building took the form of a brick octagon and featured a dome with a cupola. Its castellations, Norman towers, and round-headed windows gave it the look of a small fortress. Contemporaries irreverently called it the "Coffee Grinder," but it was the first of several houses of worship to seek a creative image in remembrance of the traditions of the Jewish people.

Though St. Louis had its share of educated, cultured residents, there was no official museum until the Museum of Fine Arts was completed in 1881. Designed by Robert Peabody and John Stearns, the handsome stone building was located at Locust and Nineteenth Streets. The building also served as a school for the arts.

The Museum of Fine Arts was a very early example of the Italian Renaissance Revival style and was viewed by Lawrence Lowic as a precursor of McKim, Mead and White's design for the Boston Public Library, the acknowledged source of the Renaissance Revival style that swept the country.

The Museum was dedicated to Wayman Crow, a major financial benefactor, on May 10, 1881. It was greeted with great enthusiasm by patrons of the arts, students, and the local newspapers, especially the *Spectator*. Articles in that publication lavishly praised the polished wood finishes and the quality of the galleries with their high ceilings, their generous and wide spaces, and the light admitted by numerous large windows. The red tile roof and elegant stone work of the exterior were also praised. The windows were an important feature of the design. The facade was adorned with bas-relief busts of Raphael, Michelangelo, and Phidias, which were the work of sculptor Howard Kretschmar.

After the Louisiana Purchase Exposition of 1904, the City acquired Cass Gilbert's handsome building on Art Hill for use as an art museum. The original Museum of Fine Arts was demolished in 1906.

The concept of a renewed riverfront and down-

ornamentation with finials and buttresses. Its interior, which boasted a capacity of 1,200, was decorated with stained glass windows. It was demolished in June, 1895, and its site is the location of the Century/Syndicate Trust Building.

The newly formed Roman Catholic parishes of the era appeared to favor the Gothic also, though several were built in the Romanesque Revival style.

The decade's most unusual ecclesiastical building, whose exotic style was loosely connected with the Romanesque Revival, was St. Louis' first permanent Jewish synagogue. Located at Sixth and Cerre Streets, the synagogue served the B'nai-El congregation, which was the result of the merger of two of the city's early Jewish congregations — the B'nai Brith and the

The DeMenil Building. *Courtesy Missouri Historical Society.*

The Title Guaranty Building. *Courtesy Missouri Historical Society.*

town incorporating a "City Beautiful" mall dates from the turn of the century. Countless city planning documents have included variations on the theme, but none has won consensus — much less approval.

Designers wanted to clear an axis along Market Street which would provide an uninterrupted view to the Old Courthouse and the riverfront beyond, and Eero Saarinen's catenary arch was designed as a focal point of this amorphous axis. However, the economics of proposed plans have stymied their proponents, and critics have questioned the wisdom of creating vast stretches of empty space in a downtown already suffering from a dearth of people and an overabundance of surface parking lots.

The controversy over the Gateway Mall came to a head in 1982, when four alternative plans for the redevelopment of the four blocks bounded by Market, Chestnut, Sixth, and Tenth Streets were presented to the City. Three of them integrated historic structures into plans that called for new structures, open spaces, and renovations. The fourth mandated the demolition of four historic buildings including the Buder, International, Western Union, and Title Guaranty Buildings.

The Community Development Agency reported to the Mayor and the Board of Aldermen recommending the City pursue an "acceptable compromise" between the proposals. If no compromise was possible, CDA recommended a plan which preserved the historic buildings as the preferable alternative.

Those recommendations notwithstanding, three important downtown buildings — the DeMenil, the Title Guaranty, and the Buder — were demolished. It was an example of the effect that economic forces, real and alleged, powerful private real estate interests, and misguided notions of progress can have on historic structures.

An internationally recognized lineup of four buildings, the three that were demolished and the Wainwright Building, was described as "significant examples of St. Louis architecture and are the work of significant St. Louis architects....[They] comprise an incomparable commercial row, perhaps unique in our American architectural heritage."

The DeMenil Building, located at Seventh and Pine Streets, was completed in 1894. Designed by Isaac Taylor and Oscar Enders, it was built of Missouri red granite, brick, stone, and terra cotta. Its lobby and floors were of one-inch-thick white Italian marble.

In the mid-1970s, the building was scheduled for

The Buder Building. *Courtesy Missouri Historical Society.*

demolition to accommodate the conversion of the Wainwright Building to a state office complex.

An organization of preservationists, Citizens to Save the DeMenil Building, fought to save the structure, which had been described by one architect as forming "an integral, vital part of the Wainwright Building's historic and architectural context." The Missouri Board of Public Buildings was not convinced. The St. Louis Chapter of the American Institute of Architects turned down the resolution of its own Historic Preservation Committee that an appeal be made for a reconsideration of the DeMenil Building's fate. It was demolished in 1976.

In 1897, Eames and Young designed the Title Guaranty Building, built as the Lincoln Trust Building, in an "H" configuration. Located at Seventh and Chestnut Streets, it rose 12 1/2 stories, as tall as permitted by an 1897 ordinance. It was an integral part of the row that renowned architectural historian Vincent Scully said constituted "a major architectural achievement of St. Louis in present no less than historical terms....As a group, [they] form a truly overwhelming and irreplaceable work of civic art....Together, espe-

A frieze from the Title Guaranty Building. *Courtesy Landmarks Association.*

cially from the east, their group cannot be matched anywhere in the world. As an historian of American architecture, I count the wall they make among this country's major glories."

The Title Guaranty Building was destroyed, by implosion, in 1984. The event attracted large crowds and gleeful media attention, making it akin to a public hanging.

The dozens of terra cotta angels which adorned the frieze were removed before demolition, and one graces the cul-de-sac at West Pine Boulevard and Sarah Street.

The third casualty was the Buder Building, which was designed by W. A. Swasey and completed in 1902. Originally built as headquarters for the Missouri Pacific Railroad, it was named for one of its principal investors when the railroad moved out. Located at Seventh and Market Streets, it was the southern anchor of the row that Scully so greatly admired.

In an unsuccessful attempt to place the building on the National Register of Historic Places, the Landmarks Association of St. Louis described it as "the city's most significant example of a richly ornamented tall office building type in the Renaissance Revival style."

The Buder Building was truly a victim of one of the incarnations of the Gateway Mall plan, which prescribes an open mall and vista of the Arch. It was demolished in 1984 in the name of that plan, even though it was fully leased as promoters of the Mall Plan and the Gateway One development were urging its demise. The Gateway One building stands in place of the Buder and Title Guaranty Buildings.

In 1976, Buford Pickens, Professor Emeritus of Architecture at Washington University, wrote, "Once destroyed, the man-made environment — the fabric of our cities — cannot come back." The row of buildings that was admired nationwide is gone. Only the Wainwright Building survives. Ironically, it is the only one of the row that was not designed by a St. Louis architect.

The implosion of the Buder Building was considered a "media event" in 1984. *Courtesy Arteaga Studios.*

Chouteau's Pond:

Sylvan Scene to Railyards

A view of Chouteau's Pond, which covered 1,155 acres. *Courtesy Missouri Historical Society.*

The grand houses of the Central West End, Vandeventer Place, and Lucas Place are well known and have overshadowed their equals that once surrounded Chouteau's Pond, lining Chouteau Avenue, Gratiot Avenue, and neighboring streets. The denizens of these streets included Joshua Brant; St. Louis' twelfth mayor, James Barry; James Harrison; Dr. Joseph N. McDowell; and General John Charles Fremont. Many other prominent St. Louis figures lived there and built grand houses. Building began in this area, west of the city limits, when Chouteau's Pond was still a scenic location and continued after the pond was drained in 1851.

The early configuration of Chouteau's Pond was formed in 1765, when Joseph Taillon built a frame flour mill with one set of millstones and dammed La Petite Riviere to provide power.

Two years later, in 1767, Taillon's mill and the pond were bought by Pierre Laclede, who built a stone mill with two millstone sets, raised the dam, and enlarged the lake. Laclede asked for, and received, a 240 arpent (an arpent equaled .85 acre) land grant to accommodate the growing body of water.

In 1770, Laclede obtained the flour and meal concession for the Indian trade and assured the financial success of the mill. After Laclede's death, the mill, pond, and surrounding land were purchased by Auguste Chouteau, who built a still-larger mill and again raised the dam. All three mills stood near Ninth and Poplar Streets. Chouteau received a land grant of 1,120 arpents, and both land grants involving the mills were confirmed by the Board of Land Commissioners in 1810.

The pond, which grew each time the dam was elevated, was bounded roughly by Eighth Street on the east, Market Street on the north, Gratiot Avenue on the south, and Twenty-second Street on the west. A United States survey indicated that the Chouteau mill holding, including the pond, covered 1,155.5 acres.

Chouteau's Pond stretched from downtown to what is now the Central West End. *Courtesy Missouri Historical Society.*

Another survey by William H. Cozens, working as an assistant to civil engineer Colonel Rene Paul, describes the pond as serpentine in shape and extending from Rock Spring, located just north of present-day Clayton Avenue about 900 feet west of Vandeventer Avenue. Rock Spring was the source of La Petite Riviere, which became known as Mill Creek. "Pond" was a misnomer for this lake, which had an average width of 300 feet and spread even wider at its bends and near the dam. It reached to Eighth and Spruce Streets, Market Street between Ninth and Tenth Streets, and slightly beyond Eleventh and Spruce Streets, enveloping Ninth, Tenth, and Eleventh Streets, with intervening land, taking all of several city blocks and reaching 900 feet in width. At Market Street the lake was fed from a gully that brought it the waters of a second spring at Eighth and Market Streets and also carried surface water from as far north as Olive Street. A branch flowed north to Washington Park, site of today's City Hall.

Chouteau's Pond became a much-loved location for St. Louisans, and it was popular for boating, picnicking, swimming, and fishing. It was well stocked with bass, crappie, catfish, sunfish, silver shad, and buffalo. Its banks served as a campsite for colorful assemblages of Native Americans from the Upper Mississippi and the Far West who came to St. Louis to confer with General William Clark and call on their old friend, General William Harney.

In 1821, George Kennerly, Alexander St. Cyr, and others organized a boating club and built a boathouse near Chouteau's mill. Pyrotechnic displays were offered there on occasions such as the Fourth of July, and the famous Baptist minister John Berry Meachum performed immersion baptisms. The pond became even more popular for swimming after an ordinance prohibiting nude bathing in the Mississippi River was passed. Because Chouteau's Pond was viewed as a rural location, such activity was acceptable there.

A scant 13 years later the city had grown far enough westward to cause Auguste Chouteau's sons, Gabriel and Henri, to prohibit that innocent relief from the heat of St. Louis summer, saying that "citizens and strangers were in the habit of visiting the place and that decency requires that the rule be rigidly enforced." Gabriel Chouteau had taken over the operation of the mill after his father's death.

Born in 1805, Henri Chouteau was the third son of the city's founder, Auguste Chouteau. In 1827, he was appointed clerk of the county court, became recorder of St. Louis County, and married Clemence Coursault of Baltimore. They started a family that would grow to ten children, all of whom survived to adulthood.

In 1830, Chouteau chose to build his grand house on a high hill overlooking Chouteau's Pond, a site that is now the corner of Tucker Boulevard and Clark Street. In building his mansion in the Greek Revival style, he reinforced the trend among the leading families toward abandoning the traditional French architectural styles in favor of American forms. The main architectural feature of the Chouteau house was its prominent portico supported by four Ionic columns. There were a pair of double chimneys joined by parapets, a wide divided-band cornice, corner pilasters, straight lintels over the windows, and a front door surrounded by sidelights with a rectangular transom. It was comparable in size and style to the homes of the wealthy in eastern cities such as Boston and Philadelphia.

In 1842, Chouteau resigned his appointive offices to establish the mercantile firm of Chouteau and Riley, which soon changed to Chouteau and Valle. He became one of the leading coffee and sugar merchants in the Mississippi Valley, and it was his custom to spend his winters among the sugar planters in the South. He would often buy the entire output of a plantation and ship whole steamboat loads back to St. Louis. He was also one of the earliest exporters of local farm products and is said to have sent the first shipments to foreign markets from the Port of St. Louis.

In 1845, George Collier located his Collier White Lead Company on the shores of Chouteau's Pond. That industry was joined by a slaughterhouse, and the decline of the pond's environment was well under way. The industries and the public used Chouteau's Pond as an open sewer, and there were no zoning restrictions or other regulations to prevent dumping of noxious wastes or to mandate cleanup. The 1849 cholera epidemic that decimated St. Louis' population was thought by some to be caused by these conditions.

Dr. Joseph Nash McDowell, founder of the McDowell Medical College, was in the forefront of demands that the pond be drained for public health reasons. Public opinion won out, and the pond was drained in 1851-1852. The fact that the Mill Creek bed was an ideal site for much-needed rail and switching yards came to light later.

Henri Chouteau died in 1855 in the Gasconade River disaster when he was on the inaugural trip of the Missouri Pacific Railroad, celebrating the completion of the line as far as Jefferson City. Rainstorms had undermined the stability of the rail bridge over the Gasconade River and it collapsed when the loaded train crossed it. Some 30 passengers, including Chouteau, were killed.

The transformation of Chouteau's Pond from sylvan lake to railyard and other commercial uses made it an undesirable site for grand residential structures. After the Chouteau mansion was demolished, its site became that of the Four Courts Building.

Completed in 1871, the Four Courts Building was built to house St. Louis' four municipal courts, the Police Department, and the jail.

Orators at the dedication waxed eloquent. One called the Four Courts structure the "finest building ever erected for the administration of criminal jurisprudence in the United States." A scion of the founding family compared the building to the Louvre in Paris,

while Police Court Judge Cady said it was "the very image of the Four Courts in Dublin to remind us of the ould sod."

Published reports echoed these comparisons. It seems that the similarities were in the eyes of the beholders, depending on whether they were French or Irish.

Its architect, Thomas Walsh, said he had used some features of the Courts in Dublin, the Louvre, and buildings in other European capitals to create a grand structure in the Municipal Second Empire style.

The large buff limestone building extended the length of Clark Street from Eleventh Street to Tucker Boulevard. Three stories high, it was visible from most sections of the city, since it stood on a hill. It had much more visibility than the Old Courthouse, considered its only architectural rival.

The most prominent features of the Four Courts Building were its three high towers. The two at the east and west ends of the building featured elegant mansard roofs. The center tower was a quadrilateral dome crowned by a high cupola.

Henri Chouteau's house overlooked Chouteau's Pond. *Courtesy Missouri Historical Society.*

The Four Courts Building, which cost over $1 million, had a stone facade with tall arched windows, and its detailing was more picturesque than typical Municipal Second Empire structures. The central section, under the dome, was adorned with columns.

At the rear of the building, a huge amphitheater formed the jail, which could be reached only by passing through the main building. The jail section was constructed of iron and was considered to be as secure as man could make it.

The Four Courts Building also housed the morgue and the gallows, but newspapers of the day did not give a detailed description of either of these facilities.

It offered the Police Department a sumptuous home in the 1870s, when the city had 305 policemen and 34 officers. At that time, St. Louis had only five police districts, including the mounted patrol. At one point in the late 19th century, the city was so peaceful that the number of districts was reduced to four.

There were many famous trials at the Four Courts Building, since it was the region's center of justice. One trial in particular generated high interest among the citizens and the media, as it featured St. Louis' first gang murder. A gang member, Yellow Kid Mohrle, was gunned down in the doorway to one of the municipal courtrooms as he was about to give testimony about his comrades in crime.

Despite the grand oratory and superlatives that accompanied the dedication of the Four Courts Building, it stood for only 36 years. Its short life was influenced not by the minority of citizens who thought it was the "ugliest public building ever erected in St. Louis" but by structural problems that defied reasonable solutions.

In 1905, Building Commissioner James A. Smith announced that the three towers of "the old pile" would be removed and replaced with a flat roof because the old roof leaked badly and all attempts to repair it had been unsuccessful.

That major alteration — some said desecration — spelled the beginning of the end for the Four Courts Building. It was demolished in 1907.

Another, more notorious, institutional building, located at Ninth and Gratiot Streets, overlooked Chouteau's Pond. Built in 1847 to house the McDowell Medical College, the building was the site of ethical and social controversy, and it also served as a Civil War prison for captured Confederate soldiers.

The McDowell Medical College was founded in 1840 as the Medical Department of Kemper College with Dr. Joseph Nash McDowell as its head. The medical college was the first to be successfully established west of the Mississippi.

The Four Courts Building was built on the site of the Henri Chouteau mansion. *Courtesy Missouri Historical Society.*

McDowell's school remained aligned with Kemper College until 1847, when financial difficulties forced Kemper College to drop the program. It then became affiliated with the University of Missouri and remained so until 1857, when it became independent as the Missouri Medical School. McDowell remained a constant throughout.

Joseph McDowell, considered one of the finest physicians of his day, came from a distinguished medical family. His uncle, Ephraim McDowell, was known as the first doctor to successfully perform an ovariotomy.

Though Joseph McDowell was an excellent doctor and teacher, his personality traits gave him a reputation for having "an erratic temperament that approached insanity." Jealousy was said to be his foulest vice. When he became angry with Ephraim McDowell, he devoted great energy to doing all he could to denigrate his mentor's reputation. He was an ardent secessionist and believed that slavery was a proper institution. While well known for being generous in treating the poor, he was equally well known for his hatred of

immigrants and Roman Catholics. He would lecture on those subjects on street corners to any who would listen.

The Gratiot Street building was erected to McDowell's specifications. Its two large Greek Revival wings flanked a large octagonal tower — really a fortress — that was topped by an unusual ellipsoid around which six cannons could be placed to defend against any possible attack. The design of the tower was said to be modeled after McDowell's favorite stove, but photographs show what one architect called "a layman's attempt to marry a Bulfinch state house with Monticello."

The central column of the tower had niches which were intended to hold the remains of deceased McDowell family members in alcohol-filled copper vessels. More mundane elements of the building included a large dissecting room, a chemical hall, a laboratory, a lecture hall, a dispensary where the poor were treated free, a rooftop observatory, and offices for the teaching staff. The most remarkable room was an anatomical amphitheater that measured 75 feet in diameter and 52 feet high, featuring six Gothic windows and a 7-foot-deep Gothic cornice. McDowell also included a museum which contained specimens of 3,000 birds of America, minerals, fossils, and antiquities of North and South America. He charged a 25-cent admission to the museum, though clergy and medical men were admitted free. There were no living accommodations, and students were expected to live in neighboring boarding houses. McDowell invested $150,000 of his own money in the building, which was the largest in the United States devoted exclusively to the medical sciences.

McDowell attracted a strong faculty, including Dr. William Carr Lane, the first mayor of St. Louis. Students were required to complete two years of study, but compared to modern

The McDowell Medical College was the largest devoted to medical services in its day. *Courtesy Missouri Historical Society.*

medical students, they did not have to study much. It was possible to graduate without ever having cared for a patient. One of McDowell's famous students was the sculptor Harriet Hosmer, who met with him in his study each morning to review the day's anatomy lesson and examine specimens. Because she was a woman, she was not permitted to join the class. McDowell was best known as an anatomist and emphasized dissection as a critical learning tool, though the discipline was not required of students during the early years. It was this interest in dissection that brought notoriety to the institution and the building, as it was difficult for any medical school of the era to acquire cadavers — dissection was against the law. To obtain "material for medical study," McDowell was forced to introduce the not-so-gentle art of body snatching to St. Louis. He referred to his and his students' nocturnal forays to cemeteries as "resurrectionist activities."

Despite McDowell's semantic civilities, many citizens were horrified. The superstitious avoided going near McDowell's school and the Pope Medical College, while the more courageous could be stirred to mob action. Reports from a pair of young boys who had climbed the fence at the Pope Medical College to find a lost ball resulted in both colleges being mobbed. The disappearance of a German emigrant woman started still another riot at the McDowell College, as its head was known for his hatred of immigrants. The crowd assumed that McDowell had kidnapped and killed her for medical purposes. She was later found in Alton, Illinois, in a demented state.

McDowell dispersed one mob by turning his pet cinnamon bear loose among the crowd. It was an effective tactic; the mob scattered quickly, and the unharmed bear returned to its lair in the basement, where it lived until it died of natural causes. McDowell then had it stuffed and placed in his museum. He also kept muskets and cannons to secure his school from violence. One of the cannons was reputed to have been the bow piece on Jean LaFitte's pirate ship. In addition, McDowell wore breastplate armor, as he perceived he had political enemies.

Although McDowell was reared in the Calvinist tradition, he became a spiritualist as an adult and believed that his long-dead relatives communicated with him. He also behaved erratically about the deaths of his own children. He hated to think that they would return to dust after death, so he sought to solve the problem by buying a cave near Hannibal in the

hope that the cool air of the cave would help preserve the body of his 14-year-old daughter. It was rumored that he buried all but one of his children there in alcohol-filled containers shaped, as one eyewitness put it, like diploma cases, leaving the tower niches for other uses.

Mark Twain wrote in *Life on the Mississippi* that "there is an interesting cave a mile or two below Hannibal. In my time, the person who then owned it turned it into a mausoleum for his daughter, age 14. The body was put into a copper cylinder filled with alcohol and this was suspended in one of the dismal avenues of the cave."

As the Civil War drew closer to reality, McDowell took comfort in an arsenal, including 1,400 muskets in addition to his cannons and other arms, which he had assembled at the college with the intent of helping the Texans in their war with Mexico, capturing Northern California, or aiding the secessionist cause. McDowell had bought the muskets as government surplus for $2.50 each.

His son, Drake, joined the fighting ranks of Brigadier General Meriwether Jeff Thompson and took two cannons with him, and McDowell shipped the 1,400 muskets south in boxes labeled as polished marble. He, too, went south to serve the Confederacy as medical director of the trans-Mississippi Department. McDowell survived his war service and, after traveling and lecturing in Europe, returned to St. Louis.

In November 1861, General Henry Halleck replaced General John Charles Fremont as commander of the Union Army's Department of the West. He converted the medical school to a prison for Confederate prisoners of war.

Known as the Gratiot Street Prison, the facility was no better or worse than other prisons operated by both sides. Conditions were grim. Overcrowding, rampant disease, inadequate medical attention, short rations of food and water, and inhumane treatment were typical, and there were as many prison casualties as there were on the battlefield. The Gratiot Street Prison could accommodate 500 prisoners but held as many as 1,100 at various times.

Excerpts from the diary of one of the prisoners, Captain Griffin Frost of Quincy, Illinois, tell of bone-chilling cold — there were only two stoves for heat — and terrible food. Enlisted prisoners were fed but twice a day. "Breakfast consisted of one-fifth of a baker's loaf of bread, a small portion of bacon and a tin cup of stuff they called coffee," he wrote. "Dinner was the same amount of bread, a hunk of beef and a cup of water the beef was boiled in called soup — sometimes there were a couple of boiled potatoes. Many leave the table as hungry as when they went to it."

After the Civil War, the prison was disbanded and McDowell returned to reassemble his school. He rehabilitated the entire building but left one room as it had been in its prison days. He referred to it as "Hell," and in it he placed a rattlesnake, a crocodile, statues of Satan, and a gallows where Lincoln was hung in effigy.

After McDowell's death from pneumonia in 1868, the building stood vacant until it was demolished in 1882. McDowell was buried at Bellefontaine Cemetery as were the remains of his deceased children which were removed from the Hannibal cave.

Among the well-known families to choose

Chouteau Avenue as the location of their residences were Joshua Brant and his wife, Sarah Benton, a niece of one of the nation's most influential senators, Thomas Hart Benton.

Brant was engaged in the construction business and was one of the early contractors who had an influence on the architecture of the city. He also had large real estate holdings which were eventually subdivided and partitioned by noted surveyor Julius Pitzman. In 1858, the holdings were valued at $301,488. The lots on Main Street were valued at $750 per front foot, and the land on the levee was valued at $250 per front foot. Lots on Second Street were valued at $850 per front foot, and the lots on Washington Avenue carried the high value of $1,000 per front foot.

Brant was also one of the initial investors in the Pacific Railroad Company, along with James H. Lucas, John O'Fallon, Daniel Page, Thomas Allen, Edward

The Joshua Brant house, built in 1859, served as General John Fremont's headquarters in 1861. *Courtesy Missouri Historical Society.*

Walsh, George Collier, James Yeatman, and Wayman Crow.

The Brant house, located at Eighth Street and Chouteau Avenue, was described as "a veritable palace that dominated the street." Built in the late 1850s, the design is attributed to George I. Barnett. Its Italianate style was an early example of the more formal Renaissance Revival trend in St. Louis. Its rooms were numerous, large, and reportedly perfectly proportioned. The property surrounding the mansion stretched along the entire block from Eighth Street to Paul Street. It was the scene of many lavish and brilliant social occasions. Senator Benton was there often when he was in St. Louis, and his headstrong, beautiful daughter Jessie and her husband — explorer, Republican presidential candidate, and Civil War general — John Charles Fremont were often guests.

After Brant died in the late 1850s, his palace stood vacant for a brief time. In 1861, the Brant estate leased it to General Fremont, who used it as his residence and headquarters during the early part of the Civil War. The mansion was once again the scene of many glittering assemblages — though many of St. Louis' leading citizens did not attend, as they chose to avoid being in such intensely Union company. The government paid a rental fee of $500 per month — not an unreasonable amount for a house that could house the general and his sizable staff. But Fremont should have realized that the arrangement would cause talk of family graft, which would turn out to be among the least of his problems.

While Fremont was a well-known historic figure, he was a source of controversy — for his actions both in California and Mexico in 1848 and in Civil War St. Louis.

He was widely admired for his three expeditions to the Far West with the Army Topographical Survey, during which he established maps of Wyoming, Oregon, and parts of California. He also contributed to the scientific discoveries related to the West by retrieving botanical, biological, and geographical specimens from the Wind River Range in Wyoming, the Grand Basin, the Columbia River Valley, and the Oregon and California coasts. Kit Carson was Fremont's guide on those expeditions, and both men enjoyed a fine reputation for bravery and daring.

But Fremont's popularity was not universal and was undermined by his actions. He was court-martialed for ignoring the orders of General Stephen

Watts Kearny and was involved in subversive activities against Mexico. Fremont resigned his Army commission, even though his powerful father-in-law had persuaded President James Polk to restore it. He organized and garnered financing for a fourth expedition to the West to find and map railroad passes through the Sierra Nevada Mountains. When California became a free state in 1850, Fremont was elected to represent it. He and his wife returned to Washington, D.C., in triumph. He also became the Republican presidential candidate in 1856.

But it was his performance during the Civil War that earned him the most enemies in St. Louis and elsewhere. In 1861, President Abraham Lincoln appointed Fremont to replace General Nathaniel Lyon as commander of the Department of the West, bowing to the influence of Senator Francis P. Blair. Lyon was viewed as being too much of a hothead, and Blair perceived that Fremont would suit him and the Union cause well.

In his zeal to keep St. Louis firmly in the Union camp, Fremont imposed martial law in the city and later in the entire state. He tolerated the unauthorized seizure of private property by Union troops, suppressed some newspapers, searched private homes for contraband, and exacted fines from prominent Southern sympathizers. He even sent the wives of some Confederate sympathizers on a forced march into Confederate territory so that "they could cause no more trouble in St. Louis." It was a time when St. Louis and Missouri needed a commander with military and organizational skills, tact, and an understanding of byzantine political situations. Unfortunately, Fremont possessed none of these qualities.

Fremont's arrogance and heavy-handed tactics, including heavy fines for those carrying weapons, curfews on concert and dance halls, the requirement of an oath of loyalty to the Union for those leaving the city or the county, and the freeing of Hiram Reed — a slave belonging to Thomas Snead — were carried out before there were any laws to govern his actions. He won friends among the Germans and avid abolitionists, but nearly everyone else objected, including President Abraham Lincoln.

Fremont also proved to be inept as a field commander during the Civil War. He did, however, bring the emancipation question to the forefront as a war issue by freeing Reed. Although Lincoln eventually embraced many of the actions that Fremont took in St.

Louis, Fremont lost a great deal of support in Washington because he had jumped the gun on the president. On November 2, 1861, Fremont was served with an order from Lincoln removing him as commander of the Department of the West. His 100-day command was marked with extravagance, corruption on the part of his staff, arrogant displays by his Hungarian-led special guard of 300, and insubordination.

After the war, the Brant mansion was occupied by several tenants, including Thomas and Ann Russell Allen and a German newspaper editor. Sarah Brant chose to live in Baltimore and Lexington, Kentucky, with family members.

Toward the end of the 19th century, the wealthy residential location was beginning to decline — it remained fashionable for only 35 years. Forty years after it was established, a former resident lamented that the area was covered by railroad yards, mills, and factories.

The Brant mansion outlasted most of its counterparts. The prominent Cracker Castle lasted only until 1896, when it was destroyed in a cyclone, and many of the others were simply abandoned as their owners moved west. Though occupied, the Brant mansion deteriorated badly. The beneficiaries of the Brant estate — there were seven surviving children — were having trouble paying the taxes and other municipal expenses and made application to the circuit court in 1901 to sell it. The petition stated that the rental income was insufficient to maintain the house and that the location was no longer a residential area and was better suited to manufacturing. At the time, the mansion and its property were valued at $16,000.

The property and the house were sold at auction to the Holman Paper Box Company, and the mansion was used briefly as a warehouse. By 1904, it was razed and a factory building was erected on the site, which is now part of the Ralston Purina complex.

Of all the buildings and houses that have been lost to our generation, the so-called Cracker Castle was among the most flamboyant and well known.

Located at the corner of Chouteau Avenue and St. Ange Lane, the large brick house was built in 1868 by Jonathan O. Pierce, a cousin of Henry Clay Pierce, who later built a large mansion at No. 40 Vandeventer Place.

Jonathan Pierce was the active partner in Pierce, Dimmick and Company, a cracker-making concern located at Sixth and Pine Streets. The company did moderately well until the Civil War, when it prospered

The "flamboyant" Cracker Castle was a prominent and much-photographed landmark. *Courtesy Missouri Historical Society.*

wildly, having wangled a huge contract to sell hardtack to the Union Army.

The company and its principals made a fortune from having such a large customer and no competition, though some segments of St. Louis society did not approve of those who grew rich helping the Union cause.

Pierce, having abandoned his previous family mansion because it was in a section of town no longer considered fashionable, chose Chouteau Avenue as the location to build his new mansion and to spend some of his new-found fortune.

In those days, Chouteau Avenue was very fashionable and attracted some of the city's prominent social and financial leaders, including Madame Auguste Chouteau, William Glasgow, and Governor E. O. Stannard. Pierce chose to be in the center of things.

The huge house that Pierce built was described in 1870 as being of "undefinable architecture," though a modern architect describes it as "an elaborately detailed example of High Victorian Italianate with elements transitioning to the more Eclectic buildings to follow in the 1880s." Designed by C.P. Clarke, who had the reputation of being something of an iconoclast, the house reflected the individualism of its owner.

Two tall square towers dominated the structure. The larger of the pair had a deeply pitched slate roof with dormer windows on each of its four sides. The second was topped by a balustraded widow's walk. It also sported a gingerbread balcony at the second-floor level.

A first-floor porch, with elaborately carved and painted wooden arches, led to the entry, and the property was surrounded by a decorative fence. There were several different sizes and shapes of windows, intricate brickwork, and fantasies of Victorian wood trim designs wherever possible. There were deep, dominant cornices with large brackets at each roofline.

The Cracker Castle cost $115,000 to build, with its solid mahogany front door alone costing $2,500. It had so many rooms that guests could get lost in the various corridors and crannies.

During a wedding there, a young reporter named Walter Stevens became lost. Growing bored with the festivities and the task to which he was ill-suited, he wandered off to browse through books and paintings. He was found in a second-floor study later in the evening by a bridesmaid who led him back to the main hall — after she had given him enough notes to write his article.

The house became a major "sight to see" for visitors and natives alike, and it was much photographed.

Pierce received the attention he intended, but in the economic readjustment after the Civil War, which did not include a need for hardtack, he came to regret spending so much on his mansion.

He eventually sold it to a prominent lawyer, Fidelio Sharp, who lived there until his death. It was then sold to Major James Pearce.

Some years later, on an abnormally hot and breathless day — May 27, 1896 — a devastating tornado struck St. Louis, killing more than 600 and injuring more than 1,200 people. The storm, which did extensive damage to Tower Grove Park, partially destroyed City Hospital, the Poor House, and the Insane Asylum. It did major damage to a portion of Eads Bridge before skipping to Illinois, and it also reduced the Cracker Castle to shambles.

The damage was so severe that repair was impossible, and the remains had to be razed. The grand house of crackers and curiosity was gone. Only a few pillars of iron fence remained.

The site is now occupied by low-rise public housing units, and St. Ange Lane is part of a parking lot.

Midtown:

Mansions, Piety Hill
and the Mill Creek Valley

Interior of Pilgrim Congregational Church, one of the 42 churches destroyed during the clearance of the Mill Creek Valley. *Courtesy Missouri Historical Society.*

St. Louis' growth before and after the Civil War brought a spate of residential, commercial, and industrial growth to the Midtown section of St. Louis — an area roughly bounded by Grand Avenue on the west, Twentieth Street on the east, Easton Avenue (now Martin Luther King Drive) to the north, and the rail and switching yards that replaced Chouteau's Pond on the south.

The railroads, and the businesses that located in their proximity, brought greatly increased commerce to St. Louis, along with greatly increased industrial pollution. By the 1880s, the smoke generated by the concentration of railroad companies was identified as a problem that could be deleterious to real estate values, but the warning did not deter residential and commercial development on neighboring streets.

Chouteau Avenue, with its grand mansions, had been known as a fashionable address since the 1850s. Lucas Place was in full flower, and streets such as Garrison Avenue, Lawton Avenue, Washington and Lindell Boulevards, and Pine Street were prime locations for residential building.

As people selected Midtown addresses, the churches that had been well-established in downtown

Gen. William Tecumseh Sherman's house at 912 N. Garrison. *Courtesy Missouri Historical Society.*

St. Louis followed the westward trend to be near members of their congregations. In the 1850s, an area known as Piety Hill was developing in part of the Stoddard Addition. Roughly bounded by Beaumont and Compton Avenues, Chestnut Street, and Lucas Avenue, Piety Hill welcomed the congregations of St. John's Methodist Church at the corner of Locust Street and Ewing Avenue in 1868, the Second Baptist Church in 1872, Central Presbyterian Church, completed in 1876, and St. George's Episcopal Church in 1874.

Garrison Avenue had many grand houses, among them the Second Empire stone mansion at 709 Garrison Avenue occupied by Samuel Dodd. Dodd, a bachelor, was president of the Missouri Edison Company and, later, the Wagner Electric Company. When Dodd moved to Vandeventer Place in 1904, he donated his handsome Garrison Avenue house to the YWCA, which decided to use it as a segregated facility for black women. It was called the Phyllis Wheatley Branch in honor of the first widely recognized woman poet of African descent to live in the United States.

The Wheatley Branch operated on Garrison Avenue until 1941, when it moved to 2709 Locust Street. The facility on Garrison was demolished shortly thereafter, as its neighborhood was in decline.

Garrison Avenue's most famous resident was William Tecumseh Sherman, one of this nation's most renowned military figures.

After Sherman graduated from the United States Military Academy at West Point, he fought the Seminole Indians in Florida and then served as adjutant to General Persifor Frazier Smith in California. It was in the latter capacity that Sherman announced, to Washington and the world, the 1848 discovery of gold at Sutter's Mill.

In 1853, Sherman resigned his commission and went to work for James H. Lucas. He worked in California for Lucas, Turner and Company at their San Francisco office, then in New York and finally in St. Louis. He managed to leave California, in debt by $13,000, after the gold rush crash. In St. Louis, Sherman worked as manager and president of the St. Louis Railway, one of the city's eight streetcar lines.

But Sherman was inept as a businessman and struggled to make a living. He accepted a post as commandant of a new military academy in Alexandria, Louisiana. He loved the academic and military life but felt compelled to resign when it became clear that Louisiana would secede from the Union. Sherman returned to St. Louis with his family to again work for Lucas.

On May 10, 1861, war came to St. Louis with the Battle of Camp Jackson, which took place on the site of today's Frost Campus of St. Louis Univer-

The Samuel Dodd/YWCA mansion at 709 N. Garrison. *Courtesy Missouri Historical Society.*

sity. A large crowd of spectators watched that day, just as they would later that summer at the First Battle of Bull Run.

Francis Grierson described the scene: "Here all was forgotten save youthful vanity, impossible ambitions, flirtations, and life, as it looked at this fashionable rendezvous, was something worth living. The ladies came in hundreds with all the delicacies of the season. War, if there was to be a war, would be a splendid pageant, headed by a military band, and members of Company A, the Washington Guards, the Missouri Guards, the Laclede Guards, and others."

No one was taking the hostilities seriously at the beginning when General Nathaniel Lyon and his troops moved to capture a large arsenal from General Daniel Frost's Confederates, but 30 spectators were killed or wounded that day. Two of the onlookers — Sherman and U.S. Grant — were unharmed.

A few days later, Sherman received his orders and a commission as colonel in the Union infantry, and started on his road to fame as an architect of modern warfare and of the eventual destruction of the Confederacy.

He went with reluctance because of his genuine affection for the South, which was superseded by his loyalty to the Union. He also dreaded the inevitable carnage of untrained young men and bitterly denounced politicians for not understanding that "war is hell."

Sherman had a nervous breakdown after the Battle of Bull Run and returned briefly to St. Louis to recover. He was soon able to outline his battle strategies for friends at the Planter's House. Those plans eventually brought about the capture and burning of Atlanta and the march across Georgia to the sea that broke the Rebel backbone and led to the war's end.

Sherman returned to St. Louis as a hero to many. In 1866, the *Missouri Republican* printed copies of letters between Sherman and a group of citizens including I. L. Garrison, William McPherson, John Yore, John How, and Barton Able. The letters indicated that the group was giving Sherman $30,000 to buy a "St. Louis residence" and that the gift was in gratitude for his service. Sherman bought the house at 912 Garrison at Bell Avenue from David Nicholson.

The property had 84 front feet on Garrison Avenue. The Italianate brick house and its central tower were square and generous, if not palatial, in size. A broad veranda stretched across the facade, and the house had what was purported to be the first shuttered sunporch in the city.

Sherman's house had 11 large, high-ceilinged rooms, each with a wide fireplace. A parlor, dining room, kitchen, and library were on the first floor. At his desk in this library Sherman wrote his reply to a telegram urging him to run for the U.S. presidency in 1883. "I will not run if nominated," Sherman wrote, "and will not serve if elected."

Sherman had declined the suggestion before and would continue to do so, despite his gregarious and somewhat vain nature. His distrust of politics and most politicians was complete. He also wanted to stay in St. Louis, where he was much admired and where his Army salary went further to support his wife and six children than it would have gone elsewhere.

At the time, Sherman held the post of General of the United States Army and was the top military officer of the land. The Army Headquarters were at Tenth and Locust Streets, and Sherman performed many military and ceremonial duties, including dedicating the statue of his old friend Francis P. Blair in Forest Park.

Sherman was a military genius, but making and managing money were difficult for him. In 1885, he went to Washington, D.C., to solicit help from former President U.S. Grant to avoid having all his property confiscated. Through various connections, he was able to generate income as a paid speaker.

In 1887, Sherman left St. Louis to live in New York. One account has it that he moved because of a dispute over a utility bill, while another says he chose New York because one of his daughters and her family were there, a son was attending Yale University, and his wife wanted to be near her grandchildren. Sherman saw the move as necessary, but he kept the Garrison Avenue house.

Sherman died at 71 in 1891, and a military procession and funeral were held in St. Louis on February 21. One of the largest crowds ever to assemble in the city lined Grand Avenue and other streets along the procession route to see the flag-draped casket and dignitaries including Rutherford B. Hayes; Interior Secretary John W. Noble; various senators including the general's brother Thomas, an Ohio senator; cabinet members; and military brass.

Sherman was buried with full military honors in Calvary Cemetery beside his wife and one son. Another son, a Jesuit priest, said the last rites. A new

Church of the Messiah, Unitarian. *Courtesy Missouri Historical Society.*

ritual — the playing of "Taps" — was carried out. Its haunting melody had come out of the Civil War and was first used officially at the funeral of U.S. Grant. It became custom after Sherman's rites.

The Sherman house on Garrison remained in the possession of his surviving children until 1900, when they finally sold it. The house then changed hands several times and was owned for some years by Missouri Baptist Hospital, which used it as a nurses' residence.

Garrison Avenue declined as a prime residential area along with the rest of the Midtown neighborhood. In 1943, newspaper accounts said Sherman's house had been divided for multifamily use and made it clear that the units were substandard housing.

Today, the site of Sherman's house is part of the new Lucas Heights development — nothing of the

hero's house remains.

Garrison Avenue was also home to grand churches. The Central Presbyterian Church was located at the corner of Lucas and Garrison for many years, and the Unitarian congregation of the Church of the Messiah followed the tide west when it built its third church at 508 Garrison Avenue. Built in 1881 and designed by Boston's Peabody and Stearns, the stone Gothic Revival church was one of the finest of its era. Based on the English Gothic, or Perpendicular, style, it had a graceful stone spire and lancet windows and included an elegant hammer beam construction.

The nomadic Unitarians moved even farther west in 1907, and the Garrison Avenue church was used by several congregations. In 1981, the apostolic congregation of the First Cathedral Church owned the building and was planning to restore the stained glass windows, the deeply spalled sandstone trim of the facade, and the 142-foot steeple. There were also plans to repair the interior. Their hopes and plans were dashed, however, when the church was badly damaged by fire in the mid-1980s. The damage was too extensive to save the building, and it was razed in 1987.

Over the years, the site at the southwest corner of Jefferson Avenue and Washington Boulevard has been a prominent one. In St. Louis' early years it was part of the estate of Dr. William Beaumont, the famous physician who was the first to observe the action of gastric juices in the stomach.

In 1852, the property was sold to Joseph Uhrig, a brewer whose plant was on the site of Union Station. Uhrig used the property's underlying large cave to cool and age his product, as the chilly and constant temperatures were ideal for lagering his beer. Uhrig sought to increase sales by inviting customers to sip his product in the cave, which proved to be too cold for even the most enthusiastic imbibers.

Uhrig then followed the tradition of the Vauxhall Gardens, established in St. Louis in 1823, when he went above ground to introduce his beer garden and dance hall. He built an elaborate establishment where

he catered picnics and family parties and offered entertainment for young and old.

In the late 1860s, Uhrig sold his enterprises and cave to Chris Nuntz, who conceived the idea of turning the place into an al fresco opera house. Among other entertainments, Gilbert and Sullivan's *H.M.S. Pinafore* was performed for an appreciative and mellow audience.

In 1881, a saloon keeper named Tom McNeary leased the cave site and then bought it for $50,000 in 1884. McNeary rearranged the beer tables to provide seating for 1,600, hired the Spencer Opera Company, and gained worldwide fame as a sponsor of light opera. He added three separate music pavilions so that his customers could be entertained nonstop by relays of fine orchestras. Phalanxes of waiters served his cave-cooled beer, wine, and large platters laden with food. No detail was overlooked — there were "retiring women" to help the ladies with their wraps and groomsmen to attend the carriages of those who drove there to enjoy the music and fresh air. Uhrig's Cave was a bona fide success.

But there were those who were critical of Uhrig's Cave and saw it as a den of iniquity. J.J. Jennings wrote in his 1886 treatise, *Theatrical and Circus Life*, that "the masher finds ample field for the sport he indulges

Uhrig's Cave was one of the early St. Louis beer gardens. *Courtesy Missouri Historical Society.*

in. A girl in red tights created a great commotion among the swell mashers who frequented Uhrig's Cave....during the summer of 1881, and in that connection there could have been revelations that would carry grief into a few homes, and bring disgrace upon not young and irresponsible men, but upon prominent citizens who were foolish enough to be fascinated by the crimson symmetricals."

When Tom McNeary died in 1893, he left his estate, including the cave property, to his brothers, John and Frank. The Uhrig's Cave closed — one account says because the proprietor lost his liquor license. By 1900, the cave had retrogressed from arias and fashionable beer parties to mushroom growing.

The 1906 demolition of the Exposition and Music Hall prompted the Business Men's League to raise $345,000 through stock subscriptions and the issuance of bonds to lease land and build a new facility to attract conventions and large entertainment events. The St. Louis Coliseum Company was formed and acquired a 99-year lease on the southwest corner of Washington Boulevard and Jefferson Avenue from the McNeary estate. The lease was set at $11,500 per year.

The large brick and stone building, designed by Frederick C. Bonsack in an eclectic and monumental Renaissance style, was completed in 1908 at a cost of $450,000. It was the intention of its backers that the Coliseum would be to St. Louis what Madison Square Garden was to New York.

The Coliseum got off to a grand start when the famed evangelist Gypsy Smith was the first to book there with his revival meetings in 1909. Smith attracted capacity crowds of 10,000 for each meeting, with total attendance of 221,000. One of his basket collections yielded over $10,500.

There were horse shows and police circuses at the Coliseum. Billy Sunday implored his zealots to oppose iniquity in its auditorium, and many a proud and glittering Veiled Prophet Ball was held there. Helen Traubel, John McCormack, and Enrico Caruso sang to thrilled audiences; flower shows bloomed. During the 1925 Christmas season, Max Reinhart staged *The Miracle*, starring Lady Diana Manners, said to be a member of British royalty. It played to packed houses for four weeks.

Woodrow Wilson was renominated when the Coliseum hosted the 1916 Democratic convention; Billy Tilden played tennis there, and Johnny Weismueller performed in what was billed as the world's largest indoor swimming pool. Among the most popular events was the 1927 wrestling match between Joe Stecker and Ed "Strangler" Lewis. Every one of the 10,000 seats was sold for the two-out-of-three-fall match — ringside seats cost $25 — and the crowd got its money's worth of wrestling. The bout went on until the wee hours of the morning, with Lewis finally emerging as the victor.

Despite all the activities and events at the Coliseum, the building was never a financial success. As early as 1914, The St. Louis Coliseum Company was cited for back taxes of over $10,000, and it was behind in its rental payments. Ownership of the building reverted to the McNeary estate, which held it until 1925, when a New York syndicate bought and renovated it. The new owners installed a huge swimming pool — 197 feet long and 88 feet wide — modeled after the natatorium at Madison Square Garden. It could be covered by a moveable floor that was installed when arena space was needed.

The construction of the St. Louis Arena in 1929 and the Kiel Auditorium complex in 1934 drew many of the larger events away from the Coliseum, and changing tastes in entertainment did not favor the old building. Further, there was a lack of room for parking in an age when the automobile was in its ascendancy.

Kiel Auditorium and the Arena eventually drew many events away from the Coliseum. *Courtesy Missouri Historical Society.*

The last event held at the Coliseum was a wrestling match in 1939, when the building was showing its age and wear. During World War II it was used for storage of $250,000 worth of new automobiles "frozen" by the government.

In 1944, Samuel Melman of the Melman Fixture Company and his partner Edward K. Schwartz bought the Coliseum for "over $100,000." On January 29, 1953, City Building Commissioner A.H. Baum, Jr., condemned the building as unsafe. "The building will have to be torn down or cleaned up and repaired," Baum said. "If it remains standing, it will have to be made safe, which it isn't now."

Schwartz was quoted in the *St. Louis Post-Dispatch* on January 30, 1953, saying that he did not know whether the Coliseum would be razed or repaired. He said there were "several irons in the fire."

The Coliseum was demolished later in 1953, to the regret of those who remembered the grand spectacles there and to the relief of those too young to remember anything but a derelict building.

The corner then was used as the site of the Jefferson Bank and Trust Company, which is well-known as the scene of the seven-month-long demonstration organized by the Congress of Racial Equality (CORE) to force the hiring of four African-American clerical workers. The demonstrations ended on March 31, 1964, when the bank hired five black clerical workers.

The decline of the Midtown area began in the early 1900s. Despite the strong anchors provided by its plethora of churches and by St. Louis University, smoke and pollution took their tolls, and the ever-fickle, well-to-do population moved west to cleaner air and quieter environments.

There were the beginnings of discussions of comprehensive zoning codes for the St. Louis and several other U. S. cities at that time, and New York City was the first to embrace one. When zoning legislation was finally passed in St. Louis in 1918, the city became the second in the United States to have a comprehensive code.

The 1918 code reflected current usages and did nothing to help the residential areas of Midtown. It mandated five use categories, five building-height categories, and four area categories. The most restrictive, single-family residential use was assigned to relatively few areas in the city with high-value homes,

including the Central West End, North city and South St. Louis. The second use category, which permitted multifamily dwellings, hotels, churches, hospitals, clubs, and boarding houses, made up the bulk of residential zoning. The commercial-use category included retailers, wholesalers, studios, and fire and police stations. Much of the area adjacent to the Mill Creek Valley as far west as Grand Avenue was zoned for industrial uses which did not produce undue levels of smoke, gas, odors, or noise. The Mill Creek Valley, along the west belt of the Terminal Railroad, and the Mississippi Riverfront were locations where anything, no matter how obnoxious, was permitted.

Any chances that Midtown residential neighborhoods near the Mill Creek Valley could prosper or be sustained were obliterated by the new code. The area that contained 43 churches and hundreds of houses — many of them designed for civic leaders by famous architects — was headed into a slow, painful slide. Residents of the neighborhood's heyday included architect George I. Barnett, 2605 Lawton Avenue; banker William H.H. Pettus and his wife, Amelia Saugrain, 2834 Lawton Avenue; Missouri's first entomologist, Charles V. Riley, 2130 Clark Avenue; William Gregg, who built a 30-room house at 3019 West Pine; and *Missouri Republican* owner Col. John Knapp, at Pine and Leffingwell. The Right Reverend Charles F. Robertson, Bishop of the Episcopal Diocese of Missouri, lived at 2727 Lawton Avenue until his death in 1896, when the house was occupied by his successor, Bishop Daniel S. Tuttle and his family. In 1903, the diocese sold the house to a real estate company, as the neighborhood was no longer considered viable.

Edward Walsh, a prominent manufacturer, merchant and capitalist, lived in an elegant mansion at 2721 Pine Street. The Walsh house was built in 1858 for Robert Funkhouser, a pioneer merchandise broker and banker. Designed in the Greek Revival style, the facade featured four tall Corinthian columns made of brick that supported the two-story portico. The columns were set in wrought iron, and a railing of the same material surrounded the porch. Even the window ledges were said to be of wrought iron. Atop the slate roof were a widow's walk and four chimneys.

The interior decorations were considered the epitome of elegance. The parlor mantels, fashioned from Italian marble, were made to order for Funkhouser in Rome. All the interior paneling and embellishments were walnut, and the parlor and dining room ceilings were painted with elaborate frescoes.

Funkhouser had lived in the house for only a year when he sold it to Walsh, who moved his large family there from a small brick house in Walsh's Row, which he had developed. The only survivor of that Row is the Eugene Field House Museum.

During the Walshes' tenure, the house was the scene of many parties and receptions, and it was reported that Prince Albert Edward, later King Edward VII, was a guest there.

When Walsh died in 1866, he willed the mansion to his son, Julius, who occupied it until 1885. It was then leased to the University Club, which was forced to vacate its quarters in the Jaccard Building, whose owners had decided to raze it.

The club had receptions at the mansion and even invited ladies — a move which was considered "a great innovation upon the fundamental idea of a club designed for gentlemen."

The handsome grounds surrounding the house were planted with formal gardens, some of which were removed for construction of two tennis courts for members to play the fashionable new game that had become popular in St. Louis.

The University Club moved to the northwest corner of Grand and Washington in 1896, and the Walsh house was then occupied by the St. Louis Republican Club until 1909. It remained vacant until 1913, when it was bought by St. Elizabeth's Catholic Church for $20,000.

The Reverend John McGuire, pastor of St. Elizabeth's, was a strong civil rights advocate and planned to use the mansion as a settlement house and social center for his flock, who were being displaced from their former neighborhoods by industrial expansion.

In 1943, newspapers reported an unusual activity at the mansion. While the top floors were being utilized as the church's parsonage, auditorium, and other traditional uses, the basement was devoted to a chicken-raising venture! The modern plant established there produced a weekly average of 1,000 chickens, used to help feed the needy.

Even when it was the site of a chicken farm, the mansion retained a good portion of its elegance. The

The Walsh Mansion on West Pine Boulevard was once site of the University Club. *Courtesy Missouri Historical Society.*

frescoes were reported to be in good condition and the paneling remained beautiful. The formal gardens suffered, however.

The Walsh mansion was torn down in the 1950s — one more casualty of urban renewal.

By 1940, much of Midtown was considered a slum. Most of the residential properties had not been adequately maintained and were being used as substandard rental housing for the poorest of the poor in St. Louis. African-American sharecroppers who had left their homes in southeast Missouri, rural Mississippi, and eastern Arkansas because farm mechanization had displaced them, came to St. Louis. Some stayed because it was an intended destination, and others remained because they could not afford to reach Chicago or Detroit in search of jobs. Many settled near the Mill Creek Valley, where housing was cheap, if abominable. A 1954 survey by the Land Clearance for Redevelopment Authority defined conditions that were well-known — 99 percent of the residential buildings were in need of major repair, 80 percent were without private bath and toilet facilities, and 67 percent lacked running water. The infant mortality rate was twice that of the rest of the city, and outdoor toilets fouled the air.

In May 1955 city voters passed a $110 million bond issue for civic improvements which included the construction of three expressways: the Daniel Boone (U.S. 40/I-64), the Mark Twain (I-70), and the Ozark (I-55). The path of the new Daniel Boone Expressway rumbled straight through the Mill Creek Valley area, which was already slated for clearance.

In 1959 the Land Clearance for Redevelopment Authority (LCRA), headed by Charles Farris, began clearing "slum homes and ancient buildings" in the 454 acres between Lindell/Olive and Scott Avenues,

St. Paul's African Methodist Episcopal Church. *Courtesy Missouri Historical Society.*

Twentieth Street and Grand Avenue. A writer in the October 18, 1959, *St. Louis Post-Dispatch* reflected that the buildings represented in "all the pretty pictures" planned for Mill Creek Valley's future would not go, when their time came, as the Victorian homes and mansions were going — "Quietly, like a lady."

"The old mansions have dignity," he wrote, "because a lot of pride and ambition and love, highly personal stuff that isn't included in the specifications of modern apartment buildings, went into the mansions' construction. The old houses in Mill Creek, notably those north of Market Street, have the quality of an aged beauty who once had class as well as form. The outline of beauty is still there and, seen in the twilight, still rates a whistle."

According to Charles van Ravensway in one of his Director's Reports in the Missouri Historical Society *Bulletin*, no architectural survey of historic structures was done, except for a possible effort by the St. Louis Chapter of the American Institute of Architects to survey the churches. The poorest African-Americans in the city — 1,772 families and 610 individuals — were displaced and lost their neighborhood in what one NAACP official called a Negro Removal Project. Whether or not the NAACP official was correct in his judgement, assumptions concerning the social aspects of displacement were tragically misguided. A gradual relocation had been planned, but a tornado forced what amounted to an evacuation. Relocated Mill Creek residents strained other aging neighborhoods, and more blight was created.

In executing the Mill Creek Valley project, 42 of the 43 churches located within its boundaries, including the old St. John's Methodist Church, Cumberland Presbyterian Church, Central Presbyterian Church, Temple Israel/Union Memorial African Methodist Episcopal Church, and St. Paul's African Methodist Episcopal Church were demolished. The congregation of the Berea Presbyterian Church is the only one that did not move, as the St. Louis Presbytery's Board of Church Extension asked it to remain, remodel, and enlarge.

St. Paul's African Methodist Episcopal Church, a descendant of the African Methodist Church organized in 1841, moved to its 2800 Lawton address in 1890. At the time of its construction, it was said to be the only church in St. Louis built by and for an African-American congregation. The handsome example of the 19th-century Romanesque style was demolished in the early 1960s, and its site is part of the Laclede Town development which was built in high hopes of creating model housing for low- and moderate-income families. Today, much of Laclede Town is vacant and boarded against vandals.

One of the saddest casualties of the Mill Creek Valley project was the Temple Israel building located at Leffingwell Avenue and Pine Street. Designed by Grable and Weber in the Richardson Romanesque style with polychrome exterior of rough-cut stone, it was completed in 1888.

The Temple Israel congregation moved west in

Temple Israel appeared to be in good condition immediately before its demolition. *Courtesy Landmarks Association of St. Louis.*

Temple Israel interior. *Courtesy Landmarks Association of St. Louis.*

1907, and the Union Memorial African Methodist Episcopal congregation occupied the building from 1907 to 1959, when they were told to vacate. The interior and exterior were both in pristine condition when demolition commenced, according to Carolyn Toft, executive director of the Landmarks Association of St. Louis.

The scope of demolition in the Mill Creek Valley was astounding, according to Joel Cooley, who was superintendent of the St. Louis operations of the Arrow Wrecking Company of Detroit. "Ours was one of four wrecking companies working on the project," Cooley said. "As I remember, we took down 1,200 buildings, including some 20 to 25 churches. The houses were solidly built — some of the details like marble fireplaces gave an indication of how beautiful they must have been once.

"I'll never forget the miles of beautiful wrought-iron fencing that was removed," Cooley said. "There was no protest from anyone that I know of. It was a shame, there was never an area like it in Detroit or any other midwestern city I've seen except, maybe, Cincinnati."

Cooley also said that some of the Mill Creek Valley rubble was shipped to the riverfront to make truck ramps to facilitate the pouring of the footings for the Gateway Arch.

Salvage contracts were let by both the LCRA and demolition contractors. An amazing array of architectural artifacts and decorative hardware was available for use in new housing, restorations, bars, and restaurants. An odd sort of cottage industry developed, centered in Gaslight Square, to supply architects and renovators with authentic materials, but many of the treasures left St. Louis.

Why was the Mill Creek area allowed to deteriorate to the extent it did? Why was there no building-by-building architectural and condition survey as a step to saving the better buildings? Why didn't someone address the issues of substandard housing as they would in later years in other projects?

Social service agencies had not been developed to modern standards in the 1940s and 1950s, and the collective social conscience had not yet been educated into awareness. Deterioration was the result of a large

Cumberland Presbyterian Church represented a fine example of stone work. *Courtesy Missouri Historical Society.*

number of properties being owned by absentee land-lords who put as little money as possible into the buildings.

Architectural preservation, as an acceptable notion, was in its infancy, and architectural merit was rarely considered in the late 1950s and early 1960s. There was little consensus among architects visiting St. Louis for the 1960 Central States Conference about the Mill Creek project.

Some were distressed by the totality of the demolition, while others admired the vistas of downtown that were opened by the clearance. A 1964 *New York Times* article by Ada Louis Huxtable was titled "St. Louis Tears Itself Apart." In it she wrote, "While the architects discussed the forces that shape cities in their professional programs, they saw a city that has more shapeless, bulldozed open space and more ambitious and debatable plans for renewal than almost any other

in the country." No wonder the Mill Creek area had become known locally as "Hiroshima Flats."

Historic buildings were vulnerable at every level of urban renewal. Most developers of the era did not want to tackle the challenges of planning around existing buildings and were not accustomed to thinking of older and historic properties as ornamental or marketable. Redevelopers, along with funding agencies, had the last word in making decisions concerning large-scale projects. The interested party least likely to be consulted was the general public, which had a high stake in the quality of its community.

Initiatives in urban renewal were managed by the business and political leadership who seem to have had little interest in architecture and even less in public opinion, which was invited only when a tax proposal or bond issue was in the offing.

Mill Creek Valley as it appeared during wide-scale demolition. *Courtesy Missouri Historical Society.*

Mill Creek Valley showing the totality of the clearance and the early phase of Laclede Town construction.
Courtesy Missouri Historical Society.

South St. Louis:
The Soulards, Industry & Beer

The popular beer gardens of Joseph Schnaider were the scene of musical and operatic entertainments. *Courtesy Missouri Historical Society.*

The mid-19th century was a time of great scientific, artistic, and commercial achievements in the United States, and St. Louis was in the forefront. The city often ranked among the top five in the country in tobacco manufacturing, iron production, cotton processing, milling, and brewing, and much of this industry was concentrated in various sections of South St. Louis.

The small city of Carondelet, incorporated into St. Louis in 1870, was the important site of iron and steel industries. The Vulcan Iron Works, Garrison, Chouteau and Hart Iron Works, and others were located there in close proximity to the Iron Mountain Railroad, which brought the needed ore from the mineral-rich Ozark hills.

The early settlement of the Cherokee-Lemp area was scattered because of numerous sinkholes and caves that attracted the brewing industry, which used the caves to cool and store their products. There were also quarry sites and clay pits, extending west to Kingshighway, south of Manchester Avenue, which formed the basis of St. Louis' important brick manufacturing industry.

The Near South Side neighborhoods of Lafayette Square and LaSalle Park were rapidly developed after the 1840s and were home to bankers, brewers, lawyers, and doctors. The streets around Lafayette Park were among the earliest to develop with fine mansions and townhouses. They remain relatively intact, having survived years of urban blight, because of the efforts of individual home owners who appreciated the fine architecture, even in its deteriorated state, and took advantage of depressed housing prices of the 1960s to restore them and the neighborhood.

LaSalle Park benefited from the corporate responsibility of the Ralston Purina Company, an area anchor since 1894, which formed the LaSalle Park Redevelopment Corporation to help reclaim the 140-acre historic district.

The Soulard section of South St. Louis bears the name of a prominent early family who subdivided some of their land in 1836. Antoine Soulard, born in France in 1766, came to St. Louis in 1794, having served in the French Navy. He was the King's Surveyor of Spanish Upper Louisiana, and a man of considerable wealth.

Soulard had rapidly accumulated large land holdings, including 10,000 acres in St. Charles County, 5,000 acres in Jefferson County, and considerable acreage in St. Louis. In 1795, he married Julie Cerre, the youngest daughter of the prosperous Kaskaskia merchant Gabriel Cerre. The young couple moved to a Creole poteau-en-terre house that Soulard owned in City Block 29, between Main and Second Streets, and started their family of four children.

After Madame Soulard's mother died in 1800, she inherited her father's country estate and they moved there to live in the stone house that Cerre had built. After Antoine Soulard died in 1825, his widow and children continued to live there until 1836, when the large tract was subdivided. The house and its block were left intact, and the dwelling was rented to the Vauxhall Gardens, a restaurant and "amusement place."

In 1837, Julie Soulard built an elaborate house at the intersection of Ninth and Marion Streets on land that was part of her husband's estate. Soulard had been given the acreage by Spanish Governor Charles Dehault Delassus in payment for surveying services.

Madame Soulard eschewed the Colonial French architecture she had known all her life. Her new 20-room house was built of red brick in the American Colonial style that was fashionable in Eastern cities. It was 2 1/2 stories high with a full basement containing four rooms. Additional space was available in a back wing. There were carved stone lintels over the windows, stone retaining walls surrounded it and broad steps led to an elegant, simple entry.

Julie Soulard was generous with her children, her

church, and her city in giving them property, or selling it to them at bargain rates. Her second son, Henry, bought 667 acres near the confluence of the Missouri and Mississippi Rivers for $20 per acre and was the recipient of 3.65 acres at Hamtrack Street (now Tucker Boulevard) and Soulard Street (now Lafayette Avenue), where he built a house similar to his mother's in 1841.

In 1843, she gave Benjamin, her third son, her mansion at Ninth and Marion Streets, together with its full city block of land. Benjamin and his family moved into the house but remained only until February 1844, when he sold the house and land to St. Vincent's Church. In 1845, the St. Louis Seminary occupied the mansion, and St. Vincent's Church, built on the northeast corner of the Soulard property, was dedicated on November 5, 1845.

In 1864, the Soulard mansion was rented to Edward A. Chouteau. Later, the house was divided into two dwellings, each with its own entrance, to enhance the church's income.

The house and its remaining grounds were sold in 1949 by a St. Vincent's corporation, the Society of the Congregation of the Mission, to the State of Missouri for $6,600. The State bought it for a highway right-of-way. It was demolished in 1952, with no thought of rerouting the highway or moving the house to save one of the city's oldest historic buildings.

At the time of her death, Julie Soulard retained only 5,000 acres in Jefferson County — a small percentage of the vast land holdings she had inherited. In addition to the gifts to her children, she had given two city blocks to the City for use as a public market and donated another full city block, bounded by Ninth, Decatur, Carroll, and Eighth Streets, to Bishop Joseph Rosati to be used as the site for Holy Trinity Church. The church site turned out to be in an unfortunate path. When the walls of Holy Trinity Church were nearly completed, a Mass was said on the site in hopes of raising money to complete the structure. But a cyclone struck the partly built edifice and the walls were destroyed. Later, St. Vincent's Insane Asylum was built on the site, and it was destroyed in the great cyclone of 1896 that did extensive damage in South St. Louis. In 1898, the Hamilton-Brown Shoe Company erected a factory on the site.

Julia Soulard house represented the shift to American architecture by St. Louis' Creole families. *Courtesy Missouri Historical Society.*

James B. Eads' house, Compton Hill, was originally designed for Mayor James Thomas. *Courtesy Missouri Historical Society.*

The extensive industrial mix of South St. Louis attracted a rich diversity of residents who chose to live there because of the job opportunities. The Germans and Czechs were attracted by the breweries and the iron foundries, Italians came to work in the clay pits and brick yards, and many came from the South and outstate Missouri to work in the tobacco factories. Laborers, business owners, entrepreneurs, and intellectuals all found South St. Louis to their liking.

One resident who fit the entrepreneurial and intellectual mold was James Buchanan Eads, one of the city's, and the nation's, finest engineers. He was a major contributor to the Union victory in the Civil War and to the future prosperity of St. Louis. Chief engineer of the innovative bridge across the Mississippi which bears his name, he is also credited with keeping the mouth of the Mississippi at New Orleans open for ocean-going vessels.

Eads was born in Lawrenceville, Indiana, in 1820. He came from a solid family, and his cousin, James Buchanan, would later become president of the United States. Eads and his parents came to St. Louis when he

was 12. They were impoverished, having lost all their worldly goods in a fire on the steamboat that carried them here. He was forced to drop out of school to help support the family, and he sold newspapers and apples on street corners. Four years later he found a job as a clerk in a mercantile house, and at the age of 18, he became a clerk on a steamboat. He held that job for two years, learning about the Mississippi River, its snares, and its problems. In later years he would gain international fame with some of his solutions to those problems.

In 1842, he formed a partnership, borrowed money, and started a firm that salvaged sunken boats and cargo from the river bottom. He developed a fleet of small steamboats, equipped with air hoses and hoisting gear, and made diving bells that enabled him and his crew to search the bottom for potential treasures. He charged salvage fees that ranged from 20 to 75 percent of the value of the cargo to insurance companies and individuals, depending on the relative danger of the job. Any cargo he salvaged that had been in the river for five years or more was his.

In 1845 Eads left the salvage business as a rich man

and started the first glassware manufacturing company west of the Mississippi. The venture was not entirely successful, and he returned to the salvage business in time to re-establish his fortune by salvaging in the river after the devastating fire of 1849.

As the Civil War began in 1861, Eads was called to Washington, D.C., by his friend and fellow St. Louisan Edward Bates, who was serving his country as attorney general of the United States. It was the belief of the Lincoln administration that the creation of an inland navy consisting of ironclad gunboats was critical to the Union cause, to protecting St. Louis, and to controlling the western rivers. The job fell to Eads.

He set up his marine yard in the then-independent city of Carondelet and managed to produce eight steam-powered, heavily armored and armed gunboats in 100 days by modifying existing vessels. When the ironclad *St. Louis* was launched on October 12, 1861, it was the first ironclad vessel in service for any branch of the U.S. military, preceding both the John Ericsson-designed *Monitor* and the *Merrimack* (later named the *Virginia*). The *St. Louis* was renamed the *DeKalb* and was quickly followed by the *Carondelet, Cincinnati, Louisville, Mound City, Cairo, Pittsburgh,* and *Benton,* named after Senator Thomas Hart Benton. All served the Union effectively and were instrumental in the capture of Tennessee's Fort Henry and Fort Donelson,

opening the way to Bloody Shiloh.

The gunboats averaged 175 feet in length and had a beam width of 51 1/2 feet. The depth of the hold was less than 6 feet, enabling them to navigate on any part of the river. Eads' boats were credited with making the difference for the Union at the siege of Vicksburg, at New Orleans, and at Mobile.

After the war, Eads turned his attention to the problem of building a bridge across the Mississippi at St. Louis. The project encountered byzantine political problems, in addition to financial and engineering problems, and took seven years to complete.

Eads devised a way to sink the huge supporting caissons into the bedrock of the riverbed under great air pressure. He also faced a severe medical challenge when the workers suffered a mysterious and sometimes fatal reaction to working under deep water. Bends had not been identified as a hazard at that time. In all, 13 men died of the bends, 91 were seriously afflicted, and 100 more suffered in lesser degrees. Men worked for only a half hour underwater, with six-hour rest periods, for much of that phase of the bridge's construction.

After his bridge was completed, Eads went to New Orleans to solve the problem of keeping the mouth of the Mississippi open to navigation. Dredging had been tried, but the river would quickly become blocked again with silt. Other engineers of the day scoffed at Eads' plan to build jetties that would force the river to create its own deep channel to accommodate ocean-going vessels. Eads' plan worked and earned him $10 million in contracts to maintain the system.

Eads married twice — first to Martha Dillon, who bore two daughters before she died, and then to Eunice Sarah, with whom he had three daughters. He lived as a bachelor at 1514 Chouteau Avenue, where he later began raising his family. They later lived in a townhouse at Fifth and Myrtle Avenues, rented from Theodore Green.

The boatyards of James B. Eads were the site of the construction of eight Union gunboats and the caissons for the Eads bridge. *Courtesy Missouri Historical Society.*

But the house most associated with Eads was the Italian Renaissance mansion in the recently populated common-field area known as Prairie de Noyers. The address of the four-acre tract was listed as 1607-1617 Compton Avenue, and the road that wound past the northern boundary of the property was eventually named Eads Avenue. Eads called the estate Compton Hill, as it occupied one of the highest sites in the city.

The huge mansion, designed by George I. Barnett for Mayor James Thomas, sat in a parklike setting surrounded by large trees. A wide circular driveway covered with white gravel led to the welcoming coupled-column porch. There was a loggia on the east side, and many tall windows on both the east and west caught all the summer breezes and let in light.

Compton Hill was the scene of many parties, and Eads was considered a generous and excellent host. The only trial guests endured was listening to Eads recite the work of his favorite poet, Robert Burns, in Scots dialect. Although Eads was aloof in public and considered by some to be arrogant and vain, he was much loved by his friends. He was a good public speaker, especially when his subject was the wonders that science would bring in the future. Accounts of the day leave little doubt that Eads appreciated his own worth.

Eads left St. Louis in the mid-1880s for New York

to promote his most ambitious idea, building a ship railway across the Isthmus of Panama at Tehuantepec as an alternative to the rigors of digging a canal. His scheme involved lifting a ship from the sea, placing it on a flat car, taking it by rail across the Isthmus, and depositing it in the opposite sea.

But in 1887 Eads, whose health had never been robust, died of pneumonia in Nassau, the Bahamas, where he was vacationing.

That same year, Eads' Compton Hill was sold to the Sisterhood of the Good Shepherd to house their Episcopal School, which had been located in rented quarters at 1532 Washington Boulevard. The sisters paid $50,000 for the property, which was financed through the gift of a generous donor. The school had 80 pupils that year — 24 boarders and 56 day students.

The sisters added a 30 by 40-foot schoolroom to the west side of the house. The addition was connected to the main parlor and was partitioned from it with folding doors.

In 1893, the school was renamed Bishop Robertson Hall in an effort to avoid confusion with the Roman Catholic House of the Good Shepherd. The name change did not bring prosperity to the school, and in 1908 the sisters moved it to more modest quarters at 4244 Washington Avenue. The Eads property was sold for $37,500, an amount that

Compton Heights under construction, 1890, where mansion design followed the scale of the Thomas/Eads house. *Courtesy Missouri Historical Society.*

financed the new facility but did not solve the Sisters' debt problems.

The trail of the story of Compton Hill goes cold from the time the Sisters sold it until 1945, when the land was acquired by the City of St. Louis. The house had been demolished, probably in the 1920s, and its four-acre tract is now Robert Terry Park.

Another intellectual, surveyor and engineer Julius Pitzman, left a tangible legacy to St. Louis, as he firmly established the private place concept here. Born in Halberstadt, Germany, in 1837, he came to the United States with his mother and siblings after the German Revolution of 1848. Pitzman worked as a newspaperman and as a postmaster in Wisconsin before coming to St. Louis in 1854, at the age of 17, to visit his sister, who was married to deputy county surveyor Charles E. Salomon.

After a brief stint in the mercantile business, Pitzman worked for city surveyor Henry Kayser. In 1859, he established his own firm, Pitzman Surveyors Company, which still exists.

During the Civil War, Pitzman served as a topographical engineer in the Union Army under Generals Grant, Sherman, and Halleck. He prepared battlefield maps for Sherman for engagements ranging from Corinth, Mississippi, to Memphis, Tennessee. He also mapped the Battle at Vicksburg for General Grant. Only four days after 3,000 Union troops met their deaths in the battle at Shiloh, Pitzman drew a map that indicated all the strategic battery and troop positions. It was after completing the Shiloh map that he came down with typhoid fever and was temporarily unavailable for service.

During this period, Pitzman is also credited with designing a system of earthen forts, or redans, around St. Louis to protect the city from possible hostile incursion.

He was wounded during the Civil War, though accounts of his injuries vary. One source claims he was wounded four times, while another indicates he was wounded only twice. What is certain is that the wound he sustained in 1864 was serious enough to send him home until the war's end.

With his health improving, Pitzman turned his attention to business and his personal life. In 1867 he married Emma Tittman, with whom he had three children.

In 1870 Pitzman subdivided the substantial estate of Joshua Brant, which consisted of central business district property valued at $301,488. In the same year, he also subdivided Thomas Payne's large estate, and in 1871 he divided Hamilton Gamble's Rose Hill tract, which included the land between St. Charles Rock Road and Page Avenue west of Union Boulevard. In subdividing the estates of the Harney family, Andrew Christy, Robert Holmes, Peter Weisenacker, Captain Lewis Biddle, and others, Pitzman set the stage for the growth and development of St Louis and established the pattern of much of today's layout.

In 1872, with his success assured, Pitzman built a handsome mansion for his family at 1900 Compton Avenue near the estate of James B. Eads. The Second Empire-style stone house had two stories with a red tile mansard roof and a tower at the rear on the south side. A large front portico was supported by pillars and topped with a balustraded railing. The mansion faced Compton Avenue and was surrounded by large trees and gardens.

Around the time that Pitzman built his house, his wife Emma died. He later married Caroline Marsh Wislizenus, niece of Italian

Julius Pitzman house in Compton Heights. *Courtesy Missouri Historical Society.*

ambassador George March and daughter of famed physician Adolph Wislizenus, known to devoted Union troops as "Whistling Jesus."

They had four children, and many of their descendants still live in St. Louis.

Pitzman is best known for further developing the private place concept in St. Louis beyond that of Lucas Place. It was his thought that the best way to protect grand residential areas from deleterious outside influences was to sell the land subject to stringent, long-term zoning and deed restrictions. Governance was the function of a board of trustees elected by the residents, not the developer.

The first of Pitzman's private places was Vandeventer Place. Though not the first such development in St. Louis, it was the first to feature enclosed streets and gates to restrict traffic. That Vandeventer Place had the most stringent restrictions of any of its later counterparts did not save it from eventual destruction. It is the only one of Pitzman's well-known private places to meet that fate. In 1888, Pitzman planned Westmoreland and Portland Places in the Central West End, followed by Kingsbury Place, Washington Terrace, Cabanne Place, Flora Place, Compton Heights, and Tower Grove Place. His largest private place project was Parkview Place, which he laid out in 1906. It showcases his most interesting street design, a horseshoe within a horseshoe interspersed with pocket parks. It was a revolutionary concept at the time.

In addition, Pitzman worked on Tower Grove Park and on the St. Louis Country Club and grounds when they were located on Hanley Road.

Pitzman was also instrumental as a member of the team that created the first plan for Forest Park, which was dedicated in 1876. In 1874 Pitzman, in his role as County Surveyor, was ordered to survey the park land. In May, he delivered his report that Forest Park encompassed 1,371.75 acres, 46 of which already belonged to the county in the form of public roads.

In the summer of 1874, Pitzman toured the great parks of Europe. On his return, he began working with Forest Park Superintendent Maximilian G. Kern, Henry Flad, and draftsman Theodore C. Link to create a plan that was compatible with the park's natural rugged terrain. The roads were designed for pleasant carriage rides with ample vistas, congregating opportunities, and picnic areas.

In 1912, Pitzman built a new house for his family on Kingsbury Place, and the old house on Compton Avenue was demolished. Some of the furniture from the Compton Avenue house was moved to Kingsbury Place, as was a rose bush that was transplanted from the old garden to the new one. The rose bush still blooms — symbolic of Pitzman's legacy to the City of St. Louis.

Julius Pitzman died at his Central West End home in August 1923 at the age of 86.

Brewing has proved to be the most durable of St. Louis' industries, and much of its history is shared with South St. Louis. By 1810, there were several breweries in operation — Joseph Philipson's St. Louis Brewery, which he sold to John Mullanphy in 1921, is credited with being the first. Mullanphy stayed in the brewers' ranks for a relatively short time until 1829, when his plant was destroyed by arson.

The industry continued to grow as St. Louisans joined the German population in appreciating beer. Ellis Wainwright opened the Fulton Brewery in 1831, and was followed by James and William Finney, who opened the City Brewery on Cherry Street between Second and Third Streets in 1834. A year later, Isaac McHose and Ezra English opened their brewery at Wisconsin and Wyoming Streets, along with a subterranean beer garden, claimed to be the first in the city, where they served their famous and potent "Double X" ale. By 1840, city breweries could not keep up with the demand for their products.

In 1842, William Lemp revolutionized the city's brewing industry by introducing lager beer, a pleasant, clean, bottom-fermented brew that quickly won public acclaim. By 1850, lagerbier had captured the majority share of the local market and in 1854, local breweries produced 60,000 barrels of lager beer. The *Missouri Republican* estimated that 18 million glasses of beer were consumed in St. Louis between March 1 and September 17 that year, "when the lager beer gave out."

Among the successful mid-19th-century brewers was Joseph Maximilian Schnaider, a native of Zell am Hammersbach in the province of Baden, Germany, who came to St. Louis in 1854. Schnaider had mastered the brewer's art with "characteristic German thoroughness" through a three-year apprenticeship and service as foreman of a large brewery in Strasburg.

On arriving in St. Louis, he worked as foreman for the Philadelphia Brewery for two years, then he and a

The Joseph Schnaider house was described as basically Italianate in style. *Courtesy Merrill Glassgow.*

partner built the Green Tree Brewery on Second Street. Schnaider and his partner operated successfully there for seven years and then built a larger and better-equipped facility on Sidney Street. He sold his interest to his partner in 1865 to build a new brewery on Chouteau Avenue between Mississippi and Armstrong Streets, which included a beer garden. Schnaider's Garden was highly successful and enjoyed a reputation for "high-class music," good food and cheer, and family atmosphere. A large bandstand sheltered Saengerbunds, or singing societies, when they performed along with three alternating bands.

After the Civil War, Schnaider formed a light opera company to compete with the St. Louis Browns, as the team's successes attracted many of his customers and eroded his profits. The St. Louis Grand Orchestra and the Musical Union Symphony played at Schnaider's Garden as did the Saengerbunds and popular bands. Reporter Mike McGee wrote in the July 17, 1963, *Globe Democrat* that they were the basis of the founding of the St. Louis Symphony Orchestra.

In addition to his breweries, Schnaider made other investments and served as president of the Market Street Bank. While building his fortune, Schnaider also built a large family. He and his wife, Elizabeth Sedler, had seven children who survived infancy. Family letters indicate that as many as seven more babies died. In 1873, he built a large house at 1423 Hickory Street, where it intersected Dillon Street.

The interior was described in a newspaper article which reported on the presentation of a gold-headed cane to Schnaider by the board of directors of the Market Street Bank.

"....every apartment was gorgeously and magnificently furnished — mirrors, portraits, and fancy paintings adorned the walls; and, in a word, we doubt there is a more complete and convenient family residence in the city. The wine cellar which, perhaps, is unsurpassed, was next visited, where the new board of directors found samples of the very best of foreign wines, and they agreed unanimously to hold their monthly meetings in this place thereafter."

In 1879, the Market Street Bank closed as a casualty of the Panic of 1877, not, it is assumed, as a result of the wine-cellar meetings. Schnaider incorporated all his remaining business interests as the Joseph Schnaider Brewing Company so that they could be managed in the event of his absence or death.

Schnaider died young at the age of 49, in 1881 at Heidelberg, Germany, where he had gone to recover his health. His businesses continued until after the turn of the century. The Chouteau Avenue Brewery buildings and lagering cellars were demolished in 1960.

In 1860, the same year that Adolphus Busch came to St. Louis, there were more than 40 breweries operating in the city. Busch's innovations and energies would change that.

Adolphus Busch was a native of Germany, having been born in 1842 near Mainz, capital of the Rhine-Hesse province. His father was a man of means with a successful timber business and large land holdings.

Busch was educated at the Gymnasium of Mainz, the Academy of Darmstadt, and the Collegiate Institute of Brussels, in Belgium. He spoke, in addition to German, fluent English and French and was proficient in speaking Spanish and Italian.

He arrived in St. Louis shortly before the Civil War started and served in the Union Army for 14 months. In 1861, he married Lily Anheuser, daughter of Eberhard Anheuser, owner of the small Bavarian Brewery. It was a double wedding with the second happy couple being Lily's sister, Anna, and Adolphus' brother, Ulrich.

After his military service, Busch used his patrimony from his father's estate to establish a brewers' supply business, a successful enterprise that foreshadowed Busch's later business triumphs. He continued his supply business until 1866, when he bought a controlling interest in the Bavarian Brewery and formed a partnership with his father-in-law, Eberhard Anheuser.

He started to enlarge the small brewery from its 8,000-barrel-per-year capacity at an opportune time. The Civil War had ended and the country was ready to get on with commerce. Busch responded quickly to advances in science and technology when he pioneered the use of refrigerated railroad cars to capture a large share of the Southern market for his beer. Until that time, brewing had been a local, even neighborhood, industry, but Busch had found a way to open a national market for his product.

He introduced pasteurized, bottled beer in 1873 and, in 1876, began marketing Budweiser, a bottled beer of great clarity and taste. It quickly became one of the world's leading beers. He founded the Adolphus Busch Glass Company of St. Louis and Belleville, Illinois, and the Streator Glass Company of Streator, Illinois, and remained the chief stockholder in both to keep the cost advantage for his brewery. Busch's innovations were disastrous to the small breweries. By 1900, only 19 remained in the city. Brewing had changed from being a local, neighborhood business to one that could take advantage of the economies of scale offered by the larger market.

In addition, Busch was considered a marketing genius. Aside from being well-liked wherever he went in the world, he promoted his products constantly. He gave away trinkets — pocket pen-knives and the like — with his picture and the brewery name on them, but the most effective device was the distribution of 100,000 large prints of Cassily Adams's large painting "Custer's Last Fight" with "Anheuser-Busch Brewing

Adolphus Busch house, No. 1 Busch Place (top), with private stable (inset). *Courtesy Missouri Historical Society and the Anheuser-Busch companies.*

Association" spread across the bottom margin. The poster was not great art, but it was an eye-catching and effective display for thousands of bars, and patrons were hard-pressed to forget Anheuser-Busch.

Busch and his wife, Lily, moved into the large mansion Eberhard Anheuser built in the 1850s in 1866. The Anheusers did not feel the need for such a large house after their daughters were married, and it seemed appropriate to all concerned that the younger couple live there.

The 20-room mansion, known as No. 1 Busch Place, was located in a parklike setting on the brewery grounds, along with its private stable. The entire residential complex, including a smaller, 12-room mansion built later, was approached through white stone and wrought iron gates, similar to those seen at the entries of the grand private places.

Designed by Widmann, Walsh and Boisselier, its style was a celebration of Victorian style resulting from an adroit mix of Queen Anne, Renaissance and European detailing.

Adolphus and Lily Busch enlarged the Anheuser house when they took it over to make it more suitable for their entertainment needs. The spacious public rooms were designated by their color schemes — the Rose Room, the Green Room, and the Blue room were included.

The inlaid wood floors were covered with Aubusson rugs, and stained glass windows admitted filtered light. Incredibly ornate and massive chandeliers hung in every room, and furniture and art objects covered every available inch of space. The dining room was long and narrow with a bay window at one end. According to Alice Tilton, Busch's granddaughter, "...it had to be [large] to seat the House of Busch."

In the huge main salon, the frescoed ceiling featured plump young women in filmy red garments floating across it. The walls were covered with tapestries and the works of artists of note.

Busch was an important art collector and was said be one of the first to recognize the talent of American landscape artist William Keith. Anders L. Zorn's portrait of Busch was considered one of the artist's best works and was given to the St. Louis Art Museum. In addition to German artists, Busch had a keen interest in the work of American artists, including John Singer Sargent and James Abbott McNeill Whistler, which he collected exclusively after 1913.

The Busches dispensed lavish hospitality at their mansion. Everyone of note who visited St. Louis also visited the Busches — Enrico Caruso; Theodore Roosevelt; Lotte Lehmann; Edward, the Prince of Wales; and many others. They entertained local friends often, and Busch thought nothing of bringing 20 colleagues home for lunch on the days he did not go to Tony Faust's Restaurant. Lily Busch retained the German custom of afternoon coffee parties to bring a coterie of friends together to discuss children, politics, and books, and to exchange pleasantries.

Busch loved animals, especially horses, and extended his hospitality to the beasts, as he could not tolerate their standing outside shivering under a blanket. After discharging the passengers, horses and carriage were driven to the large rotunda in the carriage house. The horses were stabled, and the coachmen could relax in the recreation room, where plenty of food and Budweiser were on hand.

Busch maintained one of the finest stables of riding and carriage horses in the United States. The stable building, located across the driveway from the mansion, could house 30 horses in roomy box stalls. He also had a collection of carriages, including tally-ho coaches, barouches, landaus, shooting wagons, depot wagons, and phaetons. The sets of gold-and-silver-mounted harnesses were kept in glass cases placed around the walls. For all his interest in horse flesh, Busch had no inclination to own race horses.

In the early years of the 20th century, Busch acknowledged that the "horseless carriage" was no longer a jest. He commissioned a magnificent Pope-Toledo automobile with a specially built body of wicker with brass trunk fittings on its top. It was one of the first seen in St. Louis.

Busch also loved children and holidays. Each year during the first week of December, a brewery watchman dressed as St. Nicholas and visited the children, leaving their stockings filled with oranges (a rarity in those days), gingerbread Santa Clauses, and sweetmeats, to start the Christmas season. On Christmas Eve, a huge tree on a revolving stand was the center of activity. The tree was topped with a large, waxen angel and was covered with ornaments and candles, which required the presence of a guardian with a large pail of water when the tree was illuminated.

Easter brought more festivity when Busch decided to have an egg hunt for his and his neighbors' children. It proved to be a great success, and each ensuing year brought larger numbers of "neighbors' " children until, one year, the event was moved to Forest Park.

Eventually, Busch's son, August, Sr., became so skillful at handling the business affairs of the Anheuser-Busch Brewing Association that Adolphus and Lily Busch could indulge in his taste for travel. He built a rail spur from trackage at the brewery so that his private railroad car, the Adolphus, could virtually be brought to his back door. The car, reported to have cost $50,000, was a gift from Anheuser-Busch stockholders. He used the car to travel all over the country, as he owned two houses in Pasadena, California, and a house in Cooperstown, New York, and he entertained friends in distant cities, including in Texas, where he owned the controlling interest in the Lone Star Brewing Company of San Antonio, the American Brewing Association in Houston, The Galveston Brewing Company in Galveston, and the Texas Brewing Company in Fort Worth.

In 1911, Lily and Adolphus Busch celebrated their 50th wedding anniversary as only they could. Because they so loved their homelife, they wanted to make sure that each of their children had a suitable house. August Busch, Sr., and his wife received the Chateauesque mansion built on land that had been U.S. Grant's farm; Edmee Reisinger and her husband, Hugo, received a mansion at 993 Fifth Avenue in New York; Clara von Gontard was given a mansion in Berlin, Germany; Mrs. J.W. Loeb received a fine house near Lincoln Park in Chicago; and Mrs. Edward A. Scharrer was given a house in Stuttgart, Germany.

There was also a huge celebration in St. Louis to mark the event, though Adolphus and Lily Busch were not present to see it, as they were in Pasadena, California, where Busch was seriously ill.

The party took place at the Coliseum where, while a 50-piece band played, 6,000 employees of the brewery paraded, sang, and waved flags. Lights played on a center fountain as it spouted a 30-foot jet of water. Altogether, some 13,000 employees and friends celebrated and danced well into the night. It was reported that 40,000 bottles of beer were consumed, along with 100,000 sandwiches. A good time was had by all in attendance.

Adolphus Busch's health did not improve, and in 1913 he visited Villa Lily, their house overlooking the Rhine River in Germany. He hoped that the brisk autumn weather would restore his health. On October 10, at the age of 76, Busch collapsed with a heart attack and died peacefully a few hours later.

After Busch's death, his widow divided her time between Europe and her house in Pasadena, with only occasional stops at No. 1 Busch Place. After her death in 1928, it had been unused and their children had divided the furniture, objets d'art, and paintings. August A. Busch, Sr., announced in 1929 that the mansion and the nearby 12-room house would be demolished to make room for a switching yard and perhaps a factory building, the latter to produce one of the many nonalcoholic products initiated by the company during Prohibition.

North St. Louis:
Estates & Fairgrounds, Sport & True Enterprise

St. Leo's Catholic Church, 23rd and Mullanphy streets, was built in 1889. It was demolished in 1978. *Courtesy Landmarks Association of St. Louis.*

For many years in the early 19th century, the area now occupied by North St. Louis was rural, and several large farms were located there. James Kennerly was among those who appreciated the North St. Louis location, away from the rigors of the central city. He built a large, comfortable house — never referred to as a mansion — on land he and his family called Cote Plaquemine, or Persimmon Hill.

Kennerly, a native of Virginia, came to St. Louis to improve his fortune and to be near childhood friends and relatives from his native state. He married Dr. Antoine Saugrain's daughter, Eliza, and built his house in 1832 on a high elevation where Taylor and Kennerly Avenues cross today and where it could command fine views all around.

The house was of the type that a Virginia gentleman who had enough stone, timber, and labor would build. The stone was quarried on land owned by his brother-in-law, William Clark, timber was cut on Kennerly's land, and the labor was supplied by his slaves.

The main house had two stories — all stone, with a steep shingled roof. Single-story wings projected from two sides, with additional wings at the back of each side wing.

Persimmon Hill was approached through heavy stone gates flanked by a pair of enormous elm trees which stood as sentinels. A wide, well-graveled driveway led up a slight grade to the house. The main door was shielded by a large portico, and a visitor could reaffirm his arrival by lifting the heavy brass knocker cast in the shape of an American eagle.

The large rooms of the main house opened onto a wide hall, and the floor plan was ideal for the constant entertaining dictated by the Kennerlys' hospitality. The furniture required large rooms — the majority was heavy, dark mahogany and included black marble-topped tables and large mirrored consoles. It was of the style popularly referred to as New Orleans furni-ture, presumably because it was designed and crafted there.

Massive bronze chandeliers also came from New Orleans, and other furniture and decorations came to St. Louis from Philadelphia on a keelboat, as cross-country shipping would cause too much damage. The brass fireplace set and much of the silver came from the Kennerly homestead in Virginia.

James and Eliza Kennerly's son, William Clark Kennerly, spent a large portion of his life at Persimmon Hill. He and his cousin, Jefferson Kearney Clark, son of the famous explorer and his second wife, Harriet Kennerly Radford, shared their childhood years there as brothers after the deaths of Clark's parents.

The country life the boys knew was vividly described in Elizabeth Kennerly Russell's article "Persimmon Hill," in which she recorded her father's memories of 19th-century St. Louis. Since children of Persimmon Hill were educated by tutors until it was time for them to go away to college, there was plenty of time to enjoy the sylvan delights that are long past for North St. Louis.

They rode their ponies and horses all over the countryside and learned to swim in General Clark's old quarry. They became accomplished hunters amid teeming game. Quail, partridge, grouse, and dove were plentiful, and the farm's proximity to the Mississippi flyway meant that all manner of ducks and geese were also in abundance, and often graced the family table.

Game abounded — from rabbits to deer. Beavers and otters frolicked in the streams that crossed the property, and the two boys often trapped small animals and tried to keep them as pets.

There were plenty of domesticated pets on the place. The bird dogs were part of the family and were privileged to share the hearth. A few hound dogs, not a full pack, gave valuable service on raccoon, opossum, and rabbit hunts. A small sheep dog brought the milk cows from their pasture twice a day, and two small terriers controlled the rats in the stables.

There were extensive orchards with apple, peach, plum, and pear trees at Persimmon Hill, along with a grove of honey locusts that stood near the house. It was said that one could chart the path of westward settlers by the stands of locusts they had brought from the east and planted on their new land. The tall persimmon trees that gave the farm its name surrounded and shaded the slave cabins, and a fig tree, carefully sheltered in the winter, also gave fruit. A large flower, herb, and vegetable garden was not as formal as the popular Saugrain garden in the city.

For all its bucolic pleasures, life at Persimmon Hill was quite sophisticated. Music and books were supplemented by dances, dinners, and visitors, including Nathaniel Boone, who gave the Kennerlys a portrait of his famous father; Thomas Hart Benton; Henry Clay; and in 1837, Daniel Webster.

Clark Kennerly and Jeff Clark had many adventures as they grew up, including a western buffalo hunt with an English nobleman and searching for gold in California. They also served in both the Mexican War and the Civil War.

Clark Kennerly returned to Persimmon Hill at the age of 35 with his bride, Florence Brooks of Mobile, Alabama. But the farm and its environs were changing rapidly. More and more homes were being built, game had disappeared, and times had changed.

Kennerly and his wife seem to have remained at Persimmon Hill until 1870, when the directory still listed their address as "country." By 1871, they had an address in the city.

It is not clear when the house at Persimmon Hill was torn down. In 1948, Elizabeth Russell wrote that there was no vestige of the farm left. "For many years after city streets had cut through the orchards," she wrote, "the two old elm trees stood like sentries on guard against encroaching bricks and mortar."

The hill is still there, offering a good westerly view. The Ville historic neighborhood, the William Ittner-designed Sumner High School, which was renovated in 1991 and added to the National Historic Register in 1988, and Homer G. Phillips Hospital, designed by Albert A. Osburg and placed on the National Historic Register in 1982, occupy the land now.

The great Whig politician and statesman, Henry Clay of Kentucky, was a popular figure in St. Louis. He had played an important part in acquiring statehood for Missouri, had served as Speaker of the House in Washington, D.C., and had been the Whig candidate for president in 1844.

Clay made a protracted visit to St. Louis in 1847 and was royally welcomed by political, business, and social leaders. In addition to politics, Clay's main reason for visiting St. Louis was to sell a large piece of property, called Old Orchard Farm, that he owned six miles north of the city, overlooking the confluence of the Mississippi and Missouri Rivers. Clay speculated in Missouri land and hoped to turn a large profit on that farm and all the other property he owned here.

When Old Orchard Farm was offered for sale at the courthouse, a large crowd was present. But they came for a glimpse of the great statesman, not to bid. When it became clear that the 323-acre farm would not bring a high price, Clay bought it back for $128 per acre.

He was not particularly

The Henry Clay mansion was located on land that is now Calvary Cemetery. *Courtesy Missouri Historical Society.*

discouraged, as he had looked carefully at St. Louis' rapid growth and progress and had formed a better opinion of the city and the potential value of his land than he had previously entertained.

Shortly before 1849, Clay built a brick country house on the farm for his son, James B. Clay, and his daughter-in-law, Susanna. James Clay was a lawyer in Louisville, and his wife was considered a great Southern belle.

The younger Clays moved into the mansion in 1851. The new dwelling was an Italianate-style, red brick house that stood two stories high, with a central tower rising from the roof. Its bricks were handmade on site by brickmakers brought from Philadelphia for the job.

The house had a broad veranda across the front facade supported by brick pillars. A square tower rising above the roof allowed one to view miles of surrounding countryside.

A spacious entry hall divided the interior, and each corner of the hall had a niche in which a statue representing one of the four seasons was placed.

The features of the mansion considered most impressive were the bathroom and the heating plant. Both were rare conveniences in the country in those days.

In the bathroom, the tub was level with the floor. It had a hinged cover with a rope and pulleys attached to raise and lower the lid. The tub had to be filled and emptied with buckets — not an inconvenience for the Clays because they owned slaves.

The heating plant consisted of a furnace in the basement that supplied heat to each room through ducts leading to brass registers in the floor. To be on the safe side, each room also had a large fireplace.

The plantation-style kitchen held a large cooking range brought to St. Louis from Louisville.

Despite all the luxuries the Clay house offered, James and Susanna Clay lived there for less than a year. It seems that Susanna found the mansion and Old Orchard Farm too isolated and remote and St. Louis society too diverse; the comforts and grandeur of the house could not compensate for the social whirl she had left behind in Louisville.

There were some indications that the younger Clays were not universally admired in St. Louis. A little-known actor wrote in his diary that James Clay had "all the manners of a gentleman except that he swears. There is little hope that he will reform the habit as his father, it is said, indulges in the practice to all excess."

In 1853, Archbishop Peter Kenrick, acting on behalf of the archdiocese, bought the mansion and its 323 acres from Henry Clay and lived there for several years. He had an Irish coachman, Dennis O'Leary, who drove him back and forth on the six-mile trip between the Old Cathedral and Old Orchard Farm. It was a rigorous schedule, especially on winter mornings when the archbishop had to officiate at the 5 a.m. Mass, when it involved his leaving the farm at 3 a.m. It took some time, but the archbishop's physician finally persuaded him to move back to the city.

In 1857, Kenrick divided the farm into two equal parts. On the eastern half he established Calvary Cemetery. He held the western half, with the mansion, in reserve for cemetery expansion.

The Carmelite Sisters were the next residents of the Clay mansion, but they stayed there only until they could find more convenient quarters in the city. The mansion then became home to a family of truck farmers who tilled the farm's remaining acreage.

The house was next turned over to a brother and sister, who acted as caretakers while the brother worked at the cemetery.

In more recent years, certainly through the 1930s, the mansion was used by the Catholic Outing Home, an organization that provided vacations to underprivileged boys and girls during the summer. Caretakers lived there during the winter months.

Electricity and real plumbing were installed when the mansion became a recreational facility. A swimming pool was built, and playground equipment was installed nearby. The fine country home that was too remote for a Southern belle ended its days giving respite to city children. The Clay mansion was demolished in the 1940s when the second half of the farm was needed for cemetery expansion.

Nineteenth-century St. Louisan John O'Fallon left as much a mark on the city as any of his contemporaries. His name can be found on schools, streets, and a park, and with his many descendants.

O'Fallon's father, James, came to this country from Athlone, a small town in Central Ireland. Trained as a physician, the elder O'Fallon served as a surgeon in Washington's army during the Revolutionary War. After that war, he went to Louisville, Kentucky, where he met and married Frances Clark, sister of two important historical figures, George Rogers Clark and William Clark.

John O'Fallon was a product of that marriage. His father died when he was a small child, and he was reared by his mother and his uncle, William, in Kentucky. He served as an officer in the Western army in the War of 1812 and rose to the rank of captain.

He came to St. Louis after that war to join William Clark, who had settled here after his famous expedition. Clark was the official Indian Agent for most of the Western United States, and O'Fallon served for a while as his assistant.

O'Fallon later became a contractor, buying and selling supplies to the army. This was clearly a profitable venture, as he amassed a considerable fortune in a short time.

O'Fallon's first wife was Harriet Stokes, an Englishwoman who had come to the United States with her brother, William, who impressed St. Louisans with the fortune in gold he brought with him. After she died of a fever, he married Caroline Sheets of Maryland, whom William Clark had met on a steamboat bound for St. Louis. O'Fallon met his Caroline at the St. Louis riverfront when he went there to pick up Clark, and they were married shortly thereafter.

O'Fallon invested his new wealth wisely and profitably. He became president of the Branch Bank of the United States and invested heavily in railroads. He was one of the promoters of the Pacific Railroad, now the Missouri Pacific; of the Ohio and Mississippi Railroad, which became the Baltimore and Ohio Railroad; and the Northern Railroad, which became the Wabash. O'Fallon was the first president of each of these railroads.

He also made extensive real estate investments, the most successful of which were two large tracts north of the city.

One was a 90-acre tract in the Common Fields that extended from North Broadway Boulevard nearly to Jefferson Avenue. He subdivided the property into lots and called it the Union Addition, and gave two full blocks to Washington University. Then he, and the University, aggressively sold the lots to newcomers to the growing city at a tidy profit for both of them.

The second tract was nearly 600 acres and lay farther north on the road to Belle Fontaine. The hilly part of the tract lay west of the road, and it was there that O'Fallon built his elaborate summer estate.

He called his mansion and estate Athlone after the Irish town where his father had been born. The massive, pillared house stood on the highest of three hills, or mounds, overlooking the Mississippi River.

When the cellar of the house was dug, many

John J. O'Fallon's "Athlone" was among the grandest houses built in North St. Louis. *Courtesy Missouri Historical Society.*

artifacts and human remains were found. Scientists of the time opined that they were not Indian — that they predated the Indian cultures here. Sadly, none were kept, thoroughly investigated, or classified.

The mansion was huge, and its Greek Revival style belonged to the 1840s. The exterior was red brick and limestone. It required five people holding hands to encircle one of the massive pillars of the portico. Two carved greyhounds that sat on the porch — one dozing and one wakeful — were life-sized replicas of those on the O'Fallon crest.

The house had some 40 rooms and a front hall so large that two square dances could be danced at the same time.

The estate lands were also impressive. Extensive gardens surrounded the house, and large, diverse orchards produced all the fruit the large household could use. A nine-acre spring-fed lake was stocked with thousands of fish. On the shore was a boathouse flanked by a deer pen that was said to be one of the joys of O'Fallon's life.

O'Fallon also maintained a large city house in the manner that was prevalent with the very wealthy families of the day. His first was located "north of the City Land Office," on a piece of land that became Broadway between Locust and St. Charles Streets when the city expanded. When the city encroached, he moved to his second city home at 1125 Washington Avenue.

It was at this winter residence that he died in 1865.

O'Fallon left his Athlone and 75 acres, along with his winter house and stocks and bonds, to his widow. He left the remainder of his holdings to his children and grandchildren. Considerable bequests were left to Washington University, the Bishop of the Episcopal Church and O'Fallon Polytechnic Institute.

But none of his direct heirs liked the will. His widow elected to take a child's share in fee, and one of the children brought suit to contest the will.

A jury eventually found that "the paper was not the last will and testament of John J. O'Fallon, deceased." After the contested will was finally adjudicated, all the heirs, including grandchildren born as late as July 1, 1876, received generous amounts of land and securities.

During his lifetime, O'Fallon had given a great deal of money and support to several charities. Washington University and St. Louis University were recipients of large gifts, and the O'Fallon Polytechnic Institute,

which O'Fallon founded, received particularly generous amounts. He was continually open-handed with the Episcopal Church, of which he was a member, and he funded the building of the Methodist Church at Fourth Street and Washington Avenue, where his wife was a member.

He also established the Pope Clinic and Medical School in support of his son-in-law, Dr. Charles A. Pope.

In 1875, the lovely manor house at Athlone caught fire and was partially destroyed. Later that year, the entire estate was sold to the City for $250,000.

The section of land east of Bellefontaine Road was subdivided into numerous city blocks and sold at great profit to the City. The section still bears reference to O'Fallon and his family. One street is called Athlone, and several, such as Carrie, Clarence, and Algernon Avenues, are named for his children. Carter and Harris are named for two of his daughters-in-law, and Pope Avenue is named for his son-in-law.

The city kept the western portion of the estate where the mansion was located and established O'Fallon Park. The remains of the mansion stood there until the 1890s.

The park commissioner's report of 1892 refers to the fire and recommends the destruction of the mansion, as it would cost too much to repair it and the City received no revenue from it. His report was heeded and the mansion was soon demolished.

In 1855, a group of young men, headed by Richard "Missouri Dick" Barrett and including Norman Coleman, who would become the nation's first Secretary of Agriculture, formed the St. Louis Agricultural and Mechanical Association. Articles of Incorporation were drawn and approved by the Missouri Legislature on December 7, 1855. The Association's purpose was to promote St. Louis industries and farmers through organization of an annual industrial and agricultural fair in St. Louis.

The Association bought 50 acres of prime land near Grand Avenue and the Natural Bridge Plank Road from Colonel John O'Fallon for $50,000. O'Fallon was said to be fair and generous concerning terms of payment. The money was raised through membership fees and public subscription. Investors were told there would be no dividends, that any profits would be used to improve succeeding fairs and to increase awards to winners of various contests. The

The fair's gallinarium, or "Chicken Palace" was a Victorian whimsy. *Courtesy Missouri Historical Society.*

needlework, and household products. Stalls and pens for livestock were built, and a fund of $10,000 was set up for premiums.

The first fair was held for a week, starting on October 13, 1856. It was a grand success, with receipts totaling over $25,000, despite bad weather. From its beginning the Fair attracted cattle breeders, show horse owners, and farmers from all over the Midwest and Midsouth. It also attracted hoards of the general public, including bishops and gamblers, matrons and pickpockets. While many of the activities embraced "every variety of interest in the mazy circle of civilization," the sideshows that gathered outside the gates were sleazy, with raucous barkers crying out the wonders of the Belgian Giant, Fat Lady, sword swallower, and other carnival attractions.

The weeklong event, held annually from 1856 to 1902 except for a Civil War hiatus, was the most successful promotion of St. Louis in the city's history. It grew each year — in 1857, the board added a permanent floral hall, a fine arts hall, and a three-story wire gallinarium, the "Chicken Palace," which had 90 compartments for displaying fowl. They also built a Ladies' Cottage, where two maids were in constant attendance.

By 1858, horse-drawn streetcars had been introduced to St. Louis, allowing fairgoers to travel easily and economically to the elaborate main entrance to the grounds that had been designed by Thomas Walsh.

only reward for investors was free entry to the fair.

The initial group of trustees did a remarkable job in creating a usable fairgrounds in less than a year. The property was enclosed with a substantial nine-foot-high wooden fence, and a reservoir was built to supply water for eight fountains, a fish pond, and watering troughs for cattle and horses. The naturally wooded grounds were landscaped. In the center, they built an amphitheater, then the largest in the United States, with two tiers of seating to accommodate 12,000 and standing room for an additional 24,000 people. Under the promenade, there were booths for 81 vendors of refreshments, a press room, and accommodations for the directors and their guests. A three-story pagoda was in the center of the arena for the use of judges, musicians, and dignitaries.

Adjacent to the amphitheater they built two large, wooden halls for machinery and mechanical exhibitions and erected a huge, circular tent to shelter displays of flowers, farm produce,

The Fairgrounds Amphitheater was the scene of horse shows, trotting races and cattle judging competitions. *Courtesy Missouri Historical Society.*

In the spring of 1860, the fairgrounds were made available — during nonfair times — to civic and charitable organizations for picnic parties. The organizations could rent the grounds for a day at a time. The popular program brought in additional revenue to the Association.

The first week of July, 1860, the grounds were given over to the Missouri Volunteer Militia — a group led by General Daniel M. Frost which supported the Confederate cause. They conducted a cheerful and sociable practice encampment, even though the reality of civil war was looming.

On July 9, 1860, The *St. Louis Republic* carried the historic announcement that the first regular game of baseball in the city would be played at 4 p.m. at the Fair Grounds. The players were members of the Cyclone and Morning Star baseball clubs, and the game was played according to the rules set out by the National Convention of Baseball Players. Apparently, no newspaper carried the results of the game, which was the beginning of St. Louis' love affair with baseball.

Fair organizers had established the custom of "Big Thursday" during the week of the Fair as a special occasion and official holiday. Schools and businesses were closed so that everyone could attend the fair, and family outings were encouraged. They traditionally staged an extra-special event for the day. As the summer of 1860 had been very dry, farm exhibits were not up to the usual standard and the board was anxious to provide a particularly unusual event. Knowing that Edward, the Prince of Wales, would be on an American tour, they invited him to visit the Fair, and he accepted. Few, if any, St. Louisans had ever seen or met a member of the British royal family, and a enthusiastic crowd of over 100,000 greeted the prince. No one cared that the agricultural produce exhibits were sub-par or that the finest art in the vicinity had been loaned for display in the recently completed Hall of Fine Arts.

The Agricultural and Mechanical Fairs were temporarily discontinued during the Civil War. The fairgrounds and some additional land became Benton Barracks, a training camp for Union soldiers established by General John Charles Fremont. Barracks were built as housing, and fair buildings were converted for use as a hospital and other needed facilities.

The Fairs were re-instituted in October 1866. In

The Carnivora House. *Courtesy Missouri Historical Society.*

The Fairgrounds' "House of Public Comfort,"or bathroom offered many more amenities than its modern counterpart. *Courtesy Missouri Historical Society.*

1870, the amphitheater was rebuilt and enlarged to a diameter of 450 feet. In 1876, a new Mechanical Hall was built, along with a new Floral Hall.   Zoological Gardens were established the same year, and they included bear pits located near a small, scenic lake, the exotic Carnivora house for lions, leopards, and tigers, and a house for primates — all modeled after the finest displays in Europe.   The Aviary displayed black, grey, and bald eagles, cockatoos, macaws, parrots, and African condors.

In 1877, a group of prominent businessmen established the St. Louis Jockey Club and built a first-class race track and clubhouse on 63 acres that had been added to the Fairgrounds. The facility was said to be among the finest in the country, outstripping those at Florida's Hialeah Racecourse, Saratoga at Saratoga Springs in New York, and Churchill Downs in Louisville, Kentucky. The latter had been founded, along with the Kentucky Derby, by St. Louisan Meriwether Lewis Clark, who grew up near the private Lucas track at Normandy.

The Jockey Club had an exclusive membership of leading citizens, headed at various times by Rolla Wells, C.C. Maffitt, Charles Green, Edward Martin, J.D. Lucas, Charles Clark, and L.M. Rumsey. Membership in the St. Louis Jockey Club was limited to 300 and included the city's elite — one writer compared the roster to Mrs. Astor's "list of 400" in New York. The annual fee of $50 included admission to the fair.

The clubhouse, which cost $50,000 to build, was a fine example of Victorian architecture with its three stories, high-peaked slate roof, gable, hipped, and eyebrow dormers, towers, cupola, and observation decks overlooking the track so that members could avoid the crowds in the adjacent grandstand. Interior appointments were all first quality and included a tenpin bowling alley and a billiard room in addition to the usual clubrooms. The elaborate interior decorations included paneled walls and ceilings, arched doorways, ornate columns flanking the large parlor fireplace, and Oriental rugs. Urns sat in a plethora of wall niches, and the windows were inset with jewel-like stained glass.

The adjacent grandstand, overlooking the one-mile

The Jockey Club played host to many of the nation's finest thoroughbred horses. *Courtesy Missouri Historical Society.*

track, seated 15,000. Its elegant design featured wrought-iron railings on all three levels that culminated in arches at the roofline. The paddock area in front of the grandstand was also delineated by a wrought-iron railing to set off the three-tiered judges stand, which was shaded by striped awnings. The infield had gazebos and gardens. The festive scene was further enhanced in 1886, when elephants were used to pull the sledges that smoothed the track after each race.

The St. Louis Jockey Club became the hub of the southwest circuit after 1885 and was comparable to the more established Eastern tracks. There were five races to each day's program with six to ten horses entered in each race. Purses usually ranged from $200 to $2,000, with larger purses offered for very special events.

The National Derby of 1886 was run at the St. Louis track, having been transferred from the Hawthorne track in Chicago. Entries included Ben Brush and Ben Elder; two of the best horses from the East; Prince Leif from Kentucky; Ramiro and Argentina from the Pacific Coast; Don Carillo, owned by Barney Schreiber of St. Louis; and Pat Dunn from

Chicago. Prince Leif was the winner by a short nose. St. Louisan Barney Schreiber was disappointed that day, but in 1902, his entry, Otis — a horse "of uncertain background," won the St. Louis Derby.

After 1890, horse racing as "the sport of kings" was waning. It became a vehicle for betting, and many small, inferior tracks, called jerichos, were established. When Joseph A. Folk ran for Governor of Missouri in 1904, the abolition of betting, and therefore horse racing, was his major campaign issue. In 1905, the Missouri House of Representatives voted overwhelmingly to abolish pari-mutuel wagering and the Senate passed the same bill by one vote. The Jockey Club track was closed, and the clubhouse and grandstand were demolished.

The Jockey Club activities had a strong influence on the future of the Agricultural and Mechanical Fair, as did the establishment of the Veiled Prophet celebrations in 1878, which were added to the events of fair week. But those who came for the excitement of the VP parade, the social prestige of the ball, and the thrill of betting on the ponies did not generate the same commerce that the farmers, housewives, mechanics, and industrialists of earlier days did. Crowds went to the races rather than purchase a new stove, washing machine, or thresher.

A movement started among civic leaders and businessmen to build an exhibition hall in town where the latest inventions, machinery, and manufactured products could be displayed. Funds were raised by public subscription, and the St. Louis Exposition and Music Hall was completed in 1884.

Fairs continued at the Fairgrounds, but the competitions for young people — forerunners of science fairs and 4H clubs — were dropped. The animals that remained in the Zoological Gardens were moved to Forest Park. Membership in the Jockey Club, once prized, became less attractive as big-time betting became the watchword.

Fair organizers did what they could to continue the tradition. The special "Big Thursday" event in 1892 was a balloon ascension. The following year, the grounds were wired for electricity, and fairs were held at night, weather permitting. A theater and a summer garden were added, to make a total area of 143 acres. The final Agricultural and Mechanical Fair in 1902

featured the first automobile races in St. Louis, when Harry S. Turner won the first race and B. G. Sykes took the second at the sizzling pace of 38 miles per hour.

In 1902, St. Louis was preparing for the Louisiana Purchase Exposition and all attention and energies were directed to that project. The racetrack closed in 1905, and in 1908, the 143-acre fairgrounds were sold to the city. The following year, after all the buildings except the bear pits were demolished, the site officially became Fairgrounds Park.

Of all the historic structures that have been demolished, Sportsman's Park evokes the most nostalgia among many of today's St. Louisans. Located for a century at Dodier Street and Grand Avenue, it embodied all that baseball meant to its fans when baseball was still a game, not big business; when it was a summertime way of life, with fans' schedules arranged around radio broadcasts and home games.

Fans had plenty of contact with the players, all of whom had to pass through a corridor to get to the clubhouses. The corridor was also open to the fans for many years; young boys could reach out to touch their

The Jockey Club race track closed in 1905. *Courtesy Missouri Historical Society.*

favorite heroes, and fans could get autographs on the specially designed popcorn boxes that had a space for treasured signatures and folded into megaphones.

In 1866, when the park was known as the Grand Avenue Grounds, local teams such as the Empires and the Morning Stars played games that often yielded scores similar to those of football. The park was surrounded by a board fence and, in addition to a rough baseball diamond, had shooting grounds for a local gun club.

The city's first professional team arrived in 1875, when the Browns, named for the color of their high stockings, came to Grand and Dodier. The team soon folded, but a young entrepreneur, Chris Van der Ahe, recognized the potential importance of the game to local commerce. He owned a grocery store combined with a saloon, located a block south of the baseball park, and noticed a marked drop in sales when the Browns failed.

Van der Ahe quickly joined with Al Spink, a sportswriter, to form the Sportsman's Club and reincarnate the Browns. He improved the park by tearing down the old grandstand and installing double-decked, covered seats behind home plate. He left the seats along the first and third baselines uncovered to keep the customers thirsty on warm summer days. Spink, who later founded *The Sporting News,* named the facility Sportsman's Park.

In 1892, the Browns joined the National League and abandoned Sportsman's Park for a new ball park that had been developed at Vandeventer Avenue and Natural Bridge Road.

Van der Ahe suffered financial reverses, and the team fell into the hands of Frank Robison, who owned the Cleveland team. Robison brought some of the best players from the Cleveland Spiders to St. Louis and sent some of the worst Browns' players to Cleveland. He changed the uniforms by making the stockings bright red, not brown, and sportswriter Willie McHale renamed the team the Cardinals.

Ten years later, in 1902, professional baseball returned to Sportsman's Park when Robert L. Hedges formed an American League franchise and resurrected the Browns' name. In 1909, Hedges increased the park's capacity to 18,000 by building the first concrete stands and a second deck. It was the beginning of a series of piecemeal improvements to accommodate growing crowds.

In 1916, the Browns and Sportsman's Park were sold to Phil Ball. Four years later, the struggling Cardinals moved to Sportsman's Park, and their facility at Vandeventer Avenue and Natural Bridge Road was sold to the city. It is now the site of Beaumont High School.

By 1922, St. Louis baseball was approaching its long heyday, and fans turned out at Sportsman's Park in record numbers. George Sisler led the Browns on a pennant chase, batting .420, but they finished the season a game behind the Yankees. The same year, the Cardinals' Rogers Hornsby won the National League triple crown when his batting average was .401, he hit 42 home runs, and batted in 152 runs. Phil Ball spent more than $600,000 to extend the grandstand and the upper decks down the baselines, build a roof on the right-field pavilion, and increase capacity to 32,000.

The Cardinals were the beneficiaries of the improvements. In 1926, they won the National League pennant and beat the Yankees in a seven-game World Series. Sportsman's Park was host to 10 World Series, three of which concluded with seventh-game victories for the Cardinals. The 1944 "Streetcar Series" pitted the Cardinals against the Browns, with the Cardinals winning in six games. The Cardinals won a total of seven world championships at the park. St. Louis fans were also treated to two All-Star games, in 1940 and 1948.

Sportsman's Park was remodeled again in 1946 at a cost of $750,000. Improvements included a rooftop press box, a penthouse, and an elevator. In 1953, when August A. Busch, Jr., bought the Cardinals and paid $1.1 million for Sportsman's Park, he spent an additional $1.5 million to spruce up the old place. He decided to change the name and, initially, favored Budweiser Stadium. He settled on Busch Stadium.

The Cardinals continued to play at Sportsman's Park, but it was clear that the old stadium was not adequate for the modern game of baseball. Parking was next to impossible, the neighborhood had been declining for some years, and the facility could not accommodate enough people. It had been improved and enlarged in a piecemeal fashion over 100 years, but it was time to consider a replacement.

When plans for the new stadium in downtown St. Louis were finalized, Busch announced that the grounds at Grand and Dodier would be donated to the Herbert Hoover Boys' Club.

The last Cardinals game at Sportsman's Park was played on May 8, 1966. When the final out was called, a helicopter swooped onto the infield, home plate was dug up, and the 'copter whisked it away to be installed at the new stadium. The park that was home to all of Stan Musial's Hall-of-Fame career, that saw Babe Ruth hit three home runs in a World Series game twice (1926 and 1928), that gave the opportunity finally to see Satchel Paige pitch in the big leagues, and that introduced fans to latter-day heroes such as Lou Brock and Bob Gibson had come to the end of its days.

Aalco Wrecking Company finished demolition of Sportsman's Park in six months. All that survive are uncountable memories and a sign with an "A" and a flying eagle that topped the scoreboard. It now stands above I-64 (Highway 40) near the Vandeventer Avenue overpass.

St. Louis was founded by entrepreneurs, and their ilk have been attracted to it ever since. Its location and business climate have been attractive, and many have made fortunes. But the vast majority to do so were white men. During the pre-Civil War days, several African-American men made a lot of money through business and real estate, but women, both black and white, were rarely involved in entrepreneurial opportunities.

In 1902, a young African-American woman named Annie Turnbo Pope Malone moved her already-successful business to St. Louis. She had developed a scalp care product to help grow and straighten black women's hair when she was a high-school chemistry student in Peoria, Illinois.

Malone first set up shop in St. Louis at 2223 Market Street to manufacture the product, which she copyrighted and called "Poro." In 1906, the business expanded to larger quarters at 3100 Pine Street.

Malone's business was prospering in 1918, when she established Poro College at the southwest corner of Billups and St. Ferdinand Avenues. Beauticians from around the country received training in the use of Poro products, and salespeople were taught techniques for marketing them.

The Poro Building was three stories high and was

Sportsman's Park held a capacity crowd during the 1948 All-Star game. *Courtesy Missouri Historical Society.*

built of brick with stone trim. Its handsomely pedimented entry faced the corner and was delineated by limestone quoins. The arched doorway was flanked by a pair of stone columns.

The building occupied an entire block and housed a beauty parlor, classrooms for the instruction of cosmetology, classrooms for teaching secretarial and bookkeeping skills, an auditorium, general office space, a cafeteria, a dining room, a tailor shop, guest rooms, a student dormitory, and two emergency rooms where first-aid treatments were dispensed. There was also a rooftop garden.

Malone's Poro system achieved international success, and by the 1920s Malone employed nearly 200 people. She also set up a financial branch to help many African Americans finance their first homes.

After a 1927 tornado, Poro College housed thousands whose homes had been damaged. They were fed and clothed, and the building served as a principal relief center for the American Red Cross.

The Poro building was a popular meeting place for many of the city's African-American social and civic organizations and was used as a community center.

By the 1930s, Malone was among the wealthiest black women in the world. She moved Poro College to Chicago in July 1930 to take advantage of its still-larger market.

The building was used for a time as a hotel, and in 1939, it became the site of the Lincoln University School of Law. Lloyd L. Gaines, a graduate of Vashon High School and Lincoln University, had applied to the University of Missouri Law School — he was the first African American to do so — and was rejected. The university advised him to investigate a state statute that provided out-of-state scholarships for blacks. Instead, Gaines enlisted the help of the NAACP. His case was rejected by the Boone County Circuit Court and, on appeal, by the Missouri Supreme Court. The United States Supreme Court ruled that the University of Missouri School of Law, then a segregated institution, would have to admit Gaines, unless the state could provide equivalent training elsewhere. Gaines announced his intention of entering the law school the following September. But the Missouri Legislature,

Annie Malone's Poro College functioned as a community center for the African-American community. *Courtesy Missouri Historical Society. Irv Schankman/Allied Photocolor Collection.*

during its 1939 session, appropriated $275,000 to establish a law school at Lincoln University. Administrators found the space in the Poro Building to their liking and opened the University's first class of 30 students of law.

In 1965, the congregation of the St. James AME Church bought the Poro Building and demolished it. They replaced it with the James House, a residential facility for the elderly.

Annie Malone died in 1957 at the age of 88. Her legacy lives on with the Annie Malone Children's Home and other charitable ventures.

Vandeventer Place

The gates to Vandeventer Place, a pair of which were placed in Forest Park, behind the Jewel Box.
Courtesy Missouri Historical Society.

It is appropriate to begin reminiscences of Vandeventer Place with "once upon a time," for it was the stuff of fairy tales and legends. It was the residential symbol of Victorian opulence — some would say excess — in St. Louis. Its gay '90s heydays are fondly remembered, even though no traces of the grand street remain at the original location.

Vandeventer Place, which extended west from Grand Avenue to Vandeventer between Enright and Bell Avenues, was home to 86 of the city's wealthiest civic leaders. The subdivision was platted by noted surveyor Julius Pitzman after William Vandeventer sold some of his farm land to three prominent citizens — Charles H. Peck, Napoleon Mulliken, and John S. McCune — in 1870. The three paid $3,750 for the land, which had been a part of St. Louis' Grand Prairie Common Fields. They immediately began to fashion their enclave, though their progress was slowed by the financial panic of 1873.

The Vandeventer Place houses were built on a grand scale not matched in St. Louis before or since. The pre-income tax days of the late 19th century saw

Bird's-eye view of Vandeventer Place looking west from Grand Avenue shows the Charles Peck house on the north side of the street and Napoleon Mulliken's on the south, bracketing the entrance from Grand Avenue. *Courtesy Missouri Historical Society.*

many St. Louisans making a great deal of money, and 86 of them spent lavishly to build their Vandeventer Place mansions.

By 1890, all 86 lots were sold and granitoid walks were laid midst a mansion-building boom. The original cast-iron gates that guarded the east and west entrances were replaced in 1894 with large semi-circular white Barre-granite gates designed by Louis Mullgardt, a well-known architect of the era. The elaborately landscaped center parkway, with a large fountain and ornamental pool at each end, provided an aura of serene spaciousness in the middle of the city.

Vandeventer Place was protected by a stringent indenture and deed restrictions that forbade tanneries, museums, breweries, and schools. Front steps had to be scrubbed twice a week, and three sets of curtains were required for each front window. The indenture mandated that a Vandeventer house must cost at least $10,000 to build and that it had to be set back 30 feet from the street. All main entrances were required to face Vandeventer Place, though some architects managed to circumvent this provision, and kitchens

had to be in the basement. No non-family member could spend more than one night at a Vandeventer Place mansion, and "for rent" or "for sale" signs were unthinkable. Since any change in the restrictions required the unanimous consent of the residents who made up the membership of the Vandeventer Place Association, any changes were close to impossible, as the owners all were successful business owners and civic leaders, and each was quite accustomed to having his own way.

Architectural styles, representing the gamut of various tastes, included the work of the era's best architects. The internationally famous architect Henry Hobson Richardson designed a mansion for John R. Lionberger. The work of the Chicago firm of Burnham and Root, the Boston firm of Peabody and Stearns, and Fuller and Wheeler of Albany, New York, was represented, as was the early work of St. Louis architects Eames and Young, Charles Ramsey, Shepley, Rutan and Coolidge, Grable and Weber, and Tully and Clark.

There were examples of Second Empire houses,

The $800,000 Henry Clay Pierce mansion at No. 40 Vandeventer Place was the most costly built there. *Courtesy Missouri Historical Society.*

Italian Renaissance villas, Colonial Revival manors, English Tudor halls, Chateauesque mansions, Romanesque castles, and other variations of style, including Queen Anne, French Eclectic and substantial Victorian whimsies. There were even a few that could be best described as "Victorian Exuberant." The mansions cost anywhere from $35,000 to nearly $1 million to build.

The largest and, to some, the most pretentious of the Vandeventer Place houses was built for Henry Clay Pierce at No. 40 from the design by Fuller and Wheeler of Albany, New York, who were well-known for their part in designing the New York State Capitol Building. Pierce had parlayed his father-in-law's whale oil business into the Waters Pierce Oil Company, which was large enough to rival Standard Oil. He also had interests in railroads, coal mines, and steamships, which helped finance and maintain his $800,000 Vandeventer Place mansion.

Construction on the rough-cut stone and brick mansion began in 1886 and took three years to complete. It had a gabled slate roof, parapeted gable dormers, and an asymmetrical plan, and a facade that was firmly founded on a Richardson Romanesque Revival theme popular at the time.

The 26-room mansion had 15 bedrooms and an elevator to take guests to the third-floor ballroom, which was enhanced with stained glass windows

designed by Louis Tiffany. The music room had a frescoed ceiling and a custom-made white mahogany grand piano. Pierce also had a huge gun room in the basement, but he displayed his hunting trophies — lamps made from deer and moose feet, a moose head, a stuffed caribou and a stuffed albino deer — in his first-floor study.

The living room featured a six-foot-wide fireplace surrounded by mosaic tile and carved wood. Above it was a bronze bas-relief of Pierce's father. A bust of Faust stood nearby.

Pierce had 22 servants, who were required to have a daily dress parade before the "master of the manor." The servants lived in a separate house, behind the main house, across the street on Enright Avenue, that was connected to the main house by an underground tunnel.

The stables and carriage house, which sheltered Pierce's opera bus, brougham, barouche, and hansom, were also across the street, as was the heating plant where steam was generated in huge boilers and then piped under Enright to the main house. In the 1920s, the estimated annual coal bill was $4,000.

After Pierce's first wife died in 1910, he moved to New York to pursue his business interests. He never lived in the Vandeventer Place mansion for a prolonged period again, though he maintained it as if he planned to return.

A bust of H.C. Pierce's father was a prominent feature in his living room. *Courtesy Missouri Historical Society.*

It was during this period that Pierce ran into trouble. He was accused of having a behind-the-scenes role in the Mexican Revolution and was indicted for massive antitrust violations. It turned out that Waters Pierce Oil Co. was in alliance with Standard Oil Company, not a competitor.

Pierce died in 1927 after spending some time in prison. Accounts concerning his will vary. Some state that he left no will at all; others state the more likely story that he was insolvent at the time of his death. In 1934, a petition filed by his son, A.C. Pierce, says that the estate was insolvent by $33,800.

In 1928, the furnishings were sold at public auction, and in 1933, the house was deeded to the U.S. Fidelity and Casualty Co. in payment for the estate's default in paying federal income taxes. The saga ended in 1936, when the fixtures were sold and the house was razed.

Among the first three Vandeventer Place houses was the lavish Second Empire-style mansion designed by George I. Barnett for Charles H. Peck in 1871. With its stone-fronted tall first and second stories and mansard third story, Barnett's design provided the transition to the popularity of the Second Empire style in St. Louis. Peck's mansion at No. 7 Vandeventer Place stood across the street from another Second Empire house built for Napoleon Mulliken. The two bracketed Vandeventer Place's eastern entrance.

A native of New York, Peck was educated as an architect and builder. He stood at the opposite end of the spectrum from H. C. Pierce in both personal and architectural terms. Peck was a staunch Presbyterian and conservative who worked hard to amass his fortune. He became a major shareholder in the St. Louis Gas and the Carondelet Gas companies, he was president of the St. Louis Mutual Fire Insurance Company, and he ran one of the largest planing mills in the United States.

Peck's personal scrapbook reflects the wide range of his interests — from clippings about the dedication of Shaw Place to receipts for the treatment of equine sores and bruises; from newspaper accounts of the Pacific Railroad controversy of 1869 to a pedigree of "Mr. Bodley's thoroughbred bull."

His lifelong interests in architecture and the size of his family — he had nine children — were reflected in his Vandeventer Place house. A 1948 appraisal of City Block 2289, acquired by the Landmarks Association, included black and white photographs, a narrative description, current taxes on the land and improvements, and the appraiser's valuation for each parcel.

The Charles H. Peck mansion was the first built on Vandeventer Place. *Courtesy Missouri Historical Society.*

The appraiser described No. 7 Vandeventer Place as "...a large brick home with stone on the front and east side walls. It is designed in the grand Victorian manner and very substantially built. Its appointments inside are reminiscent of the splendor of the post-Civil War period. The woodwork is ornately carved, every window is fitted with small louvered interior shutters and the fireplace openings are equipped with polished marble mantels. Large mirrors, some framed in walnut, some in gold leaf, adorn the drawing rooms and dining room. The first floor ceilings are 14 feet high. Carved cornices embellished with gold leaf decorate the window pediments."

The narrative continues, "The first floor contains six rooms [in addition to the] service halls, reception halls and pantry and storage closet. The second floor has six bedrooms, five baths and three dressing closets. The third floor has three bedrooms, a library, a book vault and one bath. The house contains 198,000 cubic feet.

"Auxiliary buildings include a brick storage build-ing and a two-story stable and garage building. An underground passageway, formerly a wine cellar, runs from the basement to Bell Avenue."

The appraisal concludes, "The property is well constructed, but now needs painting and repair. Due to its size and present state of repair, it is evident that this property has practically reached the end of its economic life. The utility it offers is limited and the amount of maintenance it requires leaves only a nominal net return, if any."

The dismal appraisal was backed up with the tax assessment valuation of $9,568 for the land and $5,600 for the improvements, which resulted in a 1948 real estate tax of $415.59. The appraised value of the property was $4,125 for the land and only $2,625 for the improvements.

Peck had died in 1899, having outlived the two other Vandeventer Place founders. His family continued to occupy the house. His $1 million estate was left in trust for 15 years after the death of any descendants living at the time of his demise, so that the ultimate

The J. W. Lambert house at No. 62 Vandeventer Place was designed by George I. Barnett. *Courtesy Missouri Historical Society.*

heirs were his great-grandchildren.

In 1889, George I. Barnett also designed a Victorian red brick mansion for Jordan Wheat Lambert at No. 62 Vandeventer Place. Lambert, a native of Alexandria, Virginia, was a chemist and pharmacist who came to St. Louis in 1873. He discovered an antiseptic he named Listerine and organized Lambert Pharmacal Company in 1881 with great, and rapid, financial success.

Ironically, Lambert died in 1889 of an infection. His six children were orphaned two months later when Lily Lambert died of pneumonia shortly after the birth of their youngest child.

The children were reared in the house by relatives and trust company guardians. The eldest, Albert Bond Lambert, was an aviation pioneer who put up considerable money to finance Charles Lindbergh's flight to Paris. Lambert International Airport is named for him.

Another son, Gerard, boosted the family business

to a $90 million corporation. He was also president of the Gillette Company.

In his autobiography, *All Out of Step*, Gerard Lambert described the mansion of his childhood:

"From the front hall you could enter two quite formal parlors which might be thrown together by moving sliding doors. Adjoining these parlors was a 'smoking room.' This curious 1889 addition (attributed to Eames and Young, not Barnett) to the house was dark, Oriental and depressing. A row of stained glass windows, high on the wall, served only to add to its gloom.

"In the parlors great sliding doors which disappeared into the wall gave access to the dining room. Here all the luxury and vulgarity of the period burst forth. The ceiling was of canvas, emotionally frescoed. After all these years, I have forgotten the design, but I fear there were pink and light blue angels and cupids in the corners.

"Entirely out of place in such a room, over the

The Lionberger house stood at No. 27 Vandeventer Place. *Courtesy Missouri Historical Society.*

elaborate mantelpiece, was a perfectly enormous moth-eaten dingy buffalo head with a very morose expression in its eyes. Its strange brown hair always made me think of a beard stained with tobacco juice."

The John R. Lionberger house at No. 27 Vandeventer Place is of great interest to architectural historians. It was designed in 1886 by Henry Hobson Richardson, today the best known of the Vandeventer Place architects. There is conjecture, however, that he would not have bothered with designing houses in St. Louis had Lionberger's brother-in-law, George Shepley, not worked for him and married Richardson's daughter. Richardson also designed a handsome shingle house at 5814 Cabanne Place for Henry Potter, who was married to one of Lionberger's daughters.

The Lionberger house, appropriately, resembled a compact fortress. Built of rough-cut stone, the deep round-arched entrance and loggia above it appeared to be carved into the facade in a manner that united the round corner towers on a single plane. A handsomely detailed belt course wrapped the facade above the side porch roofline, accentuating the massive feel of the first-floor level.

The Lionberger house was smaller than the Peck and Pierce houses but was generous by any standard. The first floor contained a large reception hall reached through the front entry and vestibule. A living room, study, library, butler's pantry (later converted to a kitchen), and dining room completed the public rooms of the house. A guest closet and lavatory nestled under the front stairs — a forward-thinking and unusual refinement for the era. The second floor had five bedrooms, a sitting room, three baths, and a dressing closet. The third floor had five finished rooms, a bath, and two large closets.

Lionberger, a Virginia native, had come to St. Louis in 1855 to establish a wholesale boot and shoe business, Lionberger and Shields. That company became J. R. Lionberger and Company and remained one of the city's most prosperous enterprises. Lionberger retired from his company in 1867, leaving a going concern to his successors, and pursued other interests. He became president of the Third National Bank and invested in street railroads, gas companies, and safe deposit companies. He was one of the original stockholders in the Granite Mountain Silver Mine, which yielded him a fortune, unlike some of the mine's later investors. Lionberger was also a member and

president of the Merchants' Exchange, prominent in the affairs of the Northern Missouri Railroad, and a strong supporter of the construction of Eads Bridge. His prominence and the fame of the architect served to focus a great deal of attention on No. 27 Vandeventer Place.

When Lionberger died, he left the mansion to his daughter, Mary. It and its fixtures were valued at $50,000. In 1910, the Lionberger house was sold to C.O.L. Johnson, who owned it until it was sold to the federal government so that its site could be incorporated with others as the location for a new veterans' hospital.

Among of the largest and most prominent of the Vandeventer Place houses was the one built at No. 46 for Joseph Gilbert Chapman in 1892 — it was one of the last. Designed in the "Italian Renaissance with overtones of Georgian Revival" style, the large yellow brick mansion stood at the corner of Vandeventer Place and Spring Avenue. Despite the provision in the indenture that the front entrance must face Vandeventer Place, the Chapman mansion's classically pedimented entrance faced Spring. In an effort to somewhat comply with the indenture, Eames and Young designed the Vandeventer facade with a large Palladian window flanked by a pair of two-story bows.

Chapman, a native of New York State and a graduate of Brown University, came to St. Louis to work in his father's company, Chapman and Thorp, which had extensive lumber manufacturing interests in both St. Louis and Eau Claire, Wisconsin. He married Emma Bridge, the daughter of Hudson E. Bridge — a prominent St. Louis businessman — and established himself as a leading citizen. He was a director of the St. Louis National Bank, the Bridge and Beach Manufacturing Company, and the Bellefontaine Railroad. He served as a trustee of Washington University and was the second president of the Board of Control of the St. Louis Museum and School of Fine Arts. He was also a member of the Board of the Unitarian Church of the Messiah, a founder of the University Club, and a member of the Commercial Club.

Chapman and his family moved into the yellow mansion five years before he died in 1897 at age 56. Two years later, his daughter married architect John Lawrence Mauran. They moved into the house her father had built and stayed for many years. Mauran designed a library addition on the south side of the house and may have added the shutters seen in photographs.

The Chapman/Mauran house was described in an assessor's survey as one of the largest and most elaborate in Vandeventer Place. According to the 1948 survey, it was "truly a relic of an era of opulence and splendor now past." The first-floor reception hall was entered through a vestibule, and the first floor had, in addition to a large parlor, a living room, library, dining room, sitting room — with adjoining alcove and toilet, kitchen, butler's pantry, and storage room.

"The woodwork and the mantels are superbly done and the carving of the ballroom mantel could probably not be duplicated due to the dearth of craftsmen capable of such fine workmanship," the appraiser wrote. "The polished woods, such as cherry, mahogany, and walnut, would be fabulously expensive to duplicate."

J.L. Mauran died in 1933, and his widow remained in the house to which she had moved with her parents in 1892. She was one of the few members of the original families remaining in Vandeventer Place.

Emily Tyler Eaton also remained. She had grown up at No. 80 Vandeventer Place in the house her mother, Mrs. William Tyler, had built. When she married, her husband Francis bought the mansion and they never moved.

It was in the mid-1930s that Emily Eaton launched a one-woman campaign to save Vandeventer Place. She argued that the remaining houses could be renovated and that the old place could once again be a fashionable address. "Where else could one find a location that is only ten minutes from downtown and uptown shopping, convenient and where children can play on a grassy sward? It is protected and dignified and the houses were built by famous architects," she said in a *Post-Dispatch* interview. She granted that the economy, nationwide, was a terrible problem but made

The Chapman house was described as "truly a relic of an era of opulence and splendor now past." *Courtesy Missouri Historical Society.*

the point that Vandeventer Place was just as viable as New York's Sutton Place and Boston's Beacon Street.

Eaton overlooked all the economic, environmental, and social forces working against Vandeventer Place. The creation of Portland Place, Westmoreland Place, and other private places of the Central West End offered a grand alternative to her beloved street and had started the erosion of Vandeventer Place as early as 1888.

In addition, the planners of the grand place had not thought to protect its surroundings.

A prescient article in the *St. Louis Republic* on May 5, 1895, said, "To the impartial observer at the present time it appears that the only mistake made by the projectors of Vandeventer Place was the overlooking or rather underestimating the rapid growth of the city. Vandeventer Place is now largely hemmed in by street railroads and business houses, and in the course of a few years this is liable to prove quite a detriment."

By 1922, Vandeventer Place had lost its status as a premier residential street. Many of the original residents had died, and others had moved to escape the smoke, traffic, and industry of the ever-growing city.

The first attempt to break the single-family deed restrictions occurred that year when a new owner opened a boarding house at No. 12. It was reported that shocked residents had seen men lounging in shirt sleeves on the porch — and worse, some of the men were without collars and had the audacity to roll up their sleeves! The unwelcome intrusion was shut down.

Further, Vandeventer Place's high-living style had created some resentment among those who could not share it. In the early 20th century, a threatened strike by the cooks of Vandeventer Place and rumors that the street's coachmen were demanding regular hours and overtime pay delighted some nonresidents. The residents' seeming disregard for others and their opulent lifestyle did little to garner public sympathy to save the street.

Along with Emily Eaton's efforts, which included the formation of a garden club, a few of the residents who remained in the mid-1930s considered breaking the deed restrictions, and several discussed the possibilities of an apartment redevelopment. By 1935, the City of St. Louis had acquired several properties for back

A view of the Vandeventer Place east gates taken in 1880. *Courtesy Missouri Historical Society.*

taxes and proposed that Vandeventer Place become a park and a community center which would be built by the WPA. The Vandeventer Place trustees stood firm in upholding the indenture.

By the end of the Great Depression eight houses, including H.C Pierce's opulent mansion at No. 40, the Lambert house at No. 62 that could not attract a buyer at any price, and others whose owners wanted to save taxes and maintenance costs, had already been demolished. Ten years later, the 1946 City Directory listed only 36 houses on Vandeventer Place, and four of them were vacant. Isabel Chapman Mauran remained at No. 46 and Henri Chouteau still occupied the mansion designed by Charles Ramsey for Edward Mallinckrodt at No. 26.

Emily Eaton's cogent arguments came 30 years too soon when preservation was unfashionable and money was tight, even for the very wealthy. In 1947, a generation before Congress passed Historic Preservation legislation requiring a review of federally funded projects, the Veterans Administration chose the easternmost block of Vandeventer Place as the location for a new hospital. According to the Landmarks Association's January 1985 "Landmarks Letter," contemporary accounts suggested that a location closer to Forest Park might have been preferred, but it was considered too expensive to condemn.

At the groundbreaking for the John J. Cochran Veteran's Hospital, Mayor Joseph M. Darst said that "while the necessary removal of the stately homes on this historic site occasioned a certain amount of regret in the hearts of many people — and rightly so — I am sure that we are all agreed we must move forward."

Darst's regrets were not unanimously shared. In a letter to the editor of the *St. Louis Post-Dispatch*, a writer identified as "Marxo Grouch" said that it was only just that Vandeventer Place be destroyed, as it was built to be exclusionary and it was the enclave of the elite. The writer opined that Vandeventer Place was discriminatory and that it was good to see it go.

The residents at the west end of Vandeventer Place also found argument with Darst's statement. The fate of their houses was sealed by their unwelcome new neighbor, but they stood in tatty elegance for ten more years. In 1958, the City condemned their houses and land, demolished the remaining mansions, and built the Juvenile Detention Center.

There is little more than memories left of Vandeventer Place. Charles Peck's mansion at No. 7, the first to be built, was among the last to be torn down because it did not stand in the way of new construction.

The Mullgardt gates that guarded the west entrance were moved to Forest Park, where they stand in a meadow east of the Jewel Box, leading to some occasional speculation as to their origin. One of the parkway fountains stands in Shaw Place, and the porch of the Lionberger house has been reassembled and incorporated into a house on Westmoreland Place.

Central West End:
Mansions, Institutions
& a Highlands Fling

Designed by Tom P. Barnett and completed in 1914, Cicardi's restaurant was located at the northwest corner of Euclid Avenue and Delmar Boulevard. It was razed in 1925 and provided a site for the Roosevelt Hotel. The decorative panels were created by overlaying stucco on a black surface and then carving the stucco down to the base in a manner similar to carving a cameo. *Courtesy Missouri Historical Society.*

St. Louis was a bustling and growing city as it looked forward to the 20th century. The recently established Forest Park rivaled any in the larger eastern cities. St. Louis ranked fourth in population, it had survived the decimating cholera epidemics of the mid-19th century, and it was an important center of commerce. There was every reason for its leaders to be brimming with optimism.

Growth was vigorous as the city grew west out the central corridor rather than north and south along the Mississippi River. The unplanned growth required the relocation of several cemeteries and extensions of the city limits until, in 1876, the city separated from St. Louis County to become one of only two cities in the United States not included within a county boundary.

The central corridor area west of Grand Avenue out to the city limits was known as the west end in the early days and, in the 1950s, became known as the Central West End. It was here, and in Vandeventer Place, that opulent residential and institutional architecture came to full fruition. Large and elegant houses were built on public and private streets, and Lindell Boulevard, the central spine, included fine examples of both houses and institutional buildings.

An interior view of Cicardi's restaurant. *Courtesy Missouri Historical Society.*

LINDELL BOULEVARD

The late 19th century brought a building boom to the Central West End. The city was growing rapidly, fortunes were being made, and city leaders were building mansions, clubs, private enclaves, and elegant avenues. Lindell Boulevard was the most prominent of the broad avenues, lined with mansions and stabilized — so those early builders thought — by universities, institutions, and private clubs. Its broad, yellow gravel expanse was well traveled with increasing numbers of visitors going to Forest Park and to the new grand residential areas built near it. Lindell became popular for carriage races; it was ideal for those young men who could not resist letting their horses extend themselves. It also became the site of some of the first speeding tickets issued by city government.

In 1901, civic pride engendered by the upcoming Louisiana Purchase Exposition produced a strenuous street improvement program that would greatly enhance the desirability of a Lindell Boulevard location. At that time, adjacent property owners were required to maintain Lindell and some were reluctant to spend the needed funds to repair the city's leading thoroughfare. Mayor Rolla Wells testified at a Board of Public Improvements hearing that the boulevard "has to be reconstructed, and that any property owner who cannot afford the slight cost of such improvement is living there, in my judgment, under false pretenses and should move to another street." Wells' challenge ended the debate.

The buildings and mansions of Lindell and adjacent private and public streets were a tour de force of United States architecture. The work of noted architects, both local and national, abounded. Count Apponyi of Hungary, visiting the World's Fair, extravagantly praised St. Louis residences as "more beautiful than in all of Central Europe." In 1903, a national magazine ranked St. Louis first anywhere, saying that many houses were "veritable palaces in every particular richness, appointment and setting."

Another point of view was expressed by turn-of-the-century sociologist Thorstein Veblen. Well-known for his conspicuous consumption theory, he delighted in criticizing the foibles of the rich. He could well have been thinking of St. Louis when he wrote, "The process of selective adaptations of designs to the end of conspicuous waste, and the substitution of pecuniary beauty for aesthetic beauty have been especially

effective in the development of architecture."

While Veblen's acid comments had a ring of truth, many of the houses built in the Central West End at this time were quite handsome. They showed that an amalgam of styles and evolving tastes, in the hands of a talented architect, could be extremely successful.

Lindell Boulevard was named for Peter Lindell, an early businessman who made his fortune first in trade along the Ohio River and later as a holder of extensive real estate in St. Louis.

The small path that was to become Lindell Boulevard probably started to be claimed from the prairie around 1800, when the French colonials and others made their way from town to Montaigne a Marie to drink, gossip, quarrel, and relax. The spring, then owned by Alexis Marie, was located on land now bordered by Newstead, Lindell, Maryland and Euclid.

The light glowed from the windows and the open door of the red brick and granite mansion at the corner of Spring and Lindell, welcoming guests to a wedding reception. The sounds of laughter and escalating conversation poured out into the chilly October night as they had countless times over the 75 years that the Castleman-Mackay family had given parties at 3693 Lindell.

The dining room shimmered with candlelight — the table was set with the same china, silver and linens that had been used at another family wedding in 1914 — but the year was 1971. None of the guests knew that this was to be the last of the parties — that the house had been sold. The Mackay family members knew, but even they did not suspect the ultimate fate of their house.

-From the West End Word

The Castleman-Mackay mansion was completed in 1897. It was built for Judge Arthur Castleman and his wife, Lucie Cable of Rock Island, Illinois. Her family had extensive interests in the railroad that bore that town's name.

Construction had begun in 1892 on a site formerly occupied by a white farmhouse. A carriage house and stables already stood at the back of the lot. The New York firm of Renwich, Aspinwall and Owen were the architects, though Lucie Castleman had a great influence on the final product.

She changed the original plans, demanding that a second tower at the west side of the house be removed and that the windows be made larger. Family lore tells that Mrs. Castleman retired to Europe for a grand tour during construction. Upon her return and subsequent inspection of the nearly completed mansion, she stood in the long front hall and announced that the doors leading to the dining room, parlor, and library were not of correct proportions — that they should be wider and higher to open the spaces and create room for better flow of people at large parties.

These modifications added a year to the construction time, and it was probably a good thing that all the intricately carved ceilings and paneling, marble, and other embellishments met with her approval. Her opinions registered, Mrs. Castleman returned to Europe to travel and continue buying furnishings for the house. She had rugs made to her specifications in Brussels and bought furniture wherever she went.

Judge Castleman did not live to see the house finished, and his childless widow moved in alone.

In 1911, Mrs. Castleman's niece and heir, Suzanne Benton Cable, married a young lawyer, George Castleman Mackay (no relation), and lived in a fine — if more modest — house across the street at 3680 Lindell. There is some speculation that Mrs. Castleman did not entirely approve of her niece's marriage and felt the best way to manage was to have the young couple within eyesight.

At any rate, the Mackay's two young daughters, Suzanne and Lucie, went across Lindell every day for lunch at the big house with their great-aunt. Upon Mrs. Castleman's death in 1926, the Mackays moved into 3693 Lindell.

According to Lucie Palmer Garnett, who as the daughter of Lucie Mackay Palmer also grew up in the house, the tradition of grand parties begun by Mrs. Castleman continued throughout the life of the house. "Great Aunt Lucie was well known for her parties," Mrs. Garnett said. "Grandmother and Grandfather had at least two dinner parties a week, some of which included an evening of duplicate bridge, and a New Year's Day reception for 400 guests.

"My mother and father had New Year's Eve waltzing parties after World War II — white tie and all — but with a juke box filled with Strauss waltzes because an orchestra was prohibitively expensive." Mrs. Garnett added that the house could comfortably hold 500 for a party. "After that, it got a bit crowded," she said.

Mrs. Garnett said that the house had been redecorated only twice. "In 1896 and '97, when 'Great-auntie' was doing the original, she bought double the necessary amount of green and gold brocade wallpaper. Thus when the house was redecorated in 1930, the wallpaper could be replaced exactly. There was also some work done in the late 1940s, but no major decorative changes and no structural changes were made over the years."

Talk of selling the Spring and Lindell mansion surfaced as early as 1925, when Mrs. Castleman considered selling the site and having the house moved, brick by brick, to a westerly location. The project was deemed impossible. The subject of sale came up periodically, but it was not until 1969 that family members were persuaded separately to entertain an offer from their neighbor to the east, the Scottish Rite. The generous offer contained a five-year tenancy clause. It made pragmatic sense to accept it, as George Mackay was a very old man, one of his daughters had died, and his grandchildren were all well started on lives of their own.

"It was our understand-

An interior view of the Castleman-Mackay mansion. *Courtesy Lucie Garnett.*

ing that the Scottish Rite people wanted to use the house for meetings and housing guests, but it was only a gentlemen's agreement that the house remain standing," Mrs. Garnett said. "There was nothing in writing."

The family moved out after the October 1971 wedding and the house was occupied by caretakers. A shooting and other incidents in the neighborhood influenced the decision to raze the house. Published reports in 1973 indicated that the Scottish Rite was determined to use the site for "much-needed parking" and that they needed to save the maintenance and tax expenses.

Efforts by individuals and the Landmarks Association to save the house — greatly hampered by a major newspaper strike — were unsuccessful.

The salvage rights were purchased by the Finer Metal Company, and the remains of the house were sold at auction in 1982, just before it was demolished.

St. Louis was thriving in 1891 when one of its prominent citizens, Roman Catholic Archbishop Peter Richard Kenrick, was celebrating his jubilee, or 50th anniversary as a priest. Kenrick was a strong leader for his archdiocese, having put it on a good financial basis after inheriting a $60,000 church debt. It was under his regime that many of the city's parishes were established and that the major portion of Calvary Cemetery was purchased. He possessed a wise and shrewd business sense which allowed him to sell land around the Old Cathedral judiciously, while not selling the building or its site. The Old Cathedral remains the only building in the city that has never been sold.

In celebration of Kenrick's jubilee, a truly grand house was built for him at 3810 Lindell Boulevard, in the center of the most desired residential area in the city. The mansion, replacing a very simple house on 16th Street, was impressive, even to newspaper reporters of the day.

Designed by Isaac Taylor, the Renaissance-style, two-story house was built of brick and stone and incorporated Romanesque motifs. A pair of low-level bays balanced the facade, with their peaks blending into the rest of the formed tile roof. A pair of graceful, covered chimneys soared above the roof.

A distinctive ribbon of arched-top windows formed a colonnade across the facade at the second story level. The arched carved stone entryway featured doors handsomely decorated with iron and brass forgings. The doors opened into a light, wide hall that ran the full depth of the mansion and divided it in half. Heavy portieres hung in the doorways, and the walls were lined with pictures. To the left of the hall was a large reception room with a bay window at the front of the house that made the room seem even more generous than it was. The room was paneled in oak, and the very formal furniture was elaborately carved.

At the rear of the reception room was a capacious dining room that could seat 50 people if the occasion demanded. It was paneled in white, quarter-sawn oak, and its furnishings were specially designed for the room. There were a richly carved oak sideboard and two amply proportioned cabinets along the walls, which surrounded a heavy oak extension table. A dozen or so matching carved chairs were covered with embossed leather.

A second parlor on the right side of the hall was grandly furnished in mahogany, including a heavy center table, many pedestals for statues, and large,

The Bishop's residence was an elegant tribute to Archbishop Richard Kenrick. *Courtesy St. Louis Public Library.*

comfortable chairs. The walls were covered with paintings of churchmen and friends of the archbishop.

The second floor contained the archbishop's living suite, which included a bedroom, bath, and large study. To the rear of his suite, several guest rooms were ready for immediate use at all times.

On the right of the second floor was Kenrick's private chapel, where he made his daily devotions. The chapel was Gothic in plan and paneled in oak, but there was a minimum of ornament. The room was 20 feet long and 15 feet wide with an 18-foot ceiling. The simple oak Gothic altar stood under a stained glass window.

The chapel furnishings, including the altar, were a gift from Julia Maffitt and her daughters. With the exception of some living room furniture that Kenrick brought from his previous residence, the mansion's furnishings were gifts from parishioners, friends, and clergy on the occasion of his jubilee celebration.

Pope Leo XII's gift was a portrait of himself, and the Sisters of Charity gave a set of regal gold and jeweled vestments. The Wm. Barr Company presented a handsome gold archiepiscopal chair.

One of the more elaborate offerings, presented by the Sisters of Loretto, was an exquisite dinner service of French china. Originally white, each piece was tinted, painted, and trimmed with gold by the Sisters themselves. The service had 175 pieces, not including a soup tureen, serving dishes for fish and game, vegetable dishes, and gravy and sauce bowls. There was everything needed to set a proper and lavish Victorian table.

The house and furnishings were a grand way to recognize Kenrick's great ecclesiastical career and contributions to his community.

Kenrick died in 1896, but the official residence of the prelate remained at 3810 Lindell until it moved west to the handsome rough-cut stone mansion built for William Nolker at the southwest corner of Lindell and Taylor. On October 16, 1958, permit number CC 6741 was issued to the Yaffe Iron Company to "wreck" a 2 1/2 story brick house, and Kenrick's Renaissance mansion was demolished. On its site, a large, modern office building — occupied first by IBM and now by the Salvation Army's headquarters — faces the small triangular park named for Archbishop Kenrick.

Lindell Boulevard figured prominently in the social and fraternal building boom that continued for more than 30 years, from 1893 through the mid-1920s. These organizations wanted to be near the residences of their members. Fraternal organizations such as the Scottish Rite, the Moolah Temple of the Mystic Shrine, the Masonic Temple, and the Medical Society built there, as did the St. Louis Club and the Columbian Club. These buildings, designed by leading architects, were among the most impressive in the city. Some remain so today.

The first of these massive buildings was the Columbian Club, completed in 1894. Built for an exclusive Jewish organization, it was designed by Alfred F. Rosenheim.

The Columbian Club building was huge — with a 190-foot facade facing Lindell just west of Vandeventer. The building covered the land back to McPherson, a block north of Lindell Boulevard.

Built of buff Roman brick in the Renaissance style, the Columbian Club was trimmed in buff terra cotta and Cleveland blue stone. The entrance had three large archways, each with an inset balcony.

Balustrades delineated the tops of the east and west porches and entries, the balconies and the roofline. A one-story library/solarium on the west side was balanced by a porte-cochere, called the Ladies' Entrance, on the east side.

Broad granite steps led members and their guests to the cavernous first-floor lobby with its marble floor inlaid in a mosaic pattern. The lobby also featured an oak-beamed and paneled ceiling and draped archways.

The Columbian Club was furnished in the style of the First Empire and decorated in emerald green and gold. Over $200,000 worth of gold leaf was used in the decorations.

A reporter, writing in the May 20, 1894, *St. Louis Republic*, was most impressed with its eight Samarkand rugs and "the one royal antique rug, 21 feet in length, that was more than 200 years old and was purchased at a cost of more than several hundred dollars."

The second floor had a great banquet hall that measured 110 by 50 feet. A large service room alongside was served by a series of dumb waiters that facilitated the speed and efficiency of serving elaborate meals to a large number of people.

A ballroom occupied the third floor. The walls were decorated in shades of rose and ivory, and its floor was of highly polished maple. The walls had paneled wainscoting and plaster Ionic pilasters that reached to the ceiling.

At the west end of the ballroom was a fully equipped stage for presenting amateur theatricals. Large productions were evidently expected, as four large dressing rooms were included.

One of the decorative touches on the stage was a backdrop curtain with a mural depicting the "Birth of Music." There were also ladies' and gentlemen's parlors.

The basement housed athletic facilities, including a gymnasium, a swimming pool, and four bowling alleys.

The grand opening of the Columbian Club in June 1894 was attended by 2,000 people. Lavish buffets were set and an orchestra played on each floor.

The Columbian Club occupied the building until 1928, when it was sold to the Knights of Columbus for their headquarters. They in turn sold it to the Automobile Club of Missouri in 1934.

The Automobile Club maintained the building as their headquarters at 3917 Lindell until March 14, 1975, when a fire, blamed on faulty wiring, raged through it. The top two floors were completely destroyed.

Fire, water, and structural damage to the first floor and the basement dictated that there was little to save. The remains were demolished, and a new structure now occupies the site.

Farther west on Lindell Boulevard, at the northeast corner of Lindell and Kingshighway, an eight-acre tract was the site of a large mansion built in 1885 by John W. Kauffmann.

Kauffmann, born in 1830, was a flour miller who made an enormous fortune through his daring grain speculations. He had plenty of money to spend on his house and the grounds around it.

The Columbian Club was among the grandest of Lindell Boulevard's private club buildings. *Courtesy Missouri Historical Society.*

He built a huge house of dressed stone and brick. Stylistically, it could well be described as a Victorian Exuberant, primarily Queen Anne mansion. It was designed by James Stewart and Company, whose principal was said to have supervised the construction of the powerhouse at Niagara Falls. The many steep gables, turrets, towers, dormers, and chimneys "made a picturesque silhouette," according to Charles Savage in his *Architecture of the Private Streets of St. Louis.* "However, the relationship of its parts — towers, gabled bays and porte-cochere pavilion — was clumsy, lacking in any coherent unity," Savage continued.

The estate had a large carriage house that included stables and was decorated with a clock. It was surrounded by a brick wall inset with handsome iron grillwork through which the grounds were visible to passers-by. Large, ornamental iron gates marked the entrances.

The house was situated where the Chase Hotel now stands, and the estate covered the area bounded by Lindell, Kingshighway, Maryland, and Euclid.

After Kauffmann died in 1902, his widow sold off the part of the estate east of the present-day York

Avenue to William K. Bixby. Mrs. Kauffmann sold the remainder of the holding to Bixby in 1904, after the World's Fair.

As president of the American Car and Foundry Company, Bixby was an important businessman of the day. He was a director of the St. Louis Union Trust Company, the Missouri Pacific Railroad, the St. Louis and San Francisco Railway, and the Wagner Manufacturing Company.

Bixby was also prominent in St. Louis' cultural life and served as president of the St. Louis Museum of Fine Arts, the Missouri Historical Society, and the Burns Society of St. Louis, and as a vice president of Washington University.

The property, which became known as the "Bixby Farm," was a landmark until the early 1920s, when Bixby announced his plans to move. The house and its outbuildings were razed, and Bixby auctioned some of his priceless artworks and furniture.

In 1922, the Chase Hotel was built on the site, followed by the neighboring Park Plaza in 1929. The large entry gates — all that was left of the grandeur of the Kaufmann/Bixby estate — were incorporated into

The John W. Kauffmann house stood where the Chase Hotel now occupies the corner of Lindell and Kingshighway boulevards. *Courtesy Missouri Historical Society.*

The large entry gates to the Kaufmann/Bixby estate were later incorporated into the Chase Hotel garage.

the construction of the Chase garage. In the 1950s, the garage was enlarged and the gates were removed.

According to a report of that era, a workman said the gates had been sold and were to be reassembled to guard the entrance of a county property.

WESTMORELAND & PORTLAND PLACES

In the early and mid-19th century, the land now occupied by Portland Place, Westmoreland Place, and the large mansions of Forest Park Terrace along the 5000-5200 blocks of Lindell Boulevard was the bucolic site of the Cabanne family's extensive dairy farm.

In the early 1870s, the Cabannes sold some of their huge holding to William Griswold, who had settled in St. Louis in 1871. In both 1872 and 1874, some of Griswold's land, along with that of Isabella DeMun, Charles P. Chouteau, Julia Chouteau Maffitt, Robert Forsyth, and Thomas S. Skinker, was selected as the site of a new park for the city. Legislative difficulties delayed the purchase in 1872, and the issue was revisited in 1874. The landowners fought the condemnation, but the city and proponents of the park won out and Forest Park was dedicated in 1876. The landowners were paid a total of $800,000 for 1,327 acres.

Griswold was the only litigant who ended up making money on the establishment of the park. He owned additional land north of, and adjacent to, the park, and his St. Louis Transfer Company stood to prosper from transporting St. Louisans to the new recreational facility from the heat, hustle, and filth of the city.

In 1887 Griswold was using his land north of Forest Park as pasture for the cattle he raised as a hobby. He was approached by officials of the Forest Park Improvement Association, who wanted to buy 78 acres to establish a new, exclusive residential enclave. The association was headed by Alvah Mansur and included such prominent businessmen as William L. Huse, Edwards Whitaker, George D. Capen, William H. Thompson, Ethan Hitchcock, James B. Johnson, Dwight Tredway, James McLemore, and Judson Thompson. Of the group, George Capen was the most insistent that this particular parcel of land was ideal for their new venture to establish two new private streets. The group paid Griswold $400,000 (half the amount paid for all 1,327 acres of Forest Park) for the tract bounded by Kingshighway on the east, Sarpy Carr Cabanne's farm on the north, Union Boulevard on the west, and Forest Park on the south. Capen's enthusiasm for the tract led to accusations by some "knowledgeable businessmen" of the time that he had engineered the worst real estate deal since the Indians sold Manhattan for $24 in beads and trinkets.

Capen turned out to be more shrewd than his detractors. He recognized some of the causes for the decline of Lucas Place and other exclusive enclaves, including lack of control over the development of surrounding areas. The park would protect the southern flank of this real estate project and would stimulate further positive residential real estate development, which was already being discussed, for the land adjacent to the remaining borders.

Capen was also aware that some residents of still-fashionable Vandeventer Place were beginning to consider moving, as the commercial aspects of the city had begun to encroach on that grand street's perimeters.

The Forest Park Improvement Association divided

the tract into two entities, with Forest Park Terrace included with Westmoreland Place, and approved the appointment of trustees for them. The Association also oversaw the crafting of nearly identical protective indentures for both.

The majority of the Westmoreland Place, Portland Place, and Forest Park Terrace mansions have survived the difficult economic and social changes of the mid-20th century. Agreement among the early owners that no bituminous coal could be used to heat the houses went a long way toward maintaining a clean and healthy atmosphere. That agreement, coupled with a lack of industrial development in the surrounding area, gave these streets, and the rest of the Central West End, longevity that was not enjoyed by their preceding elegant neighborhoods.

However, the Great Depression, taxes, World War II, and a changing society that made domestic help more difficult to hire combined to threaten these streets. Nine Westmoreland Place mansions, three Portland Place mansions, and two Forest Park Terrace mansions were not to survive.

FOREST PARK
TERRACE

While Forest Park Terrace (or the 5000-5200 blocks of Lindell Boulevard) has never been a private street, its houses are protected by the Westmoreland Place indenture with its strict guidelines concerning placement, style, building materials, and costs. Though residents do not enjoy the seclusion of a private place, they do have a wonderful view of Forest Park and live on one of the handsomest boulevards in the nation.

Lindell Boulevard was the site of elegant mansions for many years, and that tradition is maintained on the section west of Kingshighway. Early builders were encouraged to locate on Forest Park Terrace when Lindell was finally paved in anticipation of the 1904 World's Fair. The streetscape remains grand, though two

important houses have been demolished.

The first of the demolished Forest Park Terrace houses stood at No. 5 Forest Park Terrace (5061 Lindell). Its design was attributed to Grable and Weber, and it was distinctly Romanesque in style. Built in 1893 for cotton broker James H. Allen, it was the first house on Forest Park Terrace. The Allen mansion had rough-cut stone construction and rose 2 1/2 stories. Its main feature was a prominent conical tower that extended over a high, hipped roof. The entrance was marked by a typical Romanesque arch.

Allen's house, which had a handsome interior paneled in many different types of woods, cost $75,000 to build.

When Allen died in 1916, publication of the details of his will revealed that he had extensive and far-flung interests, including over 64,000 acres in Chiapas, Mexico. He left his estate to his wife, Lorraine, and their five children — but only after extracting a promise from the children that they would give half their legacy to "Christian and charitable purposes."

Mrs. Allen lived in the house until 1931, when she moved to Texas. The house remained empty for five years during which time it was vandalized. A spokesperson for the St. Louis Union Trust Company, which handled the Allen estate, said that the interior was so seriously damaged that "the cost of renovation would

The James Allen house, with its conical tower, is visible west of the statue of Francis Blair. The Hills mansion is to the statue's west. *Courtesy Missouri Historical Society.*

be at least double the present value of the house."

The Allen mansion was demolished in 1936 to save the costs of repair, maintenance, insurance, and taxes.

One of the grandest mansions ever built in St. Louis was located at 5065 Lindell, or, as it was known, No. 7 Forest Park Terrace. In 1899, Barnett, Haynes and Barnett designed the Beaux Arts-style house for tobacco millionaire Col. Charles Spear Hills.

Hills, born in New York state in 1834, was awarded a brevet-colonelship by Abraham Lincoln for his gallantry during the Civil War. He moved to St. Louis and earned his fortune — first in the wholesale grocery business and then as manager of the Daniel Catlin Tobacco Company. Hills retired a very wealthy man when the company was sold in 1899 to the American Tobacco Company.

Hills spent $175,000 to build his Lindell Boulevard mansion. Built of brick faced with Carthage marble, the exterior had three columned, two-story porticoes. The south portico defined the entrance, the west one functioned as a porte cochere, and the east portico covered a porch. Rich, carved ornaments were concentrated at the first- and third-floor windows, the cornices and the pediment. The first-story arched window keystones were swagged consoles. Plaques containing high-relief arabesques were placed between these windows, and the cornice dentils and modillions were also sharply defined. Oval attic windows, framed with cartouches and flanked by garlanded pedestals, were set in rectangular reveals.

The exterior hinted strongly at interior luxuries. Each of the 15 rooms was paneled in a different type of imported wood. The library was paneled in red African mahogany, the living room in white mahogany, and the dining room in a combination of

An interior view of the Hills mansion at 5065 Lindell Blvd. *Courtesy Missouri Historical Society.*

bird's-eye maple and birch.

The broad central staircase was also made of bird's-eye maple. An art glass window on the landing was illuminated at night with electric light. Further luxurious touches were found in the bathroom plumbing fixtures, which were either silver or silver plated.

The floors throughout the house were made of various colors of teakwood set in mosaic patterns. Most of the third floor was occupied by a ballroom decorated with marine scenes.

Newspaper reports of Hills' death in 1902 attributed his demise to poor health that was a result of "a thrilling experience with robbers in Assyria" in 1879.

Hills married twice but had no children. He left his estate to his second wife, who had children from a previous marriage. When she died in the late 1920s, the house was rented to James J. Maccallum, an inventor, who had expressed his intent to buy it.

Maccallum was reputedly a wealthy man. He had patented a gas gauge which he thought would supply royalties of $125,000 a year and a deed-recording device which could have earned $5 million over five years. But hard times intervened.

As an indicator of the economic difficulties that St. Louis and the nation suffered in the 1930s, Maccallum's art collection, valued at $100,000, brought only $7,500 when sold. A painting attributed to Corregio fetched $45. Maccallum moved from the house after he and his wife were divorced, and the Hills mansion was never occupied again.

Hills' stepson, Sturges Babbit Curren, won ownership of the house after successfully contesting his mother's will. He offered the house for sale at $11,000 without success and then decided to demolish it to save $277 in annual taxes.

On September 29, 1939, the wrecking firm of L.G. Zindell began demolition. They had paid $1,759, or 1 percent of the original cost, for the salvage rights.

WESTMORELAND PLACE

No. 2 Westmoreland Place was the address of a huge buff brick mansion built in 1895 for a wealthy chemical manufacturer, Henry A. Siegrist, who was married to the former Minnie Lawrence, daughter of a prominent physician, Joseph J. Lawrence. Siegrist moved to Westmoreland Place from a large mansion on West Pine, repeating the pattern that had destroyed the neighborhoods that were deemed too close to the

An exterior view of the Hills mansion. *Courtesy Missouri Historical Society.*

No. 2 Westmoreland Place was built for Henry A. Siegrist. *Courtesy Missouri Historical Society.*

An interior view of the Siegrist house. *Courtesy Missouri Historical Society.*

city's commercial areas.

The Siegrist house was designed in somewhat atypical Georgian Revival style by William Albert Swasey. In his book *Examples of Architectural Work,* Swasey wrote, "Originally built for Mrs. Siegrist, it is full of her ideas and requirements. The design was selected for a three-story colonial house, introducing two bay windows, and a low third story, with a flat tile roof and a balustrade, which the style called for.

"The tile roof, however, was finally adapted to please my client, and four feet were added to the height of the third story to provide for a ballroom not originally contemplated.

"The interior of the house is most elaborate, a different style being required for each room and no expense spared in their execution. Some of the rooms are an Elizabethan dining room, an Empire library and a Moorish smoking room. The lavishness of decoration and appropriate furnishing make it an interior hardly equaled in the West."

Photographs taken in 1900 reinforce Swasey's comments. The entrance hall was three stories high, and the two upper floors were rimmed by balustraded balconies. The floor line of the third story was studded with Tivoli lights.

Swasey failed to mention that Minnie Siegrist was a somewhat difficult client, that an "oriental nook" on the second-floor landing was guarded by a statue of a tousled angel, or that the main parlor was where the quantity and elaborateness of the furnishings outstripped most Victorian dreams.

Minnie Siegrist died young at 34, and the house was sold to a J.A. Lawrence. He in turn sold it to James Campbell, a utility financier.

In 1926, Campbell's daughter Lois, her husband Elzey G. Burkham, and their family moved in and occupied the mansion for more than 20 years. Burkham died in 1946 and his widow moved to the Senate Apartments in 1947.

The house was never lived in again. In 1961, after efforts to sell it on the part of the Burkham estate were unsuccessful, No. 2 Westmoreland Place was demolished, to the relief of its neighbors. Its large carriage house and a small playhouse remained as the only hints to the handsome house that had once dominated the site.

The Romanesque mansion at No. 11 was built for Thomas H. West, who was among the first Westmoreland Place trustees. Born in 1846 in Tennessee, West had joined the Confederate Army at age 16 and worked to become a successful cotton merchant before coming to St. Louis in 1880. He became a successful, respected businessman in his adopted city and by 1889 was selected as the founding president of the St. Louis Trust Company, the first institution of its kind west of the Mississippi River. Later, the Union Trust Company was formed. The two trust companies merged to create the St. Louis Union Trust Company and retained West as its president, making him one of the most powerful men in St. Louis.

In 1891, with his success assured, West engaged the firm of Grable and Weber to design his Westmoreland Place mansion. The house was built of rough-cut stone in the Romanesque style. It had 2 1/2 stories, a tower with decorative stonework at the east front corner, and an unusual veranda at the third-floor level of the east facade. The matching stable and carriage house sported a Syrian-arched coach door.

When West died in 1926, his estate was valued at $3 million. He left half to his second wife, Virginia, and his daughters from two marriages. The balance was left outright to his sons, including Allen T. West, who lived at No. 48 Westmoreland Place.

The West house was sold to Pierre and Lily Papin and later to Thomas and Jane M. Pettus. In 1957, a fire that swept through the second floor did extensive damage. The Pettuses moved to Washington Terrace, and the Romanesque mansion was demolished in 1958.

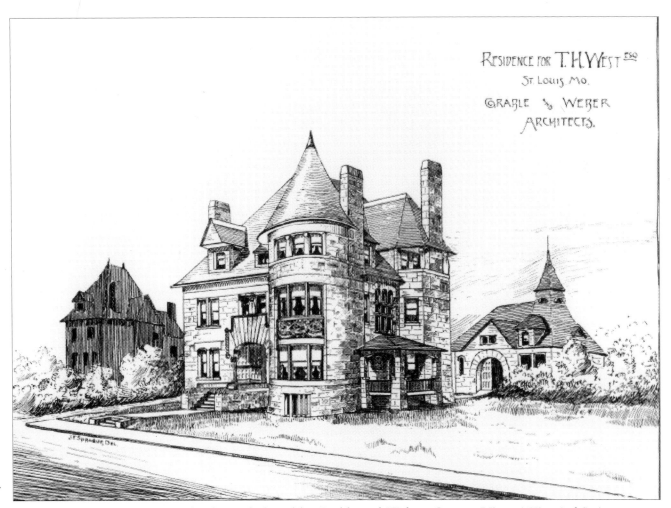

The original No. 11 Westmoreland was designed by Grable and Weber. *Courtesy Missouri Historical Society.*

Across the street from the West mansion, at No. 12 Westmoreland, stood the substantial mansion of William Bagnell. Bagnell, born in Canada in 1843, was a descendant of one of that nation's founding families. He came to St. Louis with his three brothers just before the Civil War and went into the railroad construction business. Among their projects was the construction of the St. Louis/Cape Girardeau/Fort Smith Railroad. Bagnell was also involved in banking and financial interests, real estate, and the lumber industry.

In 1879, Bagnell and his brothers incorporated Bagnell Brothers Company, which built railroads for other owners and acquired land which they sold to other railroad companies. They became closely aligned with the famous — or notorious — capitalist Jay Gould when they sold him some property. The Bagnells consequently built several railroads for him.

Shortly after 1890 — about the time that Bagnell became allied with Gould — the Bagnell brothers merged all their interests into the Bagnell Lumber Company. It was also at this time that Bagnell built his imposing mansion. He was a substantial man — both physically and financially — and his house echoed his image.

The design of the Eclectic house is attributed to William A. Lucas, though some believe it may have been the work of Lucas' employer, L. Cass Miller. The height of the terraced lawn made the three-story, 20-room mansion seem even larger than it was. Built predominantly of red brick, the Bagnell mansion was highlighted by a gabled corner turret on the east front facade. A huge Romanesque arch framed the front entrance and arched windows flanked the doorway. There were carved stone blocks on each side of the front steps, and stone pilasters graced the second-floor windows.

An 1899 addition — a large oriel window over the front door — softened the imposing facade and reinforced the Tudor style, but gave the house an even more massive presence. The addition, designed by William Lucas, was part of a larger remodeling project that may have been needed to accommodate the many social functions hosted by the Bagnells.

Bagnell was 50 when he built his house, and he lived there until he died in 1926 at the age of 83. His widow, the former Sallie Adams, moved immediately to an estate she called "Sarabelle" at 9700 Ladue Road, and his two surviving children had no inclination to live in the massive mansion.

In 1928 the house was sold to Hobart Cale and his wife, Neosha. The Great Depression took a toll, and the house was returned to the Bagnell estate in 1936. This further complicated an already-tangled probate situation, since Bagnell's estate had been disputed in 1928 on behalf of a grandchild, whose parents were divorced.

Though efforts were made to sell the mansion a second time, they were to no avail. In 1936, Bagnell's son Robert announced that the house would be demolished to avoid paying taxes on it. "The house has become run-down and unmarketable because of its old-fashioned architecture," he said.

The house that originally stood at No. 21 Westmoreland Place fulfilled the wealthy Victorian standard of being large and elaborate. Built in 1888 for Henry Levi Newman, it was one of the first on the newly established street. Designed by Peabody, Stearns and Furber, who had earlier designed a Vandeventer Place mansion for Newman, the house was initially crafted in a transitional Queen Anne style that was simpler in

No. 12 Westmoreland Place. *Michael Barfield illustration.*

No. 21 Westmoreland Place was built by cattle baron Henry L. Newman. *Courtesy Missouri Historical Society.*

silhouette than earlier houses of its ilk. The deeply recessed windows created a dignified aspect and emphasized the solidity of the structure. The walls featured a fine brick bond. The elegant parapeted gable had minimal ornamentation — simple stone bands and a simple finial.

Newman had made his mark in the cattle industry when he and his brother, E.S. Newman, were the first to prove that cattle could live and flourish year-round on the more northerly ranges of Missouri, Nebraska, Montana, and Wyoming. Their company, Newman Brothers and Farr, ran as many as 86,000 head of cattle on various properties, including a 691,200 acre ranch on the Niobrara River in Nebraska. Their revolutionary idea that cattle did not have to be driven south for the winter made the Midwestern cattle business very attractive financially. Newman also founded the National Stockyards Bank and the Joplin National

Bank and served as president of both.

In 1890, Newman sold his house to hardware magnate Edward C. Simmons and his wife, Carrie. Simmons was an important figure in St. Louis' mercantile history and was an innovator in the business world. He was among the first men in St. Louis to take note of the liberal Missouri laws relating to corporations. As a result, Simmons Hardware Company was the first mercantile establishment in the United States to incorporate. After a period of suspicion and caution, the example was enthusiastically followed by thousands of similar companies.

Simmons coined the trademark "Keen-Kutter" for his line of edge tools. He revolutionized the hardware business by packaging products conveniently for the retailer and eventually the purchaser, and issued a complete catalog of available tools and accessories. His competition, critical of some of the innovations, predicted doom for his company.

But Simmons amassed a fortune and was much admired as a self-made man (he worked 16 hours a day). Known as the dean of the United States hardware industry, he was also a civic leader in St. Louis as a director of the National Bank of Commerce and of the St. Louis Union Trust Company. He served on the Board of Police Commissioners in 1880 and 1881. That board was credited with closing all the gambling houses in St. Louis, a feat achieved in one night.

Over the years, the house at No. 21 Westmoreland Place was enlarged, including a major two-story addition in 1897. The addition was designed by Eames and Young, who also added the half-timbering to the facade that partially transformed the house from Queen Anne to a Tudor Revival. The already-large house became enormous. In 1941, the decision was made to demolish it — because it was too large. The original carriage house still stands.

A handsome new house was immediately built by members of the family to replace the original. It remained in the Simmons family until the death of Lulie Simmons Crago in 1987.

The classic house that once stood at No. 23 Westmoreland Place was built by Hudson Bridge, Jr., and his wife, Helen, in 1896. Bridge was head of his father's company, Bridge and Beach Manufacturing Company, the first stove manufacturing concern in the Midwest.

Shepley, Rutan and Coolidge designed the Hudson E. Bridge Italian Renaissance style palace in a simplified style. The Bedford limestone facade was defined with a band of rusticated stone at the first story and ashlar stone rising to the richly carved frieze above the third floor. At the second-story windows were generous bracketed cornices giving the illusion of additional height. In 1925, the house was sold to L. Warrington and Marye D. Baldwin.

In the late 1940s, the siren call to move west to St. Louis County was being heard by residents of St. Louis' older neighborhoods. The Baldwins were among those who made the move. No. 23 Westmoreland Place was demolished in 1950.

One of the largest and most beautiful of the Westmoreland and Portland Place houses was built at 26 Westmoreland Place in 1893 for George L. Allen, president of the Fulton Iron Works. The mansion was designed by the firm of Eames and Young in a Renaissance style that was more French than Italian, especially in roof shape. Standing on a double lot, the house was built of blue and buff limestone with 2 1/2 stories. The hipped slate roof was surrounded by a balustraded parapet and surmounted by a tall cupola and weather vane. The broad facade was broken by a slightly projecting center bay, articulated by a pair of pilasters supporting a pediment. Single pilasters defined the

The first No. 23 Westmoreland Place was built for Hudson Bridge, Jr. *Courtesy Missouri Historical Society.*

outer bays, and barely perceptible shadings in the limestone were placed to highlight the architectural components. Each of the four chimneys and parts of the facade were ornamented with carved garlands of flowers.

The Allen mansion had 28 rooms when it was first built. Reports vary as to the cost, with one report setting the amount at $72,000 and another at $91,000. The rooms were paneled with oak, and the central staircase was made entirely of oak. The dining room paneling was elaborately hand-carved, and the chandelier in the central hall was six feet in diameter.

After Allen died in 1924, a 34-by 60-foot ballroom was added to the back of the house at a cost of $25,000. A grated metal dome graced its entry, and the ballroom was paneled in French walnut. It was the scene of "many fashionable parties" in the late 1920s and early 1930s.

The house became vacant after Allen's widow, Lily, died in 1936. It was put up for sale, but there was little interest.

In 1938, Allen's grandson and family spokesman, Gerard B. Allen, said, "If the real estate agencies fail, it goes to the hands of the wreckers."

The 1938 valuation of the Allen house was $67,000, of which $41,000 was assigned to the improvements. By tearing down the house, the Allen estate would save $1,135 per year in taxes.

There was no buyer. By way of explanation, Gerard Allen said, "The house is simply too big and old-fashioned to attract buyers. The residential trend is toward the west — out of the smoke of the city — and any man able to afford such a house would undoubtedly want to build a new one." The house was razed in the spring of 1938.

The house built for George L. Allen at No. 26 Westmoreland Place was among the grandest of its day. *Courtesy Missouri Historical Society.*

No. 28 Westmoreland Place. *Courtesy William J. Polk, Jr.*

In 1902, George C. Hellmuth responded to the grand design by Shepley, Rutan and Coolidge for No. 23 Westmoreland Place when he designed the mansion at No. 28 for Emma C. Copelin, widow of John G. Copelin. The two mansions were quite similar and provided a grand symmetry for the streetscape of Westmoreland Place that no longer exists. Mrs. Copelin lived in her house for only a short time. In 1905, John Julius and Carolyn Mastin O'Fallon moved in and remained until 1924, when the house was sold to William Julius Polk and his wife, Sarah Chambers Polk. According to their son, William Julius Polk, Jr., the house was a happy one for his family. He, his parents and three sisters "had lots of parties, even during the Depression."

Polk reminisced that the house was quite large. The entry hall was paneled in mahogany and there was a large parlor on the right as one entered the house. "It was rather formal, with gilt furniture — Louis XV, as I remember," he said. He also recalled a massive staircase on the west side of the hall and a library that opened into the dining room. Both rooms opened to a large sunporch. "There was also a smaller room on the first floor,"

Polk said, "where my father displayed his collection of prints and etchings."

In 1938, Polk said his parents decided to give up their house "in town" and to live at Mrs. Polk's ancestral farm, Taille de Noyer, all year. "Those were very difficult times, you know," Polk said softly. No. 28 Westmoreland Place was demolished in 1939.

The talented team of Weber and Groves was hired by Charles Parsons Pettus and his wife, Georgia, to design their mansion at No. 33 Westmoreland Place in 1905. Sited at the northeast corner of Westmoreland Place and Lake Avenue, the huge Eclectic-style mansion presented an imposing presence to all who entered the private street.

The Pettus house featured intricate patterns worked into its plum-colored brick. Its stone-framed and mullioned casement windows were characteristic of Tudor Revival style, and the balustrades and belt courses were reminiscent of the Italian Renaissance style. A major element was the art gallery that extended the length of the Lake Avenue side. The

The mansion at No. 33 Westmoreland Place housed a major art collection. *Michael Barfield illustration.*

gallery was built to house a fine art collection assembled by Pettus' uncle, Charles Parsons. The collection consisted of 80 oil paintings and 360 objects that included the works of Sir Joshua Reynolds, Sir Henry Raeburn, John Hoppner, Frederick E. Church, and George Inness.

In accordance with Parsons' will, the collection became the property of Washington University upon Pettus' death in 1923. Pettus was killed falling from a horse on the R. S. Mellon estate in Ligonier, Pennsylvania. His wife, Georgia, who was an accomplished pianist, died in 1934 of a cerebral hemorrhage while playing the piano for friends who had gathered at the house for a musical evening.

The house had been vacant for over five years when James L. Ford bought it as a gift to his daughter, Elsie, and her husband, John Curby. The Curbys decided to demolish it. "The Depression and World War II had a devastating effect on efforts to maintain big houses," Mrs. Curby recalled some years later.

In 1941, the Curbys built a generous, but much smaller, house on the site.

One of the most lamented of the demolished houses stood at No. 45 Westmoreland Place. Built in 1899 for Joseph D. Bascom and his wife, Mary, it was the only house on the street designed by Frederick Bonsack.

The design was described as symmetrical French Eclectic, though the strongly bowed projections on the wall surface had little to do with Renaissance precedents. The magazine *St. Louis Builder* described the Bascom house as it was being built in 1899, proclaiming it was "destined to become one of the handsomest and most comfortable home structures in St. Louis."

The mansion was built of buff brick with a high foundation of Carthage stone. Embellishments included white terra cotta trim culminating in panels of garlands above the bay windows. The low third story was shadowed by a red tile roof.

The first-floor rooms were connected by folding doors so that they could be combined into one large reception room. The entry hall and the dining room had paneled wainscoting of mahogany, while the dining room was paneled in antique oak. There was a large billiard room in the basement, and the third-floor ballroom measured 27 by 52 feet. Design was not limited to the exterior French Eclectic style — the dining room was English, the library was Italian, and the parlor was decorated in the Louis XVI fashion.

Bascom, founder and president of the Bascom Wire Rope Company, died in 1928, and his wife died in 1932. Two different real estate agents, the Loco Realty Company and W. S. Barnickel and Company, tried to sell the mansion for four years. It was finally demolished in 1936.

PORTLAND PLACE

The mansions of Portland Place have a much better survival rate than those of Westmoreland Place, only three being victims of the "raze craze" that started in the mid-1930s.

The first mansion under construction in Portland Place stood at No. 4. Built for carpet magnate Samuel M. Kennard, it was designed in the Richardson Romanesque style by W. Albert Swasey.

Kennard's civic contributions were hard to match in his day. Born in Lexington, Kentucky, in 1844, Kennard

The design of No. 45 Westmoreland Place was described as "simplified French Eclectic." *Michael Barfield illustration.*

ran away from home to join the Confederate Army at the age of 18. He fought with distinction in many battles and held the main parapet at Vicksburg until he was captured and held prisoner by General U.S. Grant and his forces. Grant eventually paroled Kennard, who moved to St. Louis shortly after the war.

His father also moved to St. Louis, and they formed J. Kennard and Sons, said to be "the largest carpet house in the world."

The house that Kennard built in 1889 suited his position in the community and the size of his growing family. He and his wife, Annie, had six children.

The massive, 25-room house was built of rough-cut limestone with 24-inch-thick exterior walls. A pair of massive arches graced the entry, and two conical-roofed towers emphasized the solidity of the design. Swasey's design was quintessentially Victorian, with noteworthy stone transoms and detailing that were

especially typical of a Richardsonian Romanesque house, despite his comments in *Examples of Architectural Work*. Swasey said that Romanesque architecture was inappropriate for residential buildings and "should be confined to large public buildings."

The entrance hall was huge, with an impressive carved staircase that had a pair of Venetian-style arches at the landing. A passage on the landing ran between the stairs and the windows.

On the east side of the first floor, a drawing room paneled in satinwood was furnished with Adam-style chairs, couches, and tables, along with some gold opera chairs. It was restrained in decor for its era. According to one of Kennard's grandchildren, Mrs. Chapin S. Newhard, invoices for the drawing room furniture were found among Kennard's letters, and it was "appallingly expensive."

There was a conservatory, or sunroom, filled with

No. 4 Portland Place was built in 1889 for Samuel Kennard. *Courtesy Missouri Historical Society.*

plants and furniture, where the family often sat. The living room was also paneled, and though it was large, it was not unusual for its time and place.

Mrs. Newhard remembered the dining room as enormous. It, too, was paneled and had large-scale furniture with a table seating 20 for dinner. "But even at that size, the dining room could not accommodate the entire family," Mrs. Newhard reminisced. "We went there for Sunday lunch every other week, alternating with other cousins, aunts, and uncles. After lunch, the men rushed for the large couches to rest, while the ladies retired to the conservatory."

Evidently the family recovered from lunch, as the Kennards gave an open house party every Sunday evening.

The second floor featured eight connecting bedrooms and included three bathrooms, an unusual luxury for even the grandest of houses.

Aside from being president of his carpet company, Kennard was president of the St. Louis and Suburban Railway, which replaced the West End Narrow Gauge Railroad. He was president of the first Autumnal Festivities (which became the Veiled Prophet Parade and Festival), helped organize the corporation that built the "new" Planter's Hotel, was an incorporator of the Mercantile Club, and was an official of the Mississippi Valley Trust Company. He was also a trustee of Barnes

Hospital, the Methodist Orphan's Home, Kingdom House and St. John's Methodist Church.

Kennard died in 1916, and his wife died in 1930. His children were already established in other grand houses — three of which, built by Kennard for them on Pershing Place, remain standing. Accounts vary as to ownership of and attitude concerning No. 4 Portland Place over the next 28 years. One family member recalls that the house remained empty and was never sold because one of Kennard's sons could not bear to see it demolished. Another family member remembers going through it near the time of demolition and seeing "rooms painted in garish colors — each stronger than the last — it could have been a bawdy house!" A third conjecture had the Portland Place trustees buying the house and arranging for its demolition. Records in the St. Louis Assessor's office show some transfers between family and trust interests and, after 1953, three unrelated parties. There is no assessor's record of a transfer to the trustees of Portland Place.

The house was demolished in 1958 for the same reasons that many of the others were razed: it was deemed too large and too expensive to repair and maintain.

Across from the Kennard house stood No. 5 Portland Place — a monumental mansion that was also designed in the Richardsonian Romanesque style. It was built in 1896 for Thomas W. Carter, one of the original Portland Place trustees. Tom Barnett, of Barnett, Haynes and Barnett, was its architect, and his design shows strong influence by H. H. Richardson and Harvey Ellis.

The house had a monumental, rough-cut stone facade with a massive conical tower. The top-story gable had a typical tripartite window, complete with a small half-round window centered above. Barnett's trademarks, attention to detail and embellishments, could be seen in the fine stonework, especially the window that flanked the entrance.

Carter died in 1924 and his wife died in 1939. The house

No. 5 Portland Place was designed by Tom P. Barnett. *Michael Barfield illustration.*

stood vacant, awaiting a buyer, until it was razed in 1941. Its site was joined with No. 7 Portland Place in 1943.

In 1903, Breckinridge Jones, one of the leading citizens of his day, built the handsome Georgian house that once stood at No. 45 Portland Place. Its design by Weber and Groves influenced the architects who designed the second generation of Westmoreland and Portland Place houses that replaced the originals. Its Neoclassical style and its closely related Colonial Revival contemporaries would eventually eclipse all other traditional styles in popularity.

The two-story mansion was built of red brick with contrasting white trim. The design combined gabled dormers with arched windows, roofline balustrades, columned side porches, and massive end chimneys in classic Revival style. The two-story semicircular entry porch had huge Ionic columns that were a smaller version of the south portico of the White House.

Jones was a founder of the Mississippi Valley Trust Company in 1890. He served that institution successively as secretary, vice-president, counsel, president, and chairman of the board.

He was a member of the Kinloch Syndicate that formed the Union Electric Power and Light Company and the Kinloch Telephone Company. When the syndicate's interest in the light and power company was sold to the North American Company, which controlled the United States Railway of St. Louis, Jones served as a director for many years.

Jones was also elected to the Missouri State Legislature in 1882 and was interested in the development of the arts and the preservation of various cultures. He influenced his friend, E.W. Marland — president of the Marland Oil Company, which had extensive oil leases in the Osage Territory of Oklahoma — to establish a fund that would pay for compiling a dictionary of the Osage Indian language and combining it with an encyclopedia of Osage culture, rites, and ceremonies. Jones convinced Marland to make a lasting contribution to the tribe.

Jones died in 1928, two months after his wife. The house stood empty for seven years — unwanted by his heirs or potential buyers. The house was razed in 1935 — the first of the Portland and Westmoreland Place houses to go.

It is a testament to the strength of the original planning of Portland Place, Westmoreland Place, and Forest Park Terrace that the demolition of the 14 houses did not lead to total destruction, as was the case with Vandeventer Place.

The streetscapes, most dramatically on Westmoreland Place, were considerably altered. But the stringent indentures and a strong architectural heritage guided the design of the replacement structures, and where houses were not replaced, their sites were combined with neighboring ones and artfully landscaped with good results.

THE BELL PLACE PROJECT WASHINGTON TERRACE AND KINGSBURY PLACE

In 1796, Marie Louise Chouteau Papin, a daughter of St. Louis' founder, asked

No. 45 Portland Place was built in the Neoclassical style in 1903. *Michael Barfield illustration.*

the local Spanish Government for a land grant near the River Des Peres "which her slaves might cultivate to provide food for her increasing family." The Spaniards accommodated her needs with a grant of 2,720 acres that extended west to Hanley Road from Union and north to Maple Avenue from the site of the St. Louis Art Museum. The land was passed on to her ten children in 1808, and two Papin heirs sold their land to Jean Pierre Cabanne. In 1834, one of Cabanne's sons-in-law, James Kingsbury, bought a 425-acre tract that became the Kingsbury family homestead.

In 1892, Ernest Bell organized Bell Place Realty Company to develop the Bell farmstead located west of Union Boulevard and north of the Kingsbury farm. Bell and Lewis Bierman also bought the Kingsbury land. Julius Pitzman was retained to lay out a private enclave of 100 lots lining two parallel streets in a manner similar to his plans for Westmoreland and Portland Places. Washington Terrace was the first to be established in 1892 and Kingsbury Place followed in 1902.

The success and beauty of Westmoreland and Portland Places provided incentive to develop still more private streets. Bell advertised his developments as having a location "slightly higher" than the preceding places and being, therefore, healthier and cleaner. He further boasted they were as just convenient, being 15 minutes from Grand Avenue and 30 minutes from Broadway.

WASHINGTON TERRACE

Charles Savage wrote in his book *Architecture of the Private Streets of St. Louis* that "Washington Terrace was the last of the private streets with consistent scale and sustained architectural quality for its full length." Only two of the original houses have been demolished.

Unlike Vandeventer Place, Westmoreland Place, and Portland Place, Washington Terrace was not laid out with a center parkway. Other aspects, including a trust indenture that outlines responsibility for maintenance of street lights and the like, construction costs, building materials, and building lines, remained consistent with the preceding streets. The developers took the art of the entryway several steps beyond previous efforts with Harvey Ellis' 1893 design for a clock-tower gatehouse which remains a major city landmark.

The original owners in Washington Terrace hired many of the same prominent architects whose work stood in earlier private places and on Forest Park Terrace. Barnett, Haynes and Barnett designed seven houses on Washington Terrace. Of these seven, one which was considered the most impressive of the Beaux Arts palaces on any St. Louis street, is gone.

In 1902, Barnett, Haynes and Barnett designed the house at No. 5 Washington Terrace for Corwin Spencer, a grain merchant associated with Harlow, Spencer and Company and president of the Southern Electric Railway. The house was a tour-de-force of the Beaux Arts style. Of particular note were the exaggerated first-floor rustication, exuberant ornamentation at the front door and upper balcony, ornate window detailing, and handsome low-hipped tile roof.

No. 5 Washington Terrace was a tour-de-force of the Beaux Arts Style. *Courtesy Missouri Historical Society.*

For all its grandeur, No. 5 Washington Terrace changed hands quickly — Spencer sold it to David May in 1908. May and his family lived there until they sold the house to Jacob Babler, who sold it to Harry Soldini, manager of the Missouri and Maryland hotels. Babler never lived in the mansion.

Soldini lost ownership of the house in 1929 on the eve of the Great Depression. Title transferred to the Missouri State Life Insurance Company, and the house was briefly occupied by that company's president, Hillsman Taylor. Later, ownership switched to the General American Life Insurance Company. Accounts vary as to the date of demolition — one says 1943 and another 1945.

Washington Terrace lost only one other of its original houses. Elliot K. Ludington built his mansion at No. 26 Washington Terrace in 1910. Ludington was president of the Chase Bag Company, and was married to Francis Bemis, heiress to the Bemis Bag Compay.

There are no photographs available, though Martin Ludington and other family members were contacted. There is no record at city hall of its demolition, though newspaper accounts of Mrs. Ludington's funeral in 1931 say that the services were held at 26 Washington Terrace. The house was probably demolished in the 1930s, when so many mansions were destroyed because no one wanted them.

KINGSBURY PLACE

The entire private place south of Washington Terrace is commonly known as Kingsbury Place, even though it began as three separate development projects. When the Kingsbury homestead was sold to developers Ernest Bell and Lewis Bierman, it was divided in three parts. The northern section between Union and Belt was called Bell Place, the southern Bierman Terrace. The land on both the north and the south from Belt Avenue to Clara Avenue was called Kingsbury Terrace.

Around the turn of the century, architecture in St. Louis was influenced by the Revivalism movement that was prominent in both the United States and Europe. But architects were also influenced by the desires and demands of their wealthy clients. This was especially true when those building on the private places were determined to outdo each other when it came to designing their houses. Our forebears were

not immune to competition and left a rich legacy, whether or not that was their intention.

The first of the Kingsbury Place owners were wealthy, and they built large houses as evidence of their success. Among those who chose to skip west of the established private places was Charles W. Nugent, vice president of B. Nugent and Brothers Dry Goods Company.

Designed by Barnett, Haynes and Barnett in 1905, the Nugent house at No. 3 Kingsbury Place was Neo-classical, with many of the elaborations found in the earlier Classical and Greek Revival styles. It was enormous, but the space was needed as Nugent and his wife, Cora, had eight children. The house was sited on a double lot, the second accommodating the street's first private tennis court.

The three-story house stood high on a terrace and had 20 rooms, excluding the servants' quarters. There were a dozen bedrooms and six bathrooms.

The prominent semicircular entry was supported by six Ionic columns and, according to Charles Savage, may have been the architects' attempt to improve on George Hellmuth's design for the facade of the Albert Bond Lambert house at No. 2 Hortense Place. Balustrades interspersed the roofline pediment and delineated the first-floor platform porch. Four stone urns further embellished the roofline. Wide white stone steps led to the entrance. Palladian-style windows graced a porte-cochere on the west side and a graceful bow on the east side provided bays for two rooms.

Inside, in addition to the 12 bedrooms, the first floor had a large reception hall, living room, music room, library, sun room, dining room, breakfast room, and kitchen.

Charles Nugent lived in his elegant mansion for only five years. He was "stricken with apoplexy" when he climbed a steep incline near Wharf Street where his yacht was moored, and died on the way to a doctor's office.

Mrs. Nugent remained in her house for three more years, when she sold it in 1914 to James and Clara Jones for $57,000. She lost $59,500 on the initial investment of $111,500.

When Jones' second wife died, she left the house to a daughter. The mansion was considered by various speculators but remained empty for six years.

In 1936, when the title was held by real estate agent Edward Bierbower, the original No. 3 Kingsbury Place was torn down. The expenses for taxes, insur-

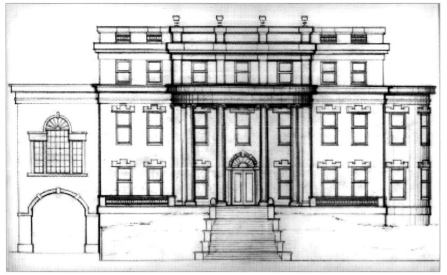

No. 3 Kingsbury Place was built for Charles W. Nugent. *Benson Tulloch illustration.*

including Italian Renaissance and French Eclectic with detailing borrowed from the Beaux Arts movement. This combination approach resulted in an innovative and handsome design that signified affluence and solid success in that era — an image many of the early residents wanted.

The house was large, with 20 spacious main rooms — an ideal place to rear a large family and to entertain.

A description of the wedding of Harrison's daughter, Florence, to Harry S. Bill details the decorations of roses, ferns, and "huge quantities of sweet peas" that decked the entrance hall, library, drawing room, and dining room.

ance, and general maintenance made it "too costly to renovate" and difficult, if not impossible, to find a buyer.

The second of the two demolished Kingsbury Place houses was also designed by Barnett, Haynes and Barnett. Built in 1902 for John W. Harrison, No. 7 Kingsbury Place was the first to be completed on the street. Born in 1840, Harrison was a native of Howard County, Missouri. He graduated from the University of Missouri in 1858 and went on to manage an iron furnace in Irondale in 1860. In that capacity, he manufactured much of the pig iron used for shot and shells by the Union Army. When Harrison moved to St. Louis, he formed the Shickel, Harrison and Howard Iron Company, of which he was president.

Having paid $20,000 for his lot in Kingsbury Place, Harrison was confident that the new private street would be in high demand. He was serving as a member of the street's first board of trustees when he commissioned Barnett, Haynes and Barnett, designers of the spectacular Beaux Arts gates to Kingsbury, to create an appropriate residence for him and his family. The massive design was a stylistic mixture of eclectic types

Harrison sold the mansion in 1911 to banker Tom Randolph. Harrison did not live long enough to witness the decline of the grand houses built by him and his peers. He died in 1923, while the rich were still amassing great fortunes and spending freely. Few were anticipating the Great Depression.

Randolph and his family moved to No. 7 Kingsbury Place from 4386 Lindell, following the

No. 7 Kingsbury Place was designed by Barnett, Haynes and Barnett, the same firm that designed the street's distinctive Beaux Arts gates. *Benson Tulloch illustration.*

westward trend established years earlier by the wealthy to escape coal fumes, traffic, and city noises.

During the seven years the Randolphs lived at No. 7 Kingsbury Place, their daughter married Harry Potter. The reception, held at home, was gloriously reported in the society columns of the day. According to the reports, the large entrance hall and drawing room were "decorated with profusions of American Beauty roses," and pink Taft roses were used in the dining room and library.

Tom Randolph died in 1918, having outlived his wife. The house changed hands again, but stayed in the family. The new owners were Ada Randolph and her husband, Harry Potter, who lived there until 1929, when they sold the house to the Burdeau Realty Company.

For 12 years, the Burdeau Company searched in vain for a buyer. The mansion was demolished in 1941.

FULLERTON PLACE

The 4300 and 4400 blocks of Westminster Place, also known as Fullerton Place, have achieved National Historic Register status because of the many houses that survived the "raze craze" that was prevalent in the 1930s and 1940s and because they represent a remark-

able showcase of the work of important St. Louis architects.

The Fullerton Place tract is roughly bounded by Taylor, Boyle, McPherson, and Olive. The land was bought in 1881 by Joseph Scott Fullerton, a Union Army general, who started the development. Fullerton, who was a lawyer, also developed one of the city's first large office buildings. He was killed in an accident in 1887 and his residential development was completed by his daughter, Anna.

Incorporated in 1882, six years before Westmoreland and Portland Places, Fullerton's Westminster Place provided a haven for the city's finest families and businessmen as the well-heeled population rushed westward.

Residents of the new street included Mr. and Mrs. Charles Cabanne, Mr. and Mrs. W. H. Walker, Mr. and Mrs. O.H. Peckham, Mr. and Mrs. Edward Walsh, Mr. and Mrs. John Carton, and Mr. and Mrs. Charles Bates. They were joined by E. H. Semple and his large family, General and Mrs. George H. Shields, and Judge Henry S. Priest.

They built large, substantial houses all of which were designed by St. Louis architects. No one hired an out-of-town firm. In the years between 1892 and 1909, 57 mansions were built representing the work of Grable and Weber, Grable, Weber and Groves, George Hellmuth, Hellmuth and Spiering, Ernst C. Janssen, Will Levy, Montrose McArdle, Edward Manny, Mauran, Russell and Garden, Louis Mullgardt, Ernst Priesler, A.F. Rosenheim, J.L. Wees, Eames and Young, and Otto Wilhelmi. But 24 of the original 57 houses were the work of two of the top local architects, W. Albert Swasey and Barnett, Haynes and Barnett, with 12 each to their credit.

All 12 of the Swasey houses, representing various styles, remain as do 11 of those designed by Barnett, Haynes and Barnett. One of the Barnett houses, along with others by Eames and Young, Ernst Janssen, J.L. Wees, and Hellmuth and Spiering have been torn down — but there is a remarkably good survival record in view of the difficult years that Fullerton's Westminster Place has

Henry S. Priest house at 4322 Westminster Place was among the few to be destroyed on that street. *Courtesy Landmarks Association of St. Louis.*

weathered.

The one house designed by Barnett, Haynes and Barnett that was lost was at 4322 Westminster Place. It was built in 1908 by Judge Henry S. Priest.

Priest, who was a relative of Texas hero Sam Houston, was born in 1853 in Ralls County, Missouri. He became a noted attorney who gained a fine state and national reputation. At various times in his early career, he was attorney for the Missouri Pacific Railroad and for the Wabash Railroad. He was appointed as U.S. District Judge by President Grover Cleveland and served in that capacity for one year before returning to private practice as a partner in the firm of Boyle, Priest and Lehman. In 1891, he was unanimously elected as president of the Missouri Bar Association.

The house that Priest built was impressive. Its style was Renaissance Revival and its sand-colored brick mass stood squarely on the site. The entryway was arched and was crowned by a second floor Palladian window and a heavy wrought iron balcony. Tall, narrow arched windows flanked the entry, and a pair of large, arched windows completed the first-floor facade. There were half-bays at the sides of the house that were crowned with elaborate iron railings at the third floor level. The flat roof was set off by handsome cornice work. There was a large, open porch on the east side of the house at ground level that was topped by a closed conservatory that was lined with leaded glass French windows. There were a side garden with a decorative pool and fountain on the east and a large yard and garden in the rear.

According to Judge Priest's grandson, long-time Central West End resident H. Sam Priest, the basement of the main house contained a large ballroom, a Turkish bath, and laundry facilities.

"All the utility systems were in the carriage house basement," Priest said. "The steam for heat and the hot water were piped underground from there to the main house."

Priest also recalled that the carriage house was huge with three full apartments and a large storage area for hay on the second floor and room for at least six cars on the first. Originally, there was probably room for five or six horses and two carriages. Priest lived at 4322 Westminster with his grandparents after his mother died in 1913. He remembered that there was a large parlor, a second parlor that opened into a generous paneled entry hall, and a large paneled dining room, in addition to a large kitchen and pantry on the first floor. He also recalled that there was a half-bath on the first floor, an unusual amenity in that era.

Priest fondly recalled his childhood days on Westminster, including the many happy hours he spent "creating" caves under the back yard — a harmless pastime unknown to his grandfather until a large, horse-drawn wagon tried to cross the back yard loaded with supplies to make repairs to the side of the house.

The wagon and horses sank deeply into the boy-made caves, causing a high level of adult consternation, Priest recalled with a chuckle.

Judge Priest was an old man when he died in 1929. The house remained empty until it was torn down in 1938. No one wanted to pay the taxes or afford the upkeep. The same year brought the identical fate to the house at 4325 Westminster Place that Eames and Young had designed for Charles F. Bates, and to the house that Ernst Janssen designed at 4312 Westminster Place. The other two houses that were deliberately razed were 4394 Westminster, which was designed by Hellmuth and Spiering and torn down in 1957, and the J.L. Wees example at 4487 Westminster which was destroyed in 1966. The sixth of the 57 original mansions was destroyed by fire in 1982.

To the credit of the residents of Fullerton's Westminster Place, all the empty sites have been landscaped so that the streetscape has no gaping holes and the losses have been minimized.

PUBLIC STREETS OF THE CENTRAL WEST END

While Lindell Boulevard and the private places flaunted more than their share of fine mansions, they were not the only Central West End locations for grand houses. Forest Park Boulevard, Maryland Avenue, West Pine Boulevard, and Washington Boulevard, among others, also had their share.

In 1876, a wide, easily traveled road headed toward Forest Park, cutting through lightly wooded, rolling farmland that had very few houses. Called Baker Avenue, its name was changed to West Pine Boulevard in the 1890s as the city sprawled westward and well-to-do citizens chose to build their houses there.

These houses were substantial and comfortable, if not as grand as those on the nearby private places. But a few of them, including a massive, buff-brick mansion built at 4545 West Pine for newspaper man Daniel Houser, could hold their own with any in the more exclusive enclaves.

The Houser/Benoist house at 4545 West Pine Blvd. sheltered four generations of the same family. *Courtesy Barbara Benoist Ring.*

Built in 1893, the Houser house was designed in the Romanesque style at a cost of $25,000. The 1 1/2-story stable was built the next year at a cost of $7,000. The building permits do not list an architect, but the permit issued for a 1903 alteration and pantry addition lists James Crawford as the architect.

The mansion was huge, with 30 rooms and 11 fireplaces and could accommodate 250 guests for a wedding or Christmas party, as it often did over the years. The space was well used, since Houser married twice and had seven children.

The large entry hall had shoulder-height mahogany paneling and a blond oak floor. A broad staircase with a large newel post and carved banisters led to the circular balcony that soared above the hall. Portieres hung in the wide doorways leading to the parlor, living room, and dining room.

The living room at the east side of the hall was lined with blond mahogany paneling carved in Italy and shipped to St. Louis, as was the rest of the house's paneling. The large fireplace and mantel were topped by a mirror that reflected the 12-light chandelier. The mantel was further crowned with carved cupids that were echoed in the wall sconces.

The window-lined conservatory was also on the east side of the house.

On the west side, the parlor had a large fireplace, and the cupids were again evident as the main theme of the room's frescoed ceiling.

In the large dining room, the high cupboards and

massive sideboard were actually set into the walls as an integral part of the paneling. The table and chairs were carved to match the walls, and a Tiffany-shaded light fixture illuminated the room.

There were a huge kitchen with its massive cooking range and a breakfast room that could accommodate a large table, 12 chairs, and a large oak sideboard. A plate warmer was built into one of the radiators. Another large room off the kitchen was used for various projects.

The second floor had seven bedrooms, six bathrooms, six fireplaces, and a full library. One of the bedrooms was completely decorated with carved gargoyles.

The grand lifestyle, unfortunately, did not bring happiness to the Houser family. One son had to move to Arizona, as his health had broken. Another's wife committed suicide, and a third died of typhoid fever at the West Pine mansion.

The Houser family sold the West Pine mansion in 1916 to Mr. and Mrs. Alan Baker, who brought to it a large and happy — if boisterous — family.

Barbara Benoist Ring, a granddaughter of the Bakers, has fond memories of life in the West Pine mansion with her mother, Mrs. Wilson Benoist, as the central figure. "At one time," Mrs. Ring said, "the house was home to four generations of the family at the same time."

The Baker/Benoist family lived in and loved every bit of the mansion. "And there were lots of animals," Mrs. Ring reminisced. "During World War II, we brought the horses and some other animals in from the farm because the gas rationing made it impossible for us to go out there.

"I exercised the horses, either in the alley or in the park every day after school. I would often meet Archbishop Glennon as he walked around the block saying his rosary. He always had a kind word and a treat for the horses."

The horses were stabled in the elegant carriage house with its carved mahogany stalls and high ceilings. Stabled with them was an adventurous goat named Tony.

Mrs. Ring recalled that Tony was not the ideal city pet and that one day he escaped. Her mother reported his disappearance to the police, who insisted on having a complete description — including height, weight, sex, and coloring — of the missing beast.

In a surprisingly short time, the authorities called with the happy news that they had located Tony. He had climbed the fire escape of the Kingsway/Ambassador Hotel, then located at Kingshighway and West Pine, and was found after an extremely agitated woman reported that "an ugly old man with a filthy beard" was leering at her through the bedroom window.

Tony's career as a peeping Tom was quickly curtailed, though he escaped again and boarded a streetcar — to the consternation of the driver, who rudely ejected him. The goat's last adventure ended with his leg being broken as he exited public transportation. He mended well, but his urban adventures were over.

The Baker/Benoist regime brought many visitors to the West Pine house for parties, weddings, and assistance. One friend, Clarkson Carpenter, Jr., brought his ailing prize gamecock to be nursed back to health. Mrs. Benoist did just that and then refused to give her patient up when the owner came to claim him to return to a fighting career. The gamecock remained on West Pine to join the rest of the animals when they greeted Pete, the milkman's horse, as he plied his daily rounds.

Mrs. Ring remembers her older sister assuring her that the ghosts of some of the Housers remained at 4545 West Pine and that an old trunk in the basement contained the bones of one of them. "I never saw a trace of a ghost, but Betty insisted there really was one — usually in the bedroom I was using," she added.

The Benoist clan's happy, if chaotic, life continued for 35 years until 1963, when the property had to be sold to pay inheritance taxes. The new owners bought the house to demolish it to make room for part of the parking lot of the Doctor's Medical Building.

The Benoists moved out the same day the salvage crews and the wreckers came in. Family members sat on the porte-cochere steps, watching numbly and offering a final champagne toast to many happy years, a sad and restless ghost, a trunk recently found to be devoid of bones, and a magnificent house.

Two blocks to the northeast of the Benoist house is the site of perhaps the most magnificent of any of the turn-of-the-century mansions. Appropriately, it was built for St. Louis' most famous citizen of the era, David Rowland Francis.

Francis had already made a fortune by the time he was thirty through the D. R. Francis Commission Company. He was also vice president of two banks, president of the Merchants' Exchange, president of the Madison County Ferry Company and had other lucrative ventures.

At that time, Francis built his house at 16 Vandeventer Place, which was a fitting backdrop for the man who was elected mayor of St. Louis in 1885. During his tenure, he had the city buy the Chain of Rocks waterworks site and brought major conventions and national recognition to St. Louis.

In 1887, President and Mrs. Grover Cleveland visited 16 Vandeventer Place. Francis met his guests' carriage and escorted them to the drawing room where he had had a solid gold chandelier installed.

In 1888, with a year remaining in his mayoral term, Francis was elected governor of Missouri and left Vandeventer Place permanently.

As governor, Francis had a major influence on the University of Missouri at Columbia. He established the bipartisan Board of Curators that remains today and took management of the university out of the political arena.

He returned to St. Louis in 1893 and bought a five-acre tract bounded by Maryland, Newstead, and Pershing Avenues. He paid $62,000 for the land that had been the site of the Nathan Coleman house since 1869.

Francis engaged the firm of Eames and Young to create a mansion that was to be known as "the most beautiful in St. Louis." In doing so, he joined the westward residential trend that would eventually bring decline to the older areas to the east.

Eames and Young retained only four rooms of the Coleman house and created a large, Corinthian columned mansion in a modified Colonial style that reminded many of the White House.

A large reception hall with a central staircase led to two balconies that overlooked the hall. A double drawing room, two living rooms, and a huge dining room were the scene of festivities and visits by presidents and foreign dignitaries.

In 1896, Francis left St. Louis for one year to serve as Secretary of the Interior. He was responsible for adding millions of acres to the nation's forest reserves.

He returned to the city in 1897 and began to assemble the Louisiana Purchase Exposition Company to run the 1903 — delayed until 1904 — World's Fair.

He was president of the 118-member board of directors.

Francis persuaded the U.S. government that St. Louis was a better location for the 100th anniversary of the Louisiana Purchase than New Orleans. He arranged financing for the fair from federal, city, and private sources. The budget was $15 million — the same amount paid to Napoleon for the Louisiana Territory.

Francis made a whirlwind tour of 19 European and Balkan countries, visiting emperors, kings, and other high officials to invite them and their exhibits to the fair. Most of them came, and all who did spent time at the house on Newstead and Maryland.

According to accounts of the time, visitors included three United States presidents — Grover Cleveland, Theodore Roosevelt, and William Howard Taft. Alice Roosevelt Longworth danced in the great reception hall. In a 1979 *West End Word* article, Elizabeth S. Benoist, a longtime Central West End

resident reminisced:

"They danced in the great reception hall which was divided into sections by marble pillars. Those pillars with their gilded Ionic pediments were things of beauty. Four on each side, they upheld a balcony off which the master bedrooms opened. Downstairs on the south was the lovely drawing room. Its walls covered with green satin brocade reflected always for me the good taste of the mistress of the house, Mrs. Francis.

"Across the reception hall from the formal drawing room were two living rooms opening into each other. One really was a great room, which in spite of its size was cozy and homelike, especially in the winter when the curtains were drawn and the two fireplaces were lighted.

"At one end of the living room was an enormous desk. It was here, and at the great dining room table across the hall, that political campaigns were mapped out, the Louisiana Purchase Exposition was planned,

David R. Francis mansion. The entrance gates still stand on Newstead Avenue one block west of Lindell Boulevard and the St. Louis Cathedral. *Courtesy Missouri Historical Society.*

and other stirring events of the day were discussed, and more often than not, settled."

In 1916, Francis again left St. Louis to serve his country when President Woodrow Wilson appointed him ambassador to Russia. World War I was being fought in Europe, and the tides of change were running high in imperial Russia. Francis arrived in Petrograd (formerly St. Petersburg, later Leningrad, and now St. Petersburg again) when Czar Nicholas II had one troubled year left in his reign.

When the American Embassy was besieged by a revolutionary mob, Francis held them off and managed to disperse them with the aid of only a shotgun and his valet. He warned Secretary of State Robert Lansing of the gravity of the Russian situation, both in terms of the War and the revolution, but even he did not forecast the fate of the czar and his family.

Francis returned to St. Louis in 1918, but not to the mansion at Maryland and Newstead. He and his family moved to the St. Regis Apartments and then to Ellenwood Avenue — far enough west to be out of the city of which he was once mayor.

The Maryland house never again had a full-time occupant, though Francis lent it to the Boy Scouts and the Junior Chamber of Commerce for meeting purposes. The last major event there was Francis' funeral in 1927.

In 1929, the St. Louis Board of Education voted to locate Central High School on the site, but the deal was never consummated. The house stood in decaying splendor until 1935, when the Sisters of Mercy acquired it. The Sisters had traded a large lot at the southwest corner of Lindell and Sarah, plus a small amount of cash, for it and planned to build a "business women's home" (McCauley Hall) on the site.

All that remains of the Francis era are the large gates that face Newstead and the memories of those like Elizabeth Benoist who knew it well.

"Now the house is long destroyed," she wrote. "But not really destroyed, for staring through the grilled iron gateway toward the curving green lawn, one can imagine

how the story of the grand old Francis house, and all the brilliant, vibrant life it sheltered, will be passed by word of mouth, from generation to generation, until at last it will become a legend."

In 1880, The Academy of the Sacred Heart, City House, joined the westward migration initiated by the well-to-do. City House had been established in 1827, 11 years before the St. Louis public schools were opened, by Mother Philippine Duchesne, a religious of the Society of the Sacred Heart. In addition to the academy for young women, Mother Duchesne founded a convent, an orphanage and a free school which thrived until the mid-1880s, when enrollment declined because of its Broadway location.

After extensive deliberation, the Sisters of the Sacred Heart bought a 6 1/2-acre tract from the Sisters of the Good Shepherd. The cost of the land in 1880 was $60,300. The property was bounded by Taylor, Berlin (now Pershing), and Maryland Avenues and abutted the property where David R. Francis built his grand house.

The Sisters commissioned a large red brick and

City House. *Courtesy of the Society of the Sacred Heart—Archives.*

stone building in institutional style that was a simplified Second Empire with Wren spire. J.H. McNamara was the architect and contractor for the original U-shaped building. His design was simple, if massive, and featured a grand, turreted entrance. The building faced Taylor and was approached via a semicircular driveway. A marble statue of Sacre Coeur stood on the lawn guarding the entrance.

Inside, there were 30 rooms on the first floor alone, including parlors, reception rooms, classrooms, and an assembly room that, until 1913, was also used as a chapel. The chapel altar and matching pedestals, designed by Louis C. Tiffany, were purchased as a gift to the new school at the Tiffany exhibit of the 1883 Chicago Exposition.

In September 1883, the building was opened to 115 students. It was shortly thereafter that parents of girls at City House asked the nuns to start a grade school for boys, as there was no private Catholic boys' school in the city. Recognizing the need, the nuns established Barat Hall.

In 1908, a new classroom addition was built on the Maryland side of the original building.

The new wing, designed by Hellmuth and Hellmuth, was begun in 1913. The main and two side chapels were on the second floor, and classrooms for Barat Hall were on the first. Each side chapel had a large stained glass window and there were 10 in the main chapel. Some of the frescoes and painted panels depicting angels and panoramas were painted by one of the nuns, Sister Mary Falley.

A gymnasium was added in 1929.

In February 1959, a tornado tore through the Central West End, and City House was in its path. The stained glass windows in the side chapels were shattered, along with many others in the building. But the real threat to City House was not severe weather. It was the climate — social, economic, and political — of the 1960s and the expensive requirements of an aging building that would lead to its destruction.

In 1966 it was announced that City House and Barat Hall would close in June 1968 because of a shortage of nuns to staff the two schools and because of the expense involved in maintaining the building. Efforts by parents, students, and alumnae to change the decision were in vain. City House was to merge with Villa Duchesne at Spoede and Conway Roads in West County, and proceeds of the sale of the Maryland and Taylor property would finance the new buildings.

Barat Hall had to find a new location. After much effort, that school did re-open in Chesterfield, but finances dictated a second closing.

The last day of school at City House was May 28, 1968. There was a large public auction on June 8 which was attended by antique dealers, collectors, and sentimental alumnae. All the furniture, along with the Tiffany altar, pews, and stained-glass windows, were sold to the highest bidders. While much of the furniture remains in the Central West End, some of the stained glass windows grace a bar in Southern California. The statue of Sacre Coeur that marked the entrance was moved and re-installed at St. Catherine of Sienna Church at Page and Ferguson.

Some of the builders of the Central West End's grand houses built other, smaller ones for their children as they married. Samuel Kennard, who built No. 4 Portland Place, built three houses on neighboring Pershing Place for some of his children, and Frederick G. Niedringhaus, president of the National Enameling and Stamping Company and the St. Louis Pressed Brick Company, built a smaller version of his Lindell mansion on the 5000 block of Washington for his daughter and her husband, J.B. Cozzens.

The Cozzens' son, Arthur, sent a detailed description of the house and turn-of-the-century life in the Central West End to Frances Stadler of the Missouri Historical Society in 1962. According to Cozzens, creature comforts were well-considered. In his family's house each of the principal rooms had a fireplace, while other rooms were equipped with gas burners consisting of a vertical sheet of copper slotted for gas and coated with asbestos fiber which glowed when heated.

Lighting in the major rooms was supplied by ornate brass ceiling fixtures which had four electric light bulbs and four gas jets shielded by fluted glass shades. Other rooms, including the maids' rooms on the third floor, had only gas jets. The indoor bathroom was lighted with electricity.

Cozzens described the electrical fixtures as being supplied with the early carbon filament bulbs that were simply pushed into position and held in their sockets by flat copper "fingers." As electric lights were thought to be hard on the eyes, gas lights or oil lamps were used for reading.

The Cozzens house even had an intercom system consisting of a tin tube that ran through the walls from the second floor hall to the kitchen. The calling device was a whistle, which swung out of the way to permit conversation.

At the turn of the century, there was no reliable, clean city water supply system, so the Cozzens family used bottled or distilled water for drinking. Occasionally, they obtained free drinking water from "Crystal Spring" in Forest Park. The spring was, however, closed later as a health hazard.

Water for cooking was supplied from a filtered tank above the sink. Water for laundry was necessarily clarified in two large iron tanks in the basement into which water was poured and allowed to stand until the mud settled. The process was hastened by the addition of lime, copperas (iron sulphate), and alum. Water was then removed from the tanks and heated for the laundry chores.

According to Cozzens, the construction of additional grand houses on the street along with the construction of three grand churches near Kingshighway and Washington, was of great interest to everyone, especially the children. Some of them made collections of the various shapes, sizes, and types of bricks used in the construction boom. They also collected horseshoes of various sizes, which possessed a distinct value other than that of mere collectors' interest.

They served as excellent missiles, and equally good were the "horse apples" which were plentiful on every street, waiting to be flipped at an unwary passer-by with a flat stick.

In 1898, the streets of the vicinity, including Washington Boulevard, were surfaced with crushed rock topped by fine brown gravel which, according to Cozzens, had a very attractive appearance. He had special memories of the occasions when sheets of rain swept diagonally across Washington, making it resemble a field of golden grain riffled by the wind.

Washington Avenue looking west from Kingshighway Boulevard, 1925. *Courtesy Missouri Historical Society.*

At the time of the World's Fair, two neighborhood streets were paved — Kingshighway with asphalt and Washington, east of Kingshighway, with brick. Shortly thereafter, the section of Washington west of Kingshighway was paved with tarred, wooden blocks, which the children found uncomfortable to cross with bare feet on St. Louis' hot summer days.

It was later discovered that the wood block surface was, to put it mildly, slippery when wet. With the installation of one of the city's first electric stop signals at Washington and Kingshighway, the newly popular automobiles frequently skidded and crashed into the curb, other cars, or both.

On rainy days, Cozzens and his friends would watch the skidding gyrations and would take guesses — or wagers — on which ones would crash. Fortunately, the speeds were low and the numbers small, so the damage was relatively minor. All agreed that modern innovations provided high entertainment.

Cozzens left a valuable account of the turn-of-the-century commerce on Delmar Boulevard which served the grand West End houses. He had fond memories of Harrigan's Livery stable at the corner of Kingshighway and Delmar. He also recalled Koehler Brothers Enterprises, a sort of early conglomerate. The brothers operated a wagon building shop, a hardware store, a grocery store, and a saloon. The saloon on the corner was off-limits to the young offspring of prominent families, as it was "a place of evil."

The Koehler grocery store was typical of its era.

Food was stocked in bulk and weighed out for each customer. The aromas of freshly ground coffee, unwrapped fresh bread, various spices, dill pickles in a large barrel, and white pine shipping boxes all contributed to a medley of scents. Only a few foods — including corn, tomatoes, beans, and peaches — were canned. Fruits such as apricots and plums were sold dried.

East of the Koehler enterprises, on the south side of Delmar, were a dry goods shop and then the shop of a glass worker who cut and polished glass in his window for all to see. Beyond this was the shop of a Mr. Dobschutz, a Swiss watch repairman and jeweler.

Farther east, there was a laundry where Chinese men, sporting long queues, ironed clothes that they sprayed, as needed, with water they held in their mouths.

Cozzens also described the Delmar Theater with its airdrome for hot weather and the Rodenberg sisters' bakery, where youngsters could usually count on being given a freshly baked cookie.

Central West End residents were also served by itinerant merchants. The ice man made his horsedrawn rounds through the alleys delivering his cooling wares. The sound of ice being chipped attracted children on hot summer days. The milk man and his horse were also fixtures of the time.

Other calls and sounds — the high, thin whistle of the popcorn man, the jingling bell of the scissors grinder, and the music of the organ grinder calling children to watch his performing monkey — were all a

Forest Park University for Women was designed by John G. Cairns. *Courtesy Missouri Historical Society.*

part of the daily fabric of living.

One of the most picturesque peddlers was the balloon man. Cozzens described him as a little round Swiss in a native costume of shorts, fancy vest, and Tyrolean hat with a brush.

Produce peddlers cried out their wares at the tops of their voices, " Watermelons and strawberries," drawing out the syllables as in a song.

Two disparate institutions, well-known to Central West End residents in the early 20th century, were located immediately south of Forest Park and shared its name. They were the Forest Park University for Women and the Forest Park Highlands.

Most of the early 20th century institutions in St. Louis were the products of the energies and imaginations of men. But there was one notable exception — the Forest Park University for Women and the College of Music, School of Art and Elocution which was the life work of Anna Sneed Cairns.

Mrs. Cairns, born in 1840, was the daughter of a minister from Louisville, Kentucky, and was unusually well educated for a woman of that era. Despite her gentle Southern background, she was an ardent abolitionist.

She was also a founding member of the St. Louis Women's Christian Temperance Union (WCTU) and made many speeches urging prohibition of drinking alcohol during the post-Civil War years, including one in front of the Missouri House of Representatives. Her efforts in the prohibitionist cause were eventually defeated at the polls, and prohibition was not adopted by constitutional amendment until many years after Mrs. Cairns abandoned her active efforts on its behalf.

She was also a leading proponent of women's rights and equality under the law.

Mrs. Cairns first started her school in 1861 as the Kirkwood Seminary, after many private schools in the state were closed as a result of the Civil War. She started with only seven scholars, little or no money, and fierce ambition. Her institution grew steadily and was the first in the United States to be chartered as being solely for the education of women.

In 1891, she moved the school to seven acres she had bought near the southwest corner of Forest Park near Clayton and Oakland Avenues. She renamed her institution the Forest Park University for Women.

The first and main building erected for the university was designed by John G. Cairns, Anna Cairns'

husband, an architect of the era. The building was completed in May 1891.

The huge, rambling stone, red brick and slate building was designed in a Richardson Romanesque style with arches, gables, turrets, and chimneys aplenty. The then-popular Queen Anne and Shingle styles were apparent in the massing and the rambling nature of the plan. Inside were a grand staircase fashioned of carved oak and beamed, paneled ceilings. The corridors were lined with quarter-sawn oak and the doorways were adorned with tartan portieres. The massive organ room was a point of pride. The building was said to have an "abundance of ideas for modern health and comfort."

One account recorded at the time of the World's Fair said that "the institution stands on high ground commanding a fine view of the park. Its grounds have been ornamented in such a manner as to make it one of the most attractive spots in St. Louis."

In 1900, Mrs. Cairns bought more land to increase the site to 12 acres. In 1901, the McKee Gymnasium was completed, and it was followed by Cairns Hall in 1903 and the College Annex in 1909.

All this progress was gained by Anna Cairns with great difficulty. She was a strong minded woman who rarely took a salary, eschewed luxury, and limited herself to one dress, one pair of shoes, and one pair of black kid gloves a year. She put all of her assets and much of her energy into her school and its success.

She met with less success in marriage. She wed John Cairns when she was 44 in 1884, but the union did not last. When he died in 1896, his obituary described him as a divorced gentleman living at the Hotel Rozier. Oddly, Mrs. Cairns referred to herself as a widow on legal documents after 1896.

During its heyday, the Forest Park University for Women had as many as 150 boarding students enrolled per term and boasted a distinguished faculty. Mrs. Cairns was especially pleased to offer a music professor as distinguished as Ernest R. Kroeger — who had gained notice as a composer and performer — to parents "who preferred to educate their daughters separately."

While Mrs. Cairns supported the concept of equality for women, she did not feel it was right for them to compete with men in the academic world. Further, the university's board of directors was composed of men only and included some of the leading clergymen of the day. Prominent women were relegated to an advisory board. So much for equality!

But Mrs. Cairns had a soft side too. She was very interested in the arts and took up painting and carving, exhibiting some talent in the latter discipline. For her private sitting room, she carved a black walnut mantel, depicting scenes from the lives of her ancestors, which was reported to be quite handsome.

The school existed for 64 years, 35 of them overlooking Forest Park. The school's longevity was due to its founder's energy and unswerving determination.

In June 1926, the buildings and land were sold to Byron Sharpe, a real estate speculator. Mrs. Cairns was forced to sell because of declining enrollment and her inability to continue as active head of the institution. She was nearly 86.

By the time Anna Cairns died on September 1, 1930, the land had been divided and resold. All tangible remnants of her life's work were gone.

The richness of the tapestry we know as the Central West End has always consisted of more than grand houses, impressive public buildings, and elegant vistas. As early as the establishment of Forest Park in 1876, people realized that life in the city had to include more than visual experience — entertainment, fun, and a measure of frivolity were essential ingredients in creating a successful business and residential area.

Forest Park was a popular success, and in 1896, a restaurant and beer garden called Forest Park Highlands opened just south of the park on Oakland Avenue between what are today St. Louis University High School and the St. Louis Arena.

The enterprise was the concept of two men known to posterity only as the Rice brothers. Their idea was better than their business skills; their business failed and was bought by Tony Stuever, a brewery owner, in 1897.

Stuever added many attractions to the beer garden and restaurant during his years of ownership. The first, a horse-drawn merry-go-round, was followed by a pagoda from the Japanese exhibition at the 1904 World's Fair.

The red lacquer pagoda, which sported gilded griffins, was used as a bandstand, and John Philip Sousa once conducted a concert there.

Other attractions at the Highlands included beauty contests, a penny arcade, a funhouse, a shooting gallery

The Forest Park Highlands was a popular attraction for 68 years. *Courtesy Missouri Historical Society.*

(in the old-fashioned sense), a Ferris wheel, a large swimming pool, and an auditorium with hand-painted curtains where vaudeville shows and boxing exhibitions by fighters such as Jack Dempsey and James Corbett were held. A mechanical carousel was added in 1939, when it was brought to St. Louis as part of a dairy show at the Arena.

Thrill rides were added, like the Bobsled and a huge roller coaster called the Comet.

A landmark feature was a 148-foot tower topped by an American flag made entirely of colored light bulbs. The tower had been built for the Fair and weighed nine tons.

A steam-powered locomotive pulled three cars around a quarter-mile track surrounding the amusement park.

By the teens of this century a spiderweb of electrical lines fed power to Highlands attractions.

The Forest Park Highlands remained a popular attraction for children and adults alike for 68 years. Young couples on dates strolled the grounds during the evening waiting for the dance music to start. Groups of teenagers would challenge one another's bravery on the roller coaster, and young children's imaginations gave life to the hand-carved horses on the carousel.

On July 19, 1963, disaster struck. A fire of undetermined origin — careless smoking or faulty wiring was the probable cause — swept through the Forest Park Highlands.

The City Fire Marshall, William Tratina, said, "Everything was highly combustible, like a tinderbox."

It took city firemen 6 million gallons of water to fight the fire, and the fire department lost $7,500 worth of equipment in the process. The St. Louis Arena Corporation, which owned the Highlands at the time, was unable to estimate the dollar amount of the loss.

Two elements of the Highlands were saved. The little steam engine, train, and tracks were placed in Tower Grove Park. The beloved carousel was sent to Sylvan Springs Park in St. Louis County.

The hand-carved horses fell into disrepair, and businessman Howard Oehlendorf bought them so that they could be restored. A group called "Friends of the Carousel" was organized in 1982 to raise money and oversee the restoration. The carousel is now happily ensconced at Faust Park, off Olive Street Road in Chesterfield.

The site of the Forest Park Highlands is now the location of the Forest Park Community College.

Cabanne & Visitation District

West Cabanne Place. *Courtesy Landmarks Association of St. Louis.*

The Cabanne/Visitation district of St. Louis, including West Cabanne Place, was at one time as fashionable a residential area as Lucas and Vandeventer Places, and it had the advantage of being located farther west than those streets. Despite its relatively rural location, the district fell on hard times.

Historically, the district has been defined by Kingshighway, Martin Luther King Drive, Delmar Boulevard, and the City Limits. In very early times, the land west of Union Boulevard from Delmar to Maple Avenue was part of Survey 378, the Spanish land grant given to the Papin family. East of Union to Kingshighway, the land was owned by various members of the Cabanne family and was part of their large dairy farm. The land north of Maple to Martin Luther King Drive and west to Hodiamont was part of a land

The Blossom house on Union Boulevard was included in the Historic American Building & Survey. *Courtesy Missouri Historical Society.*

grant given to Jean Baptiste LaFleur.

By the mid-19th century landowners in the area included J.S. Cabanne, Norman Coleman, Chalmers Blossom, James Clemens — a relative of Mark Twain's — and Emanuel de Hodiamont. They all had large parcels of land and big country houses.

Chalmers Blossom was a prominent river captain during St. Louis' steamboat era and came as close as possible to meeting the popular, romantic view of those who plied that trade. He came to St. Louis in 1839, and while on a trip upriver to Galena, Illinois, he realized that the river presented opportunities he could not overlook. He immediately launched his river career and, by 1843, was able to buy a major interest in the steamer *Monona*. He served as captain on that boat and on subsequent boats he would own.

In 1844, he bought his second steamer, the *Archer*, and six years later Blossom invested some of his considerable profits to build the famous steamer *El Paso*. In 1852, he built a second boat, the *Polar Star*. Blossom bought his fifth boat, the *Hiawatha*, in 1856 and then built the *Martha Jewett*. In all, Blossom spent 16 years on the Mississippi and Missouri Rivers during the period of highest profitability for owners and captains.

In 1858, he left his career as a riverman. Blossom was shrewd enough to realize that the high-profit glory days of Mississippi River steamboat trade were coming to an end. Railroads were offering strong competition, more and more boats were crowding the waterways, and the Civil War, with its disruption of trade, was imminent.

He left the river to become secretary of the Globe Mutual Insurance Company and established himself as an important businessman on land.

Blossom lived with his wife and children at 829 North Union Avenue on a country estate that served as his principal residence. The house faced Union — called Second Kingshighway before the Civil War — and was surrounded by gently rolling fields and pastures until the Central West End developed toward the end of the century.

The mansion was built in the Italianate style and was similar to some later designed by George I. Barnett. One source says the house was built in 1824, but that date may not be accurate, as Italianate architecture did not become popular in St. Louis until some 20 years later.

No matter when it was built, the house was handsome and impressive. It was 2 1/2 stories high and had a prominent square tower. A small, balustraded balcony was over the front door. On the south side, a large, round bay with windows extended from the corner. Two walls of elegant French windows graced the south and east sides. The arched frames and pilasters created a handsome colonnade effect.

The Blossom house had 15 rooms, including a parlor, library, dining room, and conservatory. Each room had a marble-manteled

The Blossom House parlor was representative of its era. *Courtesy Missouri Historical Society.*

fireplace.

A stucco exterior gave the house a rustic appearance that belied its sophisticated design but was appropriate for its then-rural site.

The house, a prominent landmark, is mentioned in several accounts by passengers on the West End Narrow Gauge Railroad as one of the sights they saw as they traveled from the city to outlying farms and estates.

Blossom retired in 1862 to look after his considerable investments and his Union Avenue estate. He also traveled a great deal.

Despite his brusque and dour demeanor, Blossom was liked and respected in the community. He was a staunch member of the Church of the Messiah and was considered generous to various charities. He was also a member of the Masonic Order and the King Templar for over 40 years.

Blossom's retirement lasted until he died in 1903 at the age of 84. His widow remained in the house until her death in 1908. Members of the family occupied the mansion until 1929, when Ada E. Blossom, a widowed daughter-in-law of the patriarch, died.

The house remained empty until 1942, when it was razed. Before it was destroyed, it was included in a federal survey of antebellum houses in Missouri. The detailed survey included floor plans of each house. The information is on file in the Library of Congress. The government desired to preserve the plans in hopes they could be used in the future to recreate the surveyed subjects.

The site of the Blossom house is now the location for the athletic fields of the magnet school for international studies.

To the south on Delmar stood the estate and home of Norman Colman, one of the era's best-known citizens who is barely remembered today. Colman came to St. Louis to practice law in 1853 at the age of 26, and within two years of his move here he was elected a city alderman. In later years he would serve as lieutenant governor of Missouri, a curator of the University of Missouri, United States Commissioner of Agriculture, and the first U.S. Secretary of Agriculture. He was also a well-known publisher, nurseryman, cattle breeder, and horse breeder.

In 1855, Colman bought an eight-year-old farm magazine, renamed it *Rural World and Valley Farmer*, and started a long career as editor and publisher. Through the publication, he influenced farmers all over the Western United States.

Colman's was one of the early voices to warn of the dangers of soil erosion, and in 1859, he started urging farmers to adopt plowing methods that would prevent the "precious soil from blowing away with the prairie wind."

He was also a preserver of trees — not only for soil conservation but also for aesthetic reasons. One of his editorials decried the wasteful and ugly destruction of trees as a prerequisite to building a new house.

"Many are the houses that are made every year in this, our rapidly populating country. Quite a number are being made in the forest or on timbered lands. Trees here are voted a nuisance....their destruction is the one idea of the settler."

He added that when new houses or farms are built, "they stand out in their hideous nakedness as much

The Norman Colman house was located on the 5400 block of Delmar Boulevard. *Benson Tulloch illustration.*

exposed as one of those square up-and-down dry-goods box sort of houses on a bleak, Western prairie...."

The pages of Colman's magazine contained his rules for landscaping. He stated that "for drives and walks curved lines are to be chosen rather than straight ones — and, if possible, either by forest or elevation, there should be preserved or created a background for the 'tout ensemble.' "

Colman was successful in communicating with Western and Mississippi Valley farmers because they knew that he himself was a working farmer. He owned two farms in the St. Louis area. One was near Creve Coeur Lake, where he raised cattle and trotting horses.

The other was his agrarian showplace at what would now be 5471-5499 Delmar. It was there that he maintained his main residence in a large Victorian-style stone house replete with a prominent bay and wraparound porches. Its setting complied with all of its owner's landscaping precepts and suited him and his family well.

The large house was an important landmark. Its extensive acres, which would later become known as a major part of the Cabanne section of St. Louis, were flanked by the estates of J. A. Monks and Chalmers D. Blossom and lay east of the Five Mile Tavern and Inn.

It was here that Colman established his St. Louis Nursery, where he worked to develop fruit trees that could thrive in the climatic extremes of the Mississippi Valley.

By 1861, Colman was able to produce the valley's largest selection of nursery stock, including apple, peach, pear, cherry, apricot, and nectarine trees. He also offered such fruit-bearing plants as quince, gooseberries, red and white currants, blackberries, raspberries, strawberries, and grapes, along with several varieties of evergreens.

Although Colman's nursery was successful, it was hindered by the Civil War, because he could not ship his stock throughout the Mississippi Valley.

The nursery did give him tremendous credibility with his journal's readers. Throughout the war, Colman promoted his magazine and gained a national reputation as an agronomist. Even farmers' wives owed him a debt, as he was the first trade publisher to include a women's section in his magazine. It was the closest thing to Godey's *Ladies Book* that many of the women could afford.

After the war, Colman was elected lieutenant governor of Missouri. In 1885, while working as a publisher, farmer, nurseryman, and politician, he was appointed U.S. Commissioner of Agriculture and moved to Washington, D.C., leaving his farms and magazines in the care of his sons.

Colman's national appointment came before the Department of Agriculture was considered to be of cabinet-level importance. It was largely through Colman's efforts, and those of Missouri Senator William Hatch, that the department was so recognized.

In 1889, the position of Commissioner of Agriculture was elevated to cabinet rank and Colman was named the first Secretary of Agriculture.

In his national-level posts, Colman served his country and industry well. One of his accomplishments was the effective management and eventual curtailment of pleuro-pneumonia in cattle. The disease had threatened to wipe out this country's cattle breeding and beef industries if it spread from Chicago and Missouri to the western ranges.

Colman returned to St. Louis in time to take a major role in planning the World's Fair in 1904. Shortly after he died in 1911, his Delmar estate and orchards were subdivided and the house demolished to make room for the city's expanding housing and commercial needs.

In 1877, Dr. James Sheppard Cabanne built a road through an uncultivated 75-acre meadow he had inherited from his family. The tract was bounded by Union Avenue on the east and Hodiamont on the west and lay north of Delmar Boulevard. At 60 feet wide, the road was no wagon trail — it was the beginning of his development of Cabanne Place and the later West Cabanne Place. The cleared strip was 550 feet wide and was graded in preparation for construction of a new residential enclave far from city problems. The street was macadamized, sewers were installed, and evergreen and shade trees were planted. Cabanne then dedicated the strip and its improvements to the public, via a recorded deed that made provisions for the intersecting streets he named Belt, Clara, Goodfellow, and Hamilton. The latter was named in honor of Governor Hamilton Gamble.

Cabanne Place was ready for development in 1877 — over 10 years earlier than Portland and Westmoreland Places. By 1885, some of the city's finest families had moved there. Cabanne and his wife

The Henry S. Potter residence on Cabanne Place was widely admired. *Courtesy Missouri Historical Society.*

built a large house and were joined by Mr. and Mrs. C. Bent Carr and Mr. and Mrs. W. G. McRee. The famous General William S. Harney, formerly of Lucas Place, lived there, and in 1886, Mr. and Mrs. Henry S. Potter built one of the most famous houses in St. Louis at 5814 Cabanne Place.

The great, and highly admired, Boston architect Henry Hobson Richardson designed only three houses in St. Louis: the John R. Lionberger house at No. 27 Vandeventer Place, the Isaac H. Lionberger house on Grandel Square (which remains standing in considerably altered condition), and the Henry S. Potter house. All of Richardson's work here was connected with the Lionberger family; Potter, president of the St. Louis Steel Barge Company, was married to John Lionberger's daughter, Margaret.

Richardson's widely acclaimed design for the shingle-style Potter house was completed before he died in 1886. Its style was thought appropriate for its then-rural location. Its linear plan became an L-shape when a one-story wing, which accommodated the stable, carriage house, and laundry facilities, was included. The main feature of the facade was a stair tower. When originally built, the house included a living room, dining room, and reception room in addition to the kitchen, cold room, and pantry. The

cow sheds were located at the rear of the property. There were four bedrooms on the second floor. All main rooms were oriented to the south because of climatic conditions.

The facade of the Potter house was never altered, but additions were made to the original Richardson plan. Richardson's successor firm, Shepley, Rutan and Coolidge, designed the enlargement of the cold room and pantry, added a bathroom and a billiard room, and included a wall and entry to surround the property.

Henry Potter died in 1918. The second, and last, owner of the house was noted architect Ernest J. Russell, a partner in Mauran, Russell and Garden. Subsequently, when Russell was a partner in Mauran, Russell, Crowell and Mullgardt, the firm designed an addition of two bedrooms and a bath at the rear of the third story and effected the combination of the living room and billiard room to create one large living room.

Russell also worked for Shepley, Rutan and Coolidge in Boston and was a great admirer of H. H. Richardson. He occupied the Potter house until his death in 1956. He left the house to the City of St. Louis, which demolished it in 1958.

The Potter house was the epitome of the Shingle style and encouraged the design of 10 other shingle houses on West Cabanne Place, which was being developed, west of Hamilton Avenue, by George Townsend in 1887. It also had an important influence on St. Louis architects who used elements of the design, executed in different materials, for houses built on later private places.

Townsend hired Julius Pitzman to plat West Cabanne Place. Lots were defined to have 100-foot widths and setbacks of 50 feet. Townsend touted the new private place as the "second Vandeventer Place" — a claim that never materialized. The advertisements described a semirural location made convenient by the proximity of the West End Narrow Gauge Railroad.

A remarkable number of prominent local architects who were drawn by the area's bucolic charm chose West Cabanne Place as the location of their personal residences. Charles K. Ramsey built his house at No. 6015 in 1889, Theodore Link did his earliest residential work on West Cabanne and built his own house there at No. 5900 in 1891, Robert Walsh built two houses — one for himself and one for his mother — at Nos. 5955 and 5959 in 1905, and Lawrence Ewald built at No. 6084 in 1908.

West Cabanne did not become another Vandeventer Place for various reasons. The houses were not built on as grand a scale, and the lot sizes were not maintained. When Theodore Link built his house, he did not use the entire lot, and as lot prices rose in the 1890s, others chose to buy smaller parcels, taking 50-foot lots rather than the full 100-foot lots and changing the planned scale of the street. Also, according to Carolyn Toft in *West Cabanne Place*, the earliest building period coincided with the interest of prominent St. Louis architects in designing houses within modest budgets.

The relentless residential movement to the west left the Potter house and the others on Cabanne Place mired in an area of speculation and dampened the market for those on West Cabanne Place. While some of the original context remains on West Cabanne, the Cabanne Place of the turn of the century is gone.

Of the ten shingle houses built on West Cabanne, seven remain in varying conditions.

The Visitation/Cabanne District was also home to fine institutions which located there to be near their constituents. Many, including Pilgrim Congregational Church and the Union Avenue Christian Church, remain, but some important buildings are gone.

Christian Brothers College once stood in the northeast quadrant of the district at Kingshighway and Martin Luther King Drive. CBC's beginnings were in the late 17th century free schools in Rheims, France, and in the founding of the Christian Brothers order by St. John Baptist de la Salle in 1717.

It was 100 years later that the Christian Brothers came to the United States with Bishop Louis DuBourg. Three of the brothers went first to Bardstown, Kentucky, to learn English and then traveled to Ste. Genevieve, where they began teaching in 1819. The brothers established schools in New York, Baltimore, and Canada.

In 1849, three brothers came to St. Louis from Montreal and formed a school in a building on Chestnut Street just west of the Old Cathedral. By 1851, they were teaching four primary classes and running St. Joseph's Academy, a boarding school at 16th and Market Streets.

In the same year, the brothers and students moved to a more suitable location at Eighth and Cerre Streets, where the school remained for 25 years. In 1855, the State of Missouri granted the brothers a college charter outlining powers to grant diplomas, confer degrees, and bestow literary honors.

By the beginning of the Civil War, CBC had 100 students. Though parts of their building were used by Union troops during the war, the school continued to grow, and by 1867 there were 500 students. The need for a new facility was clear. The fine families of St. Louis appreciated "an institution that offers many advantages to further the physical, moral and intellectual development of students."

The Lucas, Buder, Papin, and McBride families all sent their sons to CBC and found the "education based on pure and solid principles of morality calculated to answer the diverse views of discriminating families," as described in the catalog, to their liking.

The families willingly paid a hefty $250 tuition in 1865 for the basic curriculum and also paid an entrance fee, physician's fee, and extra charges for music, drawing, and engineering. They also paid for materials used in chemistry and natural philosophy. Uniforms were not required, and students were told they would need "three good suits and appropriate linen."

In 1871, the brothers followed the westward trend and bought a 30-acre tract at Kingshighway and Easton Avenue (now Martin Luther King Drive) for $50,000. Construction on the fine new building began in 1877, and the school was ready for occupancy in 1882.

The massive building was designed by James McGrath in the style of the Second Empire.

Built in the shape of a cross, it had a central rotunda and four ells. The structure was 370 feet wide and 200 feet deep. The central element had an elevation of 125 feet divided into three stories. The rotunda was 60 feet in diameter.

On the first floor was a magnificent vestibule finished in white marble and Philadelphia white enameled brick.

There were also four grand parlors and assorted reception rooms. The second floor of the rotunda had 30-foot ceilings and was used solely as a library. The 45-foot third story contained the college hall, which had the capacity to seat 1,000 people. The rotunda was surmounted by a glass skylight delineated by a decorative balustrade on the roof.

Each of the four wings had five floors. Rooms on the second, third, and fifth floors were used as classrooms, and the east and west wings were used as student dormitories. Each wing led to the grand rotunda. The building had all the modern conveniences of the day, including a steam-operated elevator.

By 1890, the property was valued at $500,000, and the school and the brothers' investment continued to grow until 1916, when, on October 5, a tragic fire destroyed the building. Two of the brothers, seven

firemen, and a school watchman lost their lives in the blaze, and a fine building was lost.

The survivors finished the school year at the closed Smith Academy on Cabanne that was loaned to them by Washington University.

Though efforts to rebuild were begun immediately, the college as it existed was never reconstructed. The Christian Brothers bought property on Clayton Road east of Big Bend Boulevard in 1918, and the present CBC opened there in 1922.

For many years, the major landmark of the Cabanne/Visitation district was the Academy of the Visitation, which stood on a 10-acre site at the corner of Cabanne and Belt Avenues.

The massive red brick and granite main building, designed in an ecclesiastical Chateauesque style by Barnett, Haynes and Barnett, was completed in 1892. Although it was a dark, brooding structure that could easily have been used as a movie set for a dreary Victorian orphanage, the site was well landscaped, with many large trees presenting a parklike setting.

The Academy had a long history in St. Louis before it finally located at Cabanne and Belt. It was founded in 1833 in Kaskaskia, Illinois, by Mother Mary Agnes Brent, who had traveled west from Maryland to open a school for young women at the request of Bishop Rosati of St. Louis. At the time, Kaskaskia was part of the St. Louis diocese.

By 1844, the diocesan boundaries had changed, and Kaskaskia was aligned with Chicago. But the St. Louis Catholic hierarchy wanted to keep control over the new academy, and Archbishop Peter Kenrick convinced the sisters to open an additional facility on the Missouri side of the river at Sixth and Olive Streets. Later that year, the school at Kaskaskia was flooded out and the briefly separated communities were necessarily and happily rejoined.

By 1846, the school had outgrown its space and was moved to the bishop's house

Christian Brothers College was destroyed by fire in 1916. *Courtesy Missouri Historical Society.*

on Ninth Street between Marian and Carroll Streets.

The Academy of the Visitation continued to prosper. The sisters inherited 13 acres on Cass Avenue from Anne Mullanphy Biddle, and it was there in 1858 they built their first permanent home — an impressive stone convent and school completely surrounded by a wall — appropriate for a cloistered order of nuns but somewhat restrictive for their students.

But the illusion of permanence and cloistered serenity at the Cass Avenue site was unrealistic. The industrial and commercial city was expanding rapidly, and the nuns realized that their students' families were also moving west. It had become clear that a new location was needed.

The 1892 move to Cabanne brought a physical atmosphere that was much more open than that at Cass Avenue — to the delight of the students and the concern of the nuns. The sisters also had to recognize and react to changing trends in education by reordering their curriculum. As they moved west, they also offered a much stronger academic program than before.

The academy rules, however, remained stringent. Students wore rigidly controlled uniforms — white shirtwaists and plain black cashmere skirts that had to have three box pleats both front and back. Lighter-weight black skirts were permitted during the warm months.

Students could not leave the campus without a chaperone, which the school could supply for $1.25 a day. They could receive authorized visitors only on Thursday afternoons between 1 and 5 p.m. All letters written or received by students were subject to inspection.

The academy's 1898-99 catalog lists students from all over the Midwest as well as Texas, New Mexico, and Oregon. The East was represented by students from New York, and there was even a student from Cork, Ireland. Local students included the daughters of leading St. Louis families. The Benoists, Bakewells, Carrs, Cabannes and Papins all sent their daughters for a firm Catholic and academic education.

The cost per student in 1898 was $150 per session, which covered room, board, and basic tuition. Music lessons cost an additional $40, physical culture classes were $5, and a private room added $25 to the cost. Use of library books cost $2 per session, and there was a graduating fee of $15 per department.

Since a family could easily spend $300 per student per session, it was appropriate that the facility was elegant.

A circular drive led to the main entrance. Parents could meet their daughters in the large parlor that was stylishly decorated with American Empire furniture, brass chandeliers, religious paintings, and Oriental rugs.

The refectory, or dining hall, was a large, airy room filled with long tables set with white linen tablecloths and good china. The library had handsome reading tables and tall carved bookcases. The catalog proudly proclaimed that the building was heated by hot-air furnaces and low-pressure steam.

At the turn of the century, there were lawn tennis courts and various religious shrines on the grounds, which were impeccably maintained.

In this setting students vied for prizes honoring polite deportment, fidelity to rules, neatness and order, and Christian doctrine, in addition to scholastic achievement.

In 1911, a large gymnasium was added south of the main building. The sisters were doing their best to keep up with the times.

They opened a junior college in 1920, but it lasted for only five

The Visitation Academy on Cabanne was designed in the Ecclesiastical Chateauesque style. *Courtesy Visitation Academy Archives.*

years, since the cloistered community had trouble dealing with the problems of demanded social privileges and chaperonage.

Over the years, the Academy of the Visitation evolved and shifted its emphasis from being a boarding school to being a day school.

The academy occupied the Cabanne site for nearly 70 years — educating young women and serving as an anchor for their neighborhood. But by the late 1950s the area had deteriorated badly. The students' families had moved west, and the neighborhood was not deemed suitable for young ladies.

The sisters planned another move — this time to a site on Ballas Road near Highway 40.

In 1961, the Chateauesque structure and its outbuildings were razed and the city bought the 10-acre site for use as a park. Nearly 33 years later, the park remains as an optimistic oasis awaiting the rebirth of its neighborhood.

The Cabanne/Visitation district was attractive to schools and institutions at the turn of the century because of its suburban nature and relatively low land costs. The Principia, which had strong support from various Christian Scientists, made the district its home from 1901 to 1960.

Founded by Mary Kimball Morgan, The Principia officially opened in 1898 after a year of informal operation. The school had 15 elementary-age pupils, two teachers, and assets of 20 chairs, some park benches, and some books, all housed in a two-room storefront space on what is now the 4400 block of Enright Avenue. Its name was derived from the Latin "principium," meaning principle, and was considered indicative of the institution's educational ideal.

In 1901, the same year that The Principia's Upper School, or high school, was established, it moved to land on Page Boulevard, purchased from Lewis E. Collins located on Page Avenue. The school bought the northern section of the Collins estate — an irregular parcel measuring 725 feet in length and 237 in width — that was also the site of the Collins' grand house.

One of the conditions of the sale was that the adjacent land to the south would also be purchased. One of the members of The Principia Advisory Committee bought three lots, and the committee, as a group, bought two additional lots for the school. By 1903, through various additional transactions, the entire block bounded by Page, Minerva, Belt, and Montclair Avenues was owned, directly or indirectly, by The Principia.

The students who attended The Principia in 1901 found a spacious campus in a sparsely populated area, surrounded by unpaved streets. None of the streets west of Kingshighway were paved in 1901, and major thoroughfares, including Page Boulevard, became quagmires when it rained. There were large steppingstones across both Page Boulevard and Belt

The L.E. Collins residence was designed by W. Albert Swasey. *Courtesy The Principia Archives.*

Avenue, and, as one story has it, a female student slipped off a stone and fell literally knee-deep in mud. She was rescued by a milk-cart driver, who pulled her out, leaving her boots behind.

The 16-room Collins house, which dominated the property, was rechristened Principia Hall and served as dormitory space in the early days. Designed by W. Albert Swasey in 1893, it was a grand example of Queen Anne-style architecture, with steeply pitched roof, multiple bays, asymmetrical porches, classic grouped columns, gable ornaments, and finials. The grounds were a grassy expanse, dotted informally with trees and shrubs. A high terrace ran along the Page Avenue boundary, topped by a fence of wooden posts and iron pipes, and a hedge of thorny bushes lined the Belt Avenue side.

A second grand house, located two blocks to the south at 5501 Chamberlain Avenue, was related to The Principia property, as it was purchased in 1907 by Clarence H. Howard, a generous friend of the school and president of the Commonwealth Steel Company.

Called Maplecrest, the house was the principal residence of an estate established in the 1840s by William Gay on 50 acres bounded by today's Page Boulevard, Union, Maple, and DeHodiamont Avenues. Gay built a large plantation house that was approached from Union Avenue by a long driveway edged by an alley of trees. The gardens were extensive, and Mrs. Gay was well known as a horticulturist. She sent to Philadelphia for many fine trees and shrubs, and it is said that Henry Shaw obtained some of his original plants from her. The founder of C. Young and Son, Florists, started his business with plants from her garden.

Unfortunately, that house burned in 1858, and a year later Gay built another in a simple, dignified example of the Italianate style with overhanging eaves supported by decorative brackets.

Maplecrest, the second house built on an estate established by William T. Gay in 1840. *Courtesy of The Principia Archives.*

An interior view of Maplecrest, showing a typical Victorian room. *Courtesy of The Principia Archives.*

Gay sold his estate and house in 1876, and a series of owners, including Selah Chamberlain, altered the structure and sold parts of the land. Carrie T. Cram bought it in 1888 and made several improvements, including the installation of a modern heating plant. In 1895, Louis Chauvanet became the owner and added a third story, a large front porch, and the new western entrance. Windows with segmental-arch heads were added at this time. The Chauvanet remodeling also included enlargement of the living room, alteration of the servants' wing and kitchen, and installation of a back stairway, and construction of a coachman's cottage on the grounds.

When Clarence Howard bought the property in 1907, it had shrunk to a four-acre triangular parcel bounded by Chamberlain, Bartmer, and Belt Avenues. He added a conservatory, or palm house, where his tropical plants could flourish, a glass-roofed swimming pool, and a spacious garage with a large ballroom on its second level.

When Howard moved to a new suburban home in 1931, his grand house was given to The Principia and was used as a faculty residence until the school moved to its present location in St. Louis County in 1960. Both Maplecrest and the Collins mansion were demolished, along with all but one of the campus buildings, when the school's city properties were sold and subdivided. The only building that was not demolished was the 1910 gymnasium located at the corner of Minerva and Montclair Avenues, which was recycled into multifamily housing in 1982.

Part of the Maplecrest property is now the site of the Union Memorial African Methodist Episcopal Church and its congregation, which was forced to leave its former building because of the extensive Mill Creek Valley demolition project. The site of the Collins mansion is now occupied by the Page Park YMCA.

The palm house at Maplecrest. *Courtesy The Principia Archives.*

The Narrow Gauge Railroad
& The Plantation District

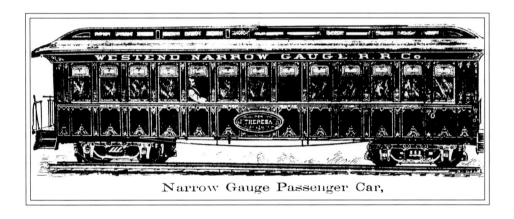

Narrow Gauge Passenger Car,

The opening of St. Louis' newest effort to establish mass transit is a reminder that "everything old is new again." The first leg of the MetroLink mimics the route used by the West End Narrow Gauge Railroad which was established in 1875 by a partnership led by Erastus Wells.

Wells established the railroad to facilitate travel from the city for those who maintained large country estates north and west of St. Louis. The thought that better transportation would enhance real estate investment opportunities opened by westerly residential expansion of the city was also a consideration. The project was a long time in its planning and met with various financial difficulties, including the panic of 1873, which had also delayed the development of Vandeventer Place.

Construction was engineered by John B. Kelly, and Fruin and Company acted as contractors. Although the railroad opened in 1875, it did not reach its terminal station at Florissant until 1878. Various stations along the route were named for the estates and locations they served.

The train's 16-mile route started at a small depot near Grand Avenue and Olive Street and traveled west to Second Kingshighway (now Union Boulevard), where passengers saw the country homes of the Waterman and Kingsbury families, mansions belonging to Daniel Bell and Chalmers Blossom, and the charming French farmhouse

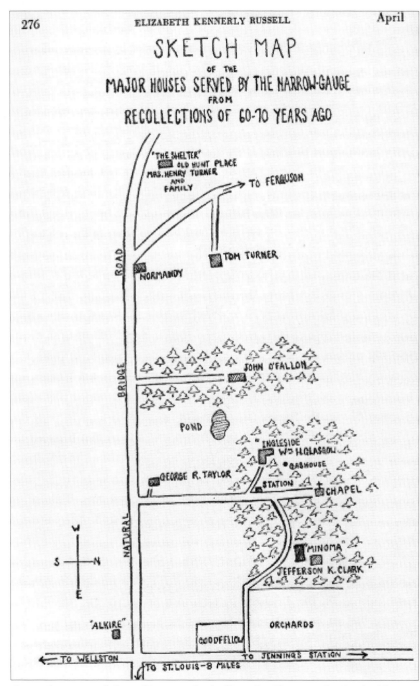

An early map of the rail route, including the Normandy, Ingleside, and Minoma estates. *Courtesy Missouri Historical Society.*

built by Emanuel DeHodiamont.

From there, the train turned west on its journey to the small city of Florissant, passing the country estates of several well-known citizens. It stopped at the Wellston station, named for its proximity to Erastus Wells' farm. The train then crossed Natural Bridge Road near the Charles McClure property, which was called Pinelawn, the country home of David R. Francis, and the large establishment of the David Goodfellow family, among others.

Then the train turned to pass Minoma, the home of Jefferson Kearny Clark — son of William Clark; Ingleside, the estate of William H. Glasgow; and the holdings of John O'Fallon. It then entered the large tract owned by various members of the Lucas family, known in its entirety as Normandy. It traversed the domain of the Mullanphy family, including the Daniel Frost estate known as Hazelwood, and ended at Florissant.

The little steam engine traveled on tracks that were only 3 feet wide (the standard, Union-gauge tracks were 4-feet-8-inches wide). Its rights of way were later used by the Hodiamont streetcar line, which also served the Central West End.

The Narrow Gauge usually ran with only two or three cars — the first of which was a smoking car for men only. One of the luxurious passenger cars was named Theresa. It was 35 feet long and had red plush seats for 46 passengers. The seats were designed so that the backs could be moved, depending on the train's direction, allowing passengers to face the direction in which they were traveling. The car weighed 9 1/2 tons and had a stove and a saloon. Air conditioning was managed with windows that opened and closed with "back-breaking ease," according to Elizabeth Kennerly Russell in her writings describing the train. The car was painted green with gold tracings.

During peak travel times, such as the beginning and end of the summer and the Christmas holidays, extra passenger cars and a baggage car were added. The train ran regular 60-minute schedules, which allowed children from the estates to attend school in the city while taking full advantage of the healthful country air, much to the envy of their town-bound classmates.

The West End Narrow Gauge Railroad was short lived. In 1884, it was sold to an Indianapolis syndicate which electrified the whole line, installed Union-gauge tracks, and called it the St. Louis and Suburban Rail-

road. It was later sold to the St. Louis Public Service Company.

MINOMA

Minoma — the name falls gently on the ear and is evocative of times long past. It refers to a large tract of land owned by explorer William Clark, northwest of the city limits. The name was bestowed on the land by Indians who visited there in the early 19th century and bespeaks the locale's abundance of fresh water springs. Minoma means "sweet water."

The tract's first owner was Joseph Alverez Hortiz, who had claim to it through an early Spanish land grant. Hortiz sold his 4,122 acres to Pierre Chouteau for $1 per acre.

Chouteau opened a trail through his land from Florissant to St. Louis. His trail crossed a limestone bridge that spanned the Rocky Branch Creek east of today's Jefferson Avenue. The well-traveled trail soon was upgraded to a plank road named for the natural bridge.

After Missouri was legally designated a territory of the United States, the land was surveyed, and all title claims were deemed clear, Chouteau sold parcels of his land, which was then known as Survey 1913. William Clark bought 1,231 acres and was followed by family and friends who purchased nearby land.

William Glasgow, David Goodfellow, Dr. Rudolph Bircher, L.C. Nelson, and John O'Fallon all bought in the area, and Dr. David Jennings bought 2,550 acres at the north of the survey.

Although Clark owned a large house in the city, he found that his role as territorial Indian agent required that he own more land. Clark's duties included negotiating treaties with various Missouri and Illinois tribes, who were represented by one or two chiefs, each of whom had an entourage of 100 or more.

Clark used his newly acquired land to provide camping grounds for hundreds of people, horses, and other domestic animals, and he eventually found it necessary to build a farmhouse for himself and his family. His Indian visitors found his country location very much to their liking, since it had plentiful water, ponds full of beaver, and forests full of game. The treaty negotiations were held on Castor Hill in a grove of trees called Council Grove.

The Tamarois, Cahokia, and Michigamia tribes all agreed to treaties at Minoma that ceded forever their ancient Missouri hunting lands to the United States in consideration of $3 million a year for ten years, to be paid in money, merchandise, and domestic stock.

When Clark died in 1838, he left his land to his sons, in specified amounts and locations. Jefferson Kearny Clark, a son of his second marriage, received the largest parcel — approximately 500 acres — which encompassed his father's house, the Council Grove, and many of the springs.

In 1856, Jefferson Clark built a large and elegant house near the old farmhouse. He had married Mary Susan Glasgow, whose family owned the neighboring estate to the west called Ingleside. Further, Clark's

half-brother, George Rogers Hancock Clark, married Mary Susan's sister, Eleanor, creating a maze of complicated family relationships.

The new house was an Italianate mansion with 26 rooms, six marble fireplaces, and 12-foot ceilings. All its brick walls were 12 inches thick. A handsome first-floor porch with full arches spanning between the supports surrounded the house, whose major architectural features included a typical large square tower that rose above the roof.

The tower was called the "armory" because of the extensive collection of weapons kept there. In the 1880s there was a spear on display which was said to be the weapon that killed the French Prince Imperial, son of Napoleon III, during Africa's Zulu Wars.

The tower also housed a private museum of artifacts from the Lewis and Clark Expedition, which had been on display at William Clark's house in the city, and there were souvenirs from his later career as well. One of the most valuable treasures was a campaign chest, fitted with silver and china eating and drinking utensils, that had been given the famous explorer by the Marquis de Lafayette in 1825.

Jefferson Clark's house was set in a park of ancient oak trees. There were orchards, gardens, and a dense forest of hickory and hard maple trees where small children were forbidden to wander alone. The side pastures were home to a flock of Southdown sheep, Jersey cows, and a "quarrelsome" Angus bull.

Life at Minoma was ordered and self-sufficient, but there was levity with many visitors and parties.

Minoma was built in 1856 and was razed in 1960. *Courtesy Missouri Historical Society.*

Friends traveled from the city for dances and weekends — by carriage until 1875 and then by rail. When a party involved dancing into the small hours of the morning, the gentlemen stayed overnight at Minoma, while the ladies slept at Ingleside. Sundays were visiting days, and Minoma was usually filled with friends and family, even during the Civil War.

Jefferson Clark and his family lived at Minoma until 1891, when he decided to move to New York. He sold his villa, along with 296 acres, for $127,000.

Minoma did not have a bright future. The acreage shrank with ensuing sales, and the house was sold twice at separate sheriff's auctions. But it survived for more than 60 years after Clark sold it.

By 1959, the end was near. All the surrounding acreage had been developed and had become the municipality of Northwoods. Minoma had a street address, 6617 Hazen, and had fallen into disrepair. The county was willing to use the house as a community center or museum if a responsible group would renovate it. But no one, including the government of Northwoods, could, or would, raise the estimated $18,000 needed to preserve history. Minoma was destroyed in 1960.

INGLESIDE

The 85-acre farm west of Minoma, called Ingleside, was owned by William Henry Glasgow, whose Scots ancestors had settled in Delaware before moving west to make their fortunes on the new frontier. He was born in Belleville, Illinois, in 1822, and in 1823, his family moved to Herculaneum, Missouri, where his father, William, Sr., operated a store and the nearby Sandy lead mines. By 1827, the family settled in St. Louis, where the senior Glasgow established the mercantile firm of Ross & Glasgow, the first of several family businesses.

By 1840, the Glasgows were among the most important figures in the dry goods business, and William H. joined his father and brother, Edward, in the family businesses. The Glasgows were dry goods and grocery merchants engaged in extensive trade in sugar, rice, tobacco, fabrics, and precious metals.

In 1842, William H. Glasgow traveled to Mexico to join his brother, who was managing their business interests in Mazatlan. They were among the early

Ingleside as it was originally built in 1854. *Courtesy of a private collection.*

pioneer traders on the Santa Fe and Chihuahua Trails. Their purpose was to improve their trade routes, open new markets in Mexico and South America, and bring fortunes in silver specie and gold bullion to St. Louis. They made several trips over the years, and in 1846, Glasgow was forced to follow the Army of the West and Colonel Doniphan's Missouri Volunteers en route to Chihuahua because of the outbreak of the Mexican War. He did not enter Chihuahua until after the Battle of Sacramento in February 1847.

William Glasgow returned to St. Louis in May 1848 and finally settled down and married his first wife, Mary Frances Wright, in 1850. In 1854, he bought the property traditionally known as Strawberry Hill and renamed it Ingleside.

The original design of the red brick manor house was late Georgian and was reminiscent of its peers in the south, with paired double interior chimneys and classic side and entry porches. It was set in a wooded parkland, and there was a large pond in the front pasture that was stocked with fish, and where ice was harvested in the winter for both the Glasgow and Clark households. There were also orchards, extensive stands of Missouri hardwood trees, and more open pastures.

The lifestyle was comfortable, if not lavish — Ingleside was a working farm — and there was plenty of help to keep it all in order. Before the Civil War there were slaves, and after the war, the same people stayed on as freemen and employees.

In 1860, when Glasgow married for the second time, to Carlota Nestor Fales of Remedios, Cuba, Ingleside was enlarged and "improved" in an effort to make it more fashionable and to include modern conveniences. A large two-story veranda was added, masking the original facade. A five-room third floor was also added, along with a second porch at the rear. Brick-colored sidewalks were another modern embellishment.

After the improvement project was completed, the house had 20 rooms, including two parlors, two dining rooms, a kitchen, a pantry, and a spacious hall running from front to back. There were eight bedrooms and two baths. Ingleside had the first built-in tin bathtub in the area, along with all possible accessories to complete the toilets and lavatories.

All the floors were carpeted in the winter — even

Ingleside remodeled. *Courtesy of a private collection.*

the stairways — and matted in the summer, as the wood used was soft.

In the early days, coal fireplaces in each room heated the house. Later, a hot air furnace was installed. Light was provided by chandeliers filled with candles, oil lamps, and gas lights. There were gas jets in every room, and family records indicate that the gas was processed on the premises. A large coal and wood oven and cooking range, built into the kitchen, helped heat the servants' quarters above.

In response to actions of the Union authorities during the Civil War, all first-floor windows were covered with iron bars. The front and back doors, also made of iron, were secured with heavy bars, along with locks and bolts.

The impressive outbuildings formed three sides of a square facing the rear of the house. Built of frame with abundant gingerbread decorations, they included a well house covering the deep well with its "old oaken bucket" and the cool troughs where the milk crocks were stored. Another sheltered the coal and wood supplies, and both were covered with wisteria and climbing roses, as was the gas house.

The children were forbidden to enter the latter, as it was considered dangerous, but they had free run of the stables where the horses and mules were housed under a huge hayloft. They also enjoyed a rope swing that hung from a primeval oak, where they could swing to "alarming heights."

In addition to the stables, there was a large barn for the cows — Glasgow was very proud of his large herd of purebred Jerseys — along with an icehouse, a greenhouse and a two-story frame residence for the gardener and his family.

Ingleside was a mecca for family and friends, according to Mary Susan Glasgow Bowling, who spent her young years there. She, her older sister Anita, and younger brother Jefferson were the children of Glasgow's second marriage. An older half-brother Edward was the child of the first marriage.

According to Mrs. Bowling's letters, their childhood experiences were wonderful. There was plenty of help, the farm produced abundant food, and there were countless opportunities for adventure with their Clark cousins and numerous friends.

The children were educated in their primary years by a live-in tutor, an Episcopal minister who also held services in the family chapel located between Ingleside and Minoma.

Later the two girls were sent to school in the city at Mary Institute, which was located on Lucas Place. They made the trip on the Narrow Gauge every day with a teacher who was given a home at Ingleside so that the girls would have a traveling companion.

All was well at Ingleside until 1879, when financial disaster befell Glasgow, Brother & Company, ending the family's 60-year prominence in the wholesale and Western trade. Ingleside was sold to William Hargadine, whose daughter Julia had married Glasgow's son, Edward, and the family moved into town.

Glasgow became president of the St. Charles Car Company, manufacturers of railroad cars, coaches, and other equipment, and eventually came to own a large portion of that company, which evolved into the American Car and Foundry Company after the turn of the century.

In 1897, while escaping St. Louis' oppressive summer heat in Manitou, Colorado, Glasgow died of typhoid fever.

Documentation of the fate of Ingleside is not as complete as that of its owner. Glasgow's grandson, William G. Bowling, remembers seeing the house in 1916 — vacant but standing. It is gone now — probably the victim of a fire.

NORMANDY

West of the Clark and Glasgow estates lay Normandy, the vast estate of the Lucas family. The holding was named for the district of France, where their patriarch Jean Baptiste Charles Lucas was born. His progeny inherited a great deal of land and continued his traditions by amassing even more. At one time, the family owned more land than any other in St. Louis.

In 1815, one of Lucas' sons, Charles, settled on part of the Normandy estate, living a bachelor's life in a large log house. But Charles, who was considered a brilliant lawyer with great promise, was killed in a duel with Senator Thomas Hart Benton.

He willed his share of the land to his sister, Anne Lucas Hunt, for whom Lucas and Hunt Road would eventually be named. She and her first husband, Theodore Hunt, built a large country house called The Shelter on the site of her late brother's cabin.

After her first husband died, Mrs. Hunt married his cousin, Wilson P. Hunt, who was postmaster of St. Louis from 1822 to 1840.

During her lifetime, Mrs. Hunt was a generous philanthropist who supported the Sisterhood and the House of the Good Shepherd, the School of St. Mary, and the Little Sisters of the Poor. In 1854, she gave land and funds to build the Church of St. Ann, where the famed missionary priest Father Peter DeSmet was pastor.

When Anne Lucas Hunt died in 1879, she left her share of the Normandy land to her daughter, who was married to Henry S. Turner. During the Turner stewardship, passengers on the Narrow Gauge used to enjoy passing the Hunt property and seeing the large herd of Shetland ponies that were pastured near the tracks.

North of The Shelter, James H. Lucas's country house was the showplace of Normandy Park. It was approached via a long driveway that wound through

Robert J. Lucas residence. *Courtesy Missouri Historical Society.*

forested park land and ended in front of the house in a large circle. The original main part of the house, two stories high, was built of brick. Two one-story wings extended back from each side.

The roof was crowned by a pair of handsome

Normandy. *Courtesy Missouri Historical Society.*

chimneys that were joined by a decorative balustrade. A broad veranda stretched across the front of the structure, shading the main parlors on the first floor. Inside, the house was stylishly furnished.

That James Lucas shared his family's love of fine, and fast, horses was shown in the large, two-story stone barn he built near his house. Conveniently, his brother Robert maintained a private racetrack on his share of the Normandy holdings.

When James Lucas died, his son, Henry V., inherited his property. Eventually, the house became the Florissant Valley Club. It met its end in 1914 when it was destroyed by fire — a fate it shared with Anne Hunt's The Shelter, which burned to the ground in 1911.

GOODWOOD

In 1890, James Lucas' son, Joseph, bought approximately 500 acres near his family's holdings and named his farm after the famed British thoroughbred breeding farm, the Goodwood Stud. It was here he maintained his private race track and raised his racehorses, emulating his uncle, Robert.

Lucas lived in a handsome Neoclassical mansion that had four tall Doric columns dominating its facade. A balustraded veranda extended across the width of the entry, and colonnaded wings reached out from both sides.

In 1912, after Joseph Lucas died of blood poison-

ing, his property was sold to C.E.M. Champ, who had come to St. Louis in 1876 to marry his bride, Sophia, and to make his fortune as a spring maker. He prospered and opened his own spring manufacturing company in 1892.

Champ kept the Goodwood name for his farm and established a dairy concern which would become well-known throughout the country.

Tragedy struck in 1916 when the mansion was severely damaged by fire. Only the chimneys remained intact. Construction on a new mansion began immediately and was completed in 1917. No attempt was made to duplicate the original house, though the new one could hold its own in terms of size and design.

The house was built of red brick in the Neoclassical style. All construction elements were masonry, in an effort to avoid its sharing the fate of its predecessor.

The Champ house was never intended to be a simple farmhouse. A large portico with Corinthian columns dominated the facade, which was approached by a tree-lined driveway. According to Norman Champ, who grew up at Goodwood, the house had 25 rooms, including an enclosed loggia that occupied the entire south side of the house on the first floor. The loggia was comfortably furnished — Oriental rugs partially covered the black and white marble floor, and comfortable seating areas alternated with formal arrangements of painted fruitwood tables and chairs. One end of the loggia was dominated by a white Italian marble fountain, the main feature of which was a cherub that stood in the top basin. Turtles and frogs sat around the rim of the larger, floor-level basin.

The entry hall had a fine double staircase with carved newel posts and banisters. The steps were covered with matching Oriental runners.

The wainscotted living room was as elegantly furnished as any found in the Central West End. Oriental rugs, 18th- and 19th-century French and English antiques, bronzes, and gilt-framed paintings combined to present a handsome and

A view of Goodwood. *Courtesy Norman Champ.*

A main feature of Goodwood's loggia was a white Italian marble fountain. *Courtesy Norman Champ.*

opulent room. A major element was an intricately carved Italian marble mantel — the only interior architectural element to survive when the original house burned.

Norman Champ recalled that the house had a huge ballroom in the basement. "But I don't recall any balls at Goodwood," Champ said. "Guests had trouble getting to Goodwood when I was growing up, because of wartime gasoline rationing. My brother and I walked across the road to Country Day School and we took buses when we were going any distance." Champ said that the ballroom, often used as a pool room, contained a large antique billiard table.

Goodwood was an important working dairy operation; it was a major supplier to the St. Louis Dairy Company, which became the Sealtest Dairy Company. There were at least 220 cows — including Jerseys, Guernseys, Ayrshires, and Holsteins — that had to be milked by hand when Champ and his brother Joe were growing up. There were also three or four bulls and from six to eight teams of draft horses — a necessity in gasoline rationing times. There were also six barns to shelter the cows and a large cruciform milking barn.

It was probably inevitable that progress — whether well-considered or not — would spell doom for Goodwood. In 1946, the city acquired 300 acres through the power of eminent domain. The expanding airport and the incursion of Highway 70 ruined the sylvan site. The highway split the acreage and separated a large, pre-Civil War farmhouse from the rest of the property. That house was used by the Holiday Hill Amusement Park for eight or ten years.

In the late 1960s, the rest of the land, the house and all the outbuildings were sold — again under the power of eminent domain — bringing an end to the farming heritage in north St. Louis County. The classic house at Goodwood was torn down in 1968. The Italian marble mantel in the living room is the only survivor, and it was included in the new Goodwood house built in Elsberry, Missouri.

The site of the old house is now covered by runways.

HAZELWOOD

One of the best known of the antebellum North County estates was Hazelwood, which stood near the intersection of Frost and Graham Roads for more than 150 years.

For most of its existence, the house and its land were owned by various members of a prominent St. Louis family. It was briefly — and uneventfully — occupied by Union troops during the Civil War, withstood visits from Indians, and was named by a prominent political figure.

When the original sections of what seems to have been an Adam-style house were built in 1807 by the Reverend William Husick, there were 1,100 acres in the estate. Shortly after the War of 1812, the house and land were bought by Major Richard Graham, who was married to St. Louis heiress Catherine Mullanphy.

The original house was enlarged substantially by

the Grahams to become a large, handsome Early Classical Revival mansion. It was built of white painted brick and had three stories. There were impressive tall wooden columns in the front and brick ones on the rear facade.

The house at Hazelwood enjoyed the reputation of being the first brick farmhouse built west of the Mississippi River, though the same claim was made for the Cabanne House, called the Pioneer Brick, which stood near today's intersection of West Pine and Kingshighway Boulevards. The Cabanne house was built in 1812, so the original parts of Hazelwood, if not the additions, may well have had the right to claim the premier honor.

The bricks with which the house was built are also the cause of debate. One local brick contractor said the bricks were made by local Indians, while historians maintain they were made by slaves. The latter theory is the more likely, as records of the era list no fewer than 40 slaves on the farm.

When Richard Graham died in 1857, the property and the house passed to his wife. When she died in 1875, the property was left to their 11 grandchildren from the marriage of their daughter and famed Con-

federate general Daniel M. Frost — who was passed over in Mrs. Graham's will after his wife died.

Frost bought the house and 200 acres in 1875 from one of his sons, John Mullanphy Frost. The elder Frost married again — to Harriet M. Chenier, a descendant of Madame Chouteau — and had two daughters, Harriet and Emily.

It is said that when Frost's dear friend, politician and orator Henry Clay, had visited the estate, he gave the house its name. Lore has it that Clay said he had never seen so many hazel bushes growing in the same place before, and suggested the name Hazelwood.

When Frost died in 1900, having married for a third time, he left Hazelwood to his daughter, Harriet, who had recently married a young lawyer named Samuel Wesley Fordyce. It was during Mrs. Fordyce's long tenure that Hazelwood became well-known to the public.

Mrs. Fordyce was a noted amateur horticulturalist, and the formal garden she created at Hazelwood gained national recognition. She was honored as the top amateur gardener in St. Louis by the St. Louis Horticultural Society for her work in developing new strains of Oriental poppies and Philippine lilies.

Hazelwood, where the original portions of the house were built in 1807. *Courtesy Missouri Historical Society.*

Hazelwood and its gardens were the scene of many elegant parties. Some were benefits for charities such as the St. Louis University Medical School, and others were simply for fun. A 1923 lawn party was the talk of the town. A movie producer making a film about St. Louis shot the final scenes at an already-scheduled fete in the garden. All the guests were extras in the film. A newspaper report said "a dozen pretty girls in bare feet and flowing garments did some artistic dancing on the lawn while cameras ground away to the delectation of the Fordyces, their friends and their house-guest, Alice Roosevelt Longworth. To top it off, while the movie was being taken, Major Albert Bond Lambert flew an airplane over from Bridgeton Field and circled about, very close to the scene."

Regrettably, the movie was not a very good one and attracted limited audiences, even in St. Louis. No copies remain.

Fordyces' guests at that party and others visited an elegant house. Additions and improvements over the years had made it a 25-room mansion with eight bedrooms and five bathrooms. There were two drawing rooms, a library, a dining room, a large kitchen, several pantries, and a servants' dining room on the first floor. All the first-floor rooms had 16-foot ceilings and were elegantly furnished with family antiques. Fifteen of the rooms had marble mantels, each with a different design and type of marble. Each of the fireplaces could accommodate four-foot cord wood.

There was a large entry hall that had a sweeping staircase with a harp-shaped newel post. The hall, which had been part of the original house, formed the center of the enlarged one.

In 1952, four years after her husband died, Mrs. Fordyce notified the Jesuits at St. Louis University that she was giving them Hazelwood. The gift was the culmination of a longtime affiliation between the institution and her family. General Frost had been the Confederate commander at the Battle of Camp Jackson, the site of which is now a part of the university's campus. For many years a statue of General Nathaniel Lyon, the Union commander at the battle, stood at the site, but it was relocated when a gift from Mrs. Fordyce established the Frost Campus.

Mrs. Fordyce stipulated that her gift of Hazelwood included 160 acres. Some 40 acres, including the house and its gardens, were to be "kept in the present condition," while the remaining 120 acres could be retained or disposed of as the university saw fit.

Hazelwood was given to St. Louis University for use as a retreat house. But in the early 1960s, after Mrs. Fordyce's death, it was perceived that the rapidly expanding aviation industry would make that use impractical. The essence of a retreat is quiet and solitude, and the roaring jets from Lambert Field and McDonnell Aircraft Company shattered the silence at regular intervals.

The university sold Hazelwood to the McCabe Powers Auto Body Company and used the proceeds to build a retreat center far to the south, away from the planes.

Before the house was demolished, several visitors toured it and its outbuildings. The mansion was in good condition, though some of its wide plank floors were covered with linoleum. The high-gabled Missouri Gothic red barn still stood — unused for many years, but sturdy. The barn had 50-foot cross timbers and was a fine example of the 19th-century barns that were once common in Missouri. There was also a cork-lined ice house that stayed wonderfully cool even on the warmest summer day.

In 1964, Hazelwood was

The garden at Hazelwood. *Courtesy Missouri Historical Society.*

torn down. It had survived 157 years of Indians, Union occupation, severe weather, and giddy parties. It couldn't survive progress.

There were many more grand houses in northern St. Louis County — L.C. Nelson's Nelsonia, Charles McClure's Pine Lawn, General William S. Harney's Harneywold, and Judge Thomas H. Thatcher's Glenn Owen, to name a few. The district was comparable to the plantation district of Natchez, Mississippi, which is now an important tourist attraction for that city. All St. Louis' architectural examples of the era are gone as a result of fire or development.

Epilogue

Although countless historic buildings have been destroyed in St. Louis, we are fortunate to have retained the number we have. The historic neighborhoods of Soulard, Lafayette Square, The Ville, the Central West End, Skinker-DeBaliviere/Parkview-Catlin Tract, and others are the envy of those who live in cities where such neighborhoods were "cleared" in the name of progress.

Traditionally, governmental policies have not been kind to preservation of historic buildings and neighborhoods. St. Louis' 1947 City Plan, developed by the City Plan Commission and guided by engineer Harland Bartholomew, proposes, as one of its stated goals, to "wipe out the obsolescent blighted areas and costly decaying slums." A map of these areas includes the Mill Creek Valley, Lafayette Square, Soulard, and old North St. Louis as "obsolete," and the Shaw neighborhood, Carondelet, the Hill, and half of the north-central portion of North St. Louis as "blighted." The plan was implemented in grim totality in the Mill Creek Valley and areas immediately north and south of downtown. Happily, no one got around to demolishing the other neighborhoods and their grand buildings.

The plan states that "new growth will take place as much or more by reconversion of existing land uses," and its proposals for Soulard and Lafayette Square show complete demolition of the grand old houses and other buildings and replacement with suburban-type clusters of multifamily buildings arranged around courtyards, facing away from the street. The Plan Commission ignored the traditional functions and form of a city. Their document shows no appreciation for historic neighborhoods and their importance to a successful city; the 1947 "Present Use" map of the Lafayette Square neighborhood notes Lafayette Park, the center of its neighborhood and the only section of the Creole Common Fields retained by the city, simply as "vacant land." Another map shows the neighborhood with predominantly high-density, multifamily zoning. The

plan suggests that Lafayette Park be extended to the east, by vacating Mississippi Avenue, to accommodate playing fields and active recreation.

The 1947 plan is a product of post-World War II thinking, and it reflects that era's popular notion that limitless access for automobiles was desirable. It forecast that St. Louis' population would grow to 900,000 by 1970, and its recommendations are based in the perceived need to house the increased numbers of people and move their vehicles efficiently. The mindset of the era was to look forward, to get rid of the old, and to ignore the past. There is no mention of urban fabric or context, much less preservation. The attitude was one that became well entrenched in the federal and state bureaucracies which they hold to this day.

The drafters of the plan also projected that construction costs would become lower, as the war was over, and they advocated public acquisition of the land so that new development and highway construction could proceed easily. Even neighborhoods that were not deemed "obsolete," such as the Central West End, were threatened by zoning changes and road "improvements." A proposed zoning map shows a large area east of Kingshighway and north of Lindell as high-density, multifamily use, with only Lenox, Pershing, and Hortense Places, along with Westminster Place from Boyle Avenue to Euclid Avenue as single-family areas. A map of proposed street improvements shows Lindell Boulevard widened to eight lanes between Kingshighway and Union Boulevards, with a grade separation at the intersection of Lindell and Kingshighway Boulevards. The map does not reveal whether the widening and grade separation would take part of Forest Park, destroy the grand houses on the north side of the street to threaten Westmoreland and Portland Places, or both.

The 1947 plan, which remains the base planning document used by the City today, is still cited in all development plan ordinances adopted pursuant to Chapters 99 and 100 of the Revised Statutes of Missouri, to assure compliance with the minimum housing standards it mandates. The language is not required in Chapter 353 developments. The concern evidenced in establishing minimum housing standards did not extend to specific thoughts as to how relocate displaced families after their old neighborhoods were destroyed.

There seems to be neither the will nor available funding to undertake the creation of a new, comprehensive, and detailed plan for the City of St. Louis to replace the old one. More recent attempts, such as the 1973 St. Louis Development Plan, developed during Mayor John Poelker's administration, in consultation with Team Four, met with overwhelming opposition from various sectors, because of lack of public input and concern for certain North St. Louis neighborhoods. As a result this plan, prepared and adopted by the City Plan Commission, was not adopted by ordinance, but is used to temper the 1947 Plan, which has never been repealed by the Board of Aldermen.

Consideration should be given to creating a new comprehensive plan. The various plans that exist for neighborhoods — redevelopment plans under Chapters 99, 100, and 353, "grass-roots" neighborhood plans generated in the context of the Operation ConServ created during the administration of Mayor Vincent C. Schoemehl, the 1976 Central Corridor Traffic Plan, the work completed to date on the Boulevards Plan, the various plans developed for neighborhood commercial districts, the Historic District plans, and others — could be examined and integrated in planning efforts for each neighborhood. After each neighborhood has a plan, developed through public process, they could be assembled as one would piece together a quilt, recognizing that some edges would have to be smoothed so that the whole fits together cogently and successfully. The optimistic news that the Heritage and Urban Design Commission has received a grant from the Missouri Department of Natural Resources to create a preservation plan for the city should be important to this effort. The grant will cover three phases — data gathering, planning, and publication — and will take three years to complete.

A process and product similar to the 1993 Downtown Strategic Plan, which involved more than 125 people from both the public and private sectors, could be helpful in setting out strategic objectives and major goals. The Downtown plan calls for, among other strategic policies, preservation and re-use of historic buildings. With such a comprehensive plan, it would be possible to repeal the sections of the 1947 plan that threaten historic neighborhoods, though it is said by many that "no one pays any attention to that part."

The 1993 Downtown St. Louis Strategic Plan will be of great help in saving some individual historic structures in the core area, west downtown area, and north downtown area, if reasonable and economically feasible uses can be found for them.

Endangered historic structures located elsewhere in the city face harder realities, including difficult economic issues and negative attitudes toward preservation. Landmarks Association of St. Louis began publishing a list of the city's most endangered buildings in 1992. The list included the Arcade-Wright Building at 800-814 Olive Street and 801-815 Pine Street, the St. Louis Arena at 5700 Oakland, the Carr School at 1412 Carr Street, Crown Candy Building/North Fourteenth Street Mall located on North Fourteenth Street between St. Louis Avenue and Warren Street, the 10-building Cupples Station Complex bounded by Highway 40-64, South Eighth, Eleventh, and Clark Streets, the Granada Theater at 4519 Gravois Boulevard, the significant Otzenberger house built in 1858 in Carondelet, the Page Avenue Police Station at the northeast corner of Page and Union Avenues, the William Rumbold-designed "Old Main" building at 5400 Arsenal Street, The Gateway (formerly the Statler) Hotel at 822 Washington Avenue, and the St. Liborius Parish Complex that dominates its neighborhood at 1835 North 18th Street. Many more are in peril.

The status of these buildings is mixed. The Arcade-Wright, with the Wright Building designed by Eames and Young and the Arcade by Tom P. Barnett in collaboration with engineer Fred C. Taxis in 1906, is vacant but standing. It seems that demolition is too costly, and it is mired in convoluted ownership and massive debt.

The Cupples Station Complex, built between 1894 and 1917, was primarily designed by the firm of Eames and Young and was considered the most advanced warehouse complex of its era. The *Inland Architect* hailed the project as "having brought warehouse design to a point where little improvement is possible," and *Scientific American* remarked on the technical prowess at a "scale of elaborateness with a perfection of detail unequaled in any other similar installation in the world." Originally, the complex had 18 buildings, but only 10 remain. The eight lost buildings were either destroyed by fire or demolished to accommodate accesses for Highway 40/64 and Busch Stadium construction. Currently owned by Blue Cross/Blue Shield of Missouri, the complex is undergoing a predevelopment feasibility study that is scheduled to be completed by the end of 1994. The study is the joint project of the owner, the National Trust for Historic Preservation, which considered it worthy of inclusion on its list of 11 most-endangered buildings nationally, the Landmarks Association of St. Louis, the City of St. Louis, and others. The study will investigate the possibilities of mixed use as offices, retail space, and housing, in accordance with the goals of the Downtown St. Louis Strategic Plan.

Sadly, the Granada Theater is history. Demolished in 1992, the theater had been designed by E.P. Rupert of Chicago and was completed in 1926. Together with its adjoining apartment buildings, it presented a resplendent terra-cotta facade in South St. Louis. The auditorium section collapsed as efforts to save the building were underway. Preservationists, unable to prevent demolition, removed interior decorative plaster and more than 1,600 terra-cotta ornaments from the facade.

It is hard to find any good news about the Page Boulevard Police Station. The building was designed in 1908, under the supervision of St. Louis Building Commissioner James R. Smith, in

a mixed Revival style to quell the protests of the burgeoning West End population.

Its era was one when public buildings were a source of civic pride. But it has been vacant since 1976 and has become of symbol of decay and indifference. In 1992, a group was formed to establish an African-American Art Museum in the building as part of a large project including artists' apartments on the top floors. The McDonnell Douglas Employees Charitable Trust granted the project $20,000, and the St. Louis Philanthropic Association pledged an additional $20,000.

The Arena's doors were closed in 1994. *Claire Ruzicka photo.*

The group leased the building from the City for $1 per year and had an option to purchase for $10,000. In 1993, fire further damaged the structure as a result of over-zealous celebration of the 4th of July. According to several sources, it will cost ten times more than the available money to make the building weather-tight, much less bring it back to its former glory.

The Carr School, viewed as a symbol of quality education and community culture, was designed by William B. Ittner in 1908. Vacant and deteriorating, the building may be saved through conversion to housing for the elderly so that senior citizens who so desire may stay in their neighborhood. A $240,000 planning grant for the second phase of the Carr Square Public Housing Reconfiguration includes funds for design development.

The St. Louis Arena at 5700 Oakland Avenue occupies one of the city's most desirable sites. It is owned by the City of St. Louis, which purchased it for $15 million from the Ornest family to prevent the Blues Hockey team's moving to Saskatoon, Saskatchewan. With the development of the Kiel Center, the hockey team will no longer play at the Arena, leaving the facility without a major tenant. In addition, the Kiel Center Partners have a non-compete agreement with the City of St. Louis that prevents any revenue-producing events competing with the Kiel Center from being conducted at the Arena. Though the loan on the $15 million purchase price has been paid down and refinanced, some $10 to $11 million is still owed to the City and the Land Clearance Redevelopment Authority.

There is great interest in the site, if not the building. According to Stan Mulvihill of the St. Louis Development Corporation, most of those interested feel the site is more desirable without the building, which is one of the area's most recognizable landmarks. Completed in October 1929, the Arena was designed by Gustel Kiewitt in association with Herman M. Sohrmann. The dome-shaped Lamella roof, an engineering marvel of its era, assured an unobstructed view from each of its 21,000 seats. Some 30 inquiries from developers have been received by SLDC, including those from the St. Louis Art Museum and the Zoo Museum District. In addition, many of those involved in the ongoing master planning process for Forest Park consider the site of critical importance to the park as a location for future institutional and facility expansion, as well as off-site parking for park users.

In the meantime, the seats and other equipment are being sold. Any adaptive re-use will have to comply with the American Disabilities Act and many other code requirements, which will be an expensive proposition. It seems that only a creative and well-funded idea will save the building.

The St. Liborius Parish Complex has survived for many years in a neighborhood that has seen epic-scale demolition. Closed by the St. Louis Archdiocese in 1992 in its efforts to consolidate the North Side parishes, the structure now serves as a warehouse for furniture and iconography from other churches. Ironically, the statues, choir stalls, confessionals, and other artifacts from St. Liborius itself were sold at auction in 1992. There does not seem to be any good news for St. Liborius in the foreseeable future.

The Crown Candy Company, a well-loved institution, is in good condition, but its neighborhood context is very troubled. It is located within the North St. Louis National Historic Register Historic District that was laid out in 1816, when the town of North St. Louis was established by Anglo-Americans from Kentucky. The Fourteenth Street commercial district, which included businesses selling furniture, appliances, hardware, clothing, confections, and groceries, was thriving at the turn of the century. When it suffered a decline in the 1950s and 1960s, the Model Cities Era solution was to create a two-block-long pedestrian mall by closing the street and demolishing rear buildings to provide for metered parking. It failed, and a plan to successfully revitalize the area is necessary if it is to be saved.

The 1858 Otzenberger house was built of local limestone is deteriorating — an example of native materials returning to native materials. The Land Reutilization Authority, which owns the house, is eager to sell it, but the prospective buyer must have the means to complete restoration.

It is positive for preservation efforts that the Landmarks Association of St. Louis continues its work as advocate and is willing to educate all who will listen. In addition, the City of St. Louis' Heritage and Urban Design Commission (HUDC) reviews all demolition proposals within the city's boundaries. They cannot save all the historic structures, but they can, and do, provide an open forum for discussion. A recent proposal by Sibag Investments, Inc., of New York and Southwestern Bell Telephone Company to demolish the International Fur Exchange, the Thomas Jefferson, and the American Zinc Company buildings on Fourth Street between Walnut and Market Streets was rejected by the Commission, based on the lack of a comprehensive, long-term development plan, as the applicants were proposing only a 156-space surface parking lot as an interim use.

It is also positive that a growing number of developers, both large and small, are seeing historic buildings as having profit potential and marketability. According to Pete Rothschild, who is renovating an 1876 Turnverein building at 2001 South Ninth Street, among several renovation projects, "It's a rewarding way to make a living, especially in the City. Bringing back beautiful buildings helps stabilize the city and makes it a better place to live."

The Union Station complex was an enormous, and seemingly successful, historic renovation project. The "back-to-the-city" movement of the 1970s and early 1980s, fueled by the National Preservation Act of 1966, did a great deal to save historic structures and neighborhoods. The extensive DeBaliviere Place project, implemented by Leon Strauss' Pantheon Corporation, is an excellent example. But such activity was curtailed nationally, as a casualty of the 1986 Tax Reform Act, which removed rehabilitation tax credit advantages. In the July 28 issue of the *Southtown Word*, Representative Richard Gephardt said, "We are trying to bring back the historic rehab [tax] credit, so that people will put money into older homes and areas. One of our great needs is to get capital reinvested in older buildings." Gephardt added that at the end of this year, he intends to include introduction of the tax credit re-establishment on the 1995 agenda.

Selected Bibliography

Blythe, Jeanne C., and Cunningham, Mary B.: *The Founding Family of St. Louis.* Midwest Technical Publications, St. Louis, MO, 1977.

Bryan, John Albury: *Missouri's Contribution to American Architecture.* St. Louis Architectural Club, St. Louis, MO, 1928.

Canaday, John: *Mainstreams of Modern Art.* Simon and Schuster, New York, 1959.

Compton, Richard J., and Dry, Camille N.: *Pictorial St. Louis, 1875.* Reprinted by Harry M. Hagen, 1971. Knight Publishing Company, St. Louis, MO, 1971.

Devoy, John: *A History of the City of St. Louis.* John Devoy, St. Louis, MO, 1898.

Edwards, Richard, and Hopewell, M.D.: *Edwards's Great West and Her Commercial Metropolis, Embracing a General View of the West* and *Complete History of St. Louis from the Landing of Liguest, in 1764, to the Present Time.* Edwards's Monthly, St. Louis, MO, 1860.

Fitch, James Marston: *American Building — The Forces that Shaped It.* Houghton Mifflin Company, Boston, MA, 1948.

Gill, McCune: *The St. Louis Story.* Historical Record Association, St. Louis, MO, 1952.

Hagen, Harry M.: *This is Our...ST. LOUIS.* Knight Publishing Company, St. Louis, MO, 1970.

Hannon, Robert E.: *St. Louis: Its Neighborhoods and Neighbors, Landmarks and Milestones.* St. Louis Regional Commerce and Growth Association, St. Louis, MO, 1986.

Harleman, Kathleen M., Stuart, Georgiana B., and Tepas, Susan K.: *The Neighborhood, A History of Skinker DeBaliviere.* Residential Service of the Skinker Debaliviere Community Council, 1973.

Harris, Cyril M.: *Dictionary of Architecture and Construction.* McGraw-Hill, Inc., New York, 1975.

Hitchcock, Henry-Russell; Fein, Albert; Weisman, Winston; and Scully, Vincent — Edited by Kaufmann, Edgar, Jr.: *The Rise of American Architecture.* Published in association with the Metropolitan Museum of Art by Praeger Publishers, New York, 1970.

Hunter, Julius K.: *Kingsbury Place, The First Two Hundred Years.* The C.V. Mosby Company, St. Louis, MO, 1982.

Hunter, Julius K.: *Westmoreland and Portland Places, The History and Architecture of America's Premiere Private Streets, 1888 - 1988.* University of Missouri Press, Columbia, MO, 1988.

Hyde, William and Conrad, Howard L.: *Encyclopedia of the History of St. Louis.* The Southern History Company, New York, Louisville, and St. Louis, 1899.

Jordy, William H.: *American Building and Their Architects — Progressive and Academic Ideals at the Turn of the Twentieth Century.* Anchor Books, New York, 1976.

Loughlin, Caroline, and Anderson, Catherine: *Forest Park.* The Junior League of St. Louis and University of Missouri Press, Columbia, MO, 1986.

Lowic, Lawrence: *The Architectural Heritage of St. Louis, 1803 - 1891.* Washington University Gallery of Art, St. Louis, MO, 1982.

McAlester, Virginia and Lee: *A Field Guide to American Houses.* Alfred A. Knopf, Inc., New York, 1988.

McCue, George: *The Building Art in St. Louis: Two Centuries.* Knight Publishing Co. St. Louis, MO, 1981.

McCue, George, and Peters, Frank: *A Guide to the Architecture of St. Louis.* University of Missouri Press, Columbia, MO, 1989.

Peterson, Charles E.: *Colonial St. Louis: Building a Creole Capital.* Missouri Historical Society, St. Louis, MO, 1949.

Primm, James Neal: *Lion of the Valley - St. Louis, Missouri.* Pruett Publishing Company, Boulder, CO, 1981.

O'Gorman, James F.: *Selected Drawings: Henry Hobson Richardson and His Office.* Catalog of an exhibition in 1974 to celebrate the centennial of Richardson's move to Boston, MA. Harvard College Department of Printing and Graphic Arts, 1974.

Rodabough, John: *Frenchtown.* Sunrise Publishing Company, St. Louis, MO, 1980.

Savage, Charles C.: *Architecture of the Private Streets of St. Louis — The Architects and the Houses They Designed.* University of Missouri Press, Columbia, MO, 1987.

Smith, Page: *The Rise of Industrial America — A People's History of the Post-Reconstruction Era.* McGraw Hill Book Company, 1984.

Toft, Carolyn Hewes; Hamilton, Esley; and Gass, Mary Henderson — Edited by George McCue: *The Way We Came - A Century of the AIA in St. Louis.* Patrice Press, St. Louis, MO, 1991.

van Ravensway, Charles, edited by Candace O'Conner: *St. Louis, An Informal History of the City and Its People, 1764 - 1865.* Missouri Historical Society Press, St. Louis, MO, 1991.

Whiffen, Marcus: *American Architecture Since 1780 — A Guide to the Styles.* The M.I.T. Press, Cambridge, MA, 1969.

Wright, John A.: *Discovering African-American St. Louis: A Guide to Historic Sites.* Missouri Historical Society Press, St. Louis, MO, 1994.

Yeakle, Mahlon M.: *The City of St. Louis Today.* J. Osmun Yeakle and Company, St. Louis, MO, 1889.

In addition, the Missouri Historical Society's various collections of scrapbooks, compilations of clippings concerning historic buildings, necrologies, vertical files, and documents have been invaluable in researching the subjects for *St. Louis Lost.* Quoted material without attribution was taken from scrapbooks or other collections of documents that listed no sources.

Index

Schmitt